D0482411

C U R R E N C Y

D O U B L E D A Y

NO-EXCUSES
MANAGEMENT

NO-EXCUSES MANAGEMENT

Proven systems for starting fast, growing quickly, and surviving hard times

T. J. Rodgers

William Taylor

Rick Foreman

CURRENCY

DOUBLEDAY

New York   Toronto   London   Sydney   Auckland

A CURRENCY BOOK
PUBLISHED BY DOUBLEDAY
a division of Bantam Doubleday Dell Publishing Group, Inc.
1540 Broadway, New York, New York 10036

CURRENCY and DOUBLEDAY are trademarks of
Doubleday, a division of Bantam Doubleday
Dell Publishing Group, Inc.

BOOK DESIGN BY CLAIRE VACCARO

Library of Congress Cataloging-in-Publication Data

Rodgers, T. J.
    No-excuses management: proven systems for starting fast,
  growing quickly, and surviving hard times
  T. J. Rodgers, William Taylor, Rick Foreman.
      p.   cm.
    1. Management.   2. Success in business.   I. Taylor, William,
  1959–   .   II. Foreman, Rick.   III. Title.
  HD31.R615   1993
  658 – dc20   92-37821
                                                          CIP

ISBN 0-385-42604-6
Copyright © 1992 by T. J. Rodgers, William Taylor, and Rick Foreman
All Rights Reserved
Printed in the United States of America
May 1993
FIRST EDITION
10   9   8   7   6   5   4   3   2   1

Contents

Money

Growth

Introduction: in praise of the fundamentals

There are many ways to measure success in business, but there is only one right way—achieving what you said you would. Competition becomes more exacting and less forgiving every day. Winning is harder, the consequences of losing more severe. I know that the business world is tougher than it's ever been because I work in the toughest business in the world.

Semiconductors—computer chips—have been shrouded in wonder and adventure since their creation thirty-five years ago. Society marvels at the relentless pace of silicon progress: spectacular advances in speed, ever-accelerating reductions in size and cost. The first computer chips contained one transistor. Today's most advanced memory chips contain more than *ten million* transistors—and sell for the bargain price of 10,000 transistors per penny. To update a famous calculation, if automobiles had advanced since 1960 at the same rate as computer chips, we would all be commuting to work in cars that cost a penny, went 2,000 miles an hour, and got great gas mileage—about 1,000 miles to the ounce.

Such stunning advances in technology are the result of fierce competition in unrelenting Darwinian markets. I have spent my entire career in Silicon Valley, where I square off against a cast of flamboyant, talented, driven executives. Cypress's rivals also include some of the biggest and most powerful chip manufacturers in Japan and Korea—companies that are ten or twenty times our size. One week of self-satisfaction, one quarter of shoddy performance, and we can get our head handed to us.

So far we've held our own. Cypress was founded in 1983, went public in 1986, and listed on the New York Stock Exchange in 1988. Today we generate annual revenues of more than $250 million. We are six times bigger than we were just five years ago, and we employ almost 1,500 people.

We succeed because we outhustle, outinnovate, and outexecute other companies battling to stay on the cutting edge of the computer revolution. Our microprocessors are the "electronic brains" inside some of the world's most powerful supercomputers. Some of our ultrafast memory chips end up in some of the world's smartest "smart weapons:" the laser-guided Maverick missile, the radar-seeking HARM missile, the Patriot antimissile missile. For every product category in which we compete, our chips must be the fastest, the most specialized, the highest performance.

Most days, though, life at Cypress doesn't seem as exhilarating as all that. It's more like crawling through a muddy battlefield than soaring into cyberspace. A computer chip is the result of literally a thousand multidisciplinary tasks; doing 999 of them right guarantees failure, not success. So our watchwords must be *accountability*, *discipline*, and *painstaking attention to detail*—at every level of the organization.

Which makes us different from every other business—right? Hardly. The pace of our business may be faster than most, the rate of change more intense, but the basic challenges are familiar ones. Managers in our industry worry about the same things that worry managers everywhere. Are we hiring the right people? Are our people working on the right problems? Are we spending enough money or too much money? Are we spending money on the right things? Are we developing the right products and are we shipping them on time? Are we going to make the plan this quarter? Next year?

If we meet these challenges intelligently and effectively, we win. If we don't, we lose. So we don't bother with the latest management theories *du jour* or exotic new "paradigms" of competition. Instead, we embrace a simple proposition:

If everyone in our company makes ordinary business decisions in a commonsense way, we will be unstoppable.

The problem, of course, is that very few people in our company (or any other) make ordinary business decisions in a commonsense way. Which is why we place so much emphasis on systems.

At Cypress we apply the powerful new tools of the information age to the timeless fundamentals of business. The unsung, unglamorous, unappreciated fundamentals that ultimately determine whether a business—any business—succeeds. Most companies don't fail for lack of talent or strategic vision. They fail for lack of execution—the routine blocking and tackling that great companies consistently do well and always strive to do better. The role of our management systems is to keep us focused on the fundamentals and to alert us when things go wrong.

These systems use the latest electronic hardware and software: high-performance workstations and personal computers, relational databases, high-speed data networks. But Cypress's systems are not powerful because they are complicated. They are powerful because they are simple. Businesses come in different shapes and sizes, but most of business boils down to four things: People, Work, Money, and Growth. These are the four themes around which our management systems—and this book—are organized.

I don't use the word *systems* loosely. Each one involves holding specific meetings, maintaining computer databases, submitting detailed reports and/or summaries, and securing approvals when a lot of money is involved. For example, Cypress managers grant raises by using a software package that prompts them step-by-step through the evaluation-and-reward process. The computer recommends initial salary increases based on merit rankings, prompts managers to adjust the recommendations to reflect their in-depth knowledge and personal judgments, and alerts them instantaneously if their decisions are at odds with basic company policies.

That said, we don't confuse systems with bureaucratic planning.

In our business (and, I suspect, most businesses), five-year plans, even one-year plans, tend to become obsolete before the ink dries. So we make plans, but we don't become enslaved by them at unrealistic levels of detail. We worry less about meeting exact product-by-product forecasts than about responding quickly and effectively to unforeseen competitive developments.

We plan so that we can react. Precisely because we understand that detailed long-term forecasts are so unreliable, we collect revenue figures *daily* and review them weekly in one of the company's most intense and important meetings. At our "ship-review" sessions, held every Wednesday at five P.M., we track the week's results from our seven profit-and-loss centers, analyze how they compare with the quarterly plan, identify what we need to do to keep performance on forecast, and anticipate what problems might be looming. The sessions are candid, even combative, but they always involve hard data and substance. They focus on the nitty-gritty details that are the difference between success and failure.

This is important. Real management is about mastering details. To my mind, no CEO can claim to be in charge of the organization unless within thirty minutes—and I mean this literally—he or she can answer the following questions and others like them. What are the company's revenues per employee? How do the figures compare with the competition's? What are the revenue-per-employee figures for each of the company's leading product lines? What explains recent trends in each line? What is the average outgoing quality level in each product line? Which of the company's top twenty executives are standouts, which are low performers, and why? Which business units could recover from a major competitive shock (massive price cuts, new entrants, technological change) and which are vulnerable? What are the yields, costs, and cycle times at every manufacturing operation? What explains the company's stock-price valuation relative to its competitors?

By now, I suspect, some readers are ready to protest: What CEO can possibly generate such information within thirty minutes? I have a different question: What CEO who can't produce such information can possibly claim to be doing the job?

Being able to summon and analyze data quickly doesn't mean

interfering where you don't belong. The power of our management systems is that they allow me and other senior executives to be in *command* without being in *control.*

In 1985, when Cypress was a $50 million company, an area sales manager called me to complain that one of his key customers had not received samples of a new chip. At Cypress, not shipping samples is a cardinal sin. New products are the lifeblood of our business, and customers won't accept new products before conducting extensive tests on samples. This manager was angry, and he wanted to know what I, the president, could do to help.

I said I'd get back to him. How could I figure out what was going on? Easy. We have a modest little system called "sample czars." For each of our new chips there is one person, typically a new engineer, responsible for making sure that samples get to customers. I buzzed my secretary and asked for the latest sample-czar report. (Back then, I received the report weekly and reviewed it monthly.) The report is one page long and easy to read. I scanned the page and saw that all but one of our product lines had shipped every sample on time. The one remaining product, with thirty delinquent samples, was the subject of the irate manager's call.

I called the appropriate sample czar and got my answer: The thirty chips were ready, but the customer had requested assembly packages that we did not build ourselves. That meant going to an outside supplier, which meant the request took longer than usual to fill. But the special samples had been assembled, they were being tested and marked, and would be out the door in a few days.

Those were reasonable answers. I asked the sample czar to immediately telephone our disgruntled sales manager, fill him in on the situation, and patch things up.

I hung up the phone and looked at my watch. My entire "investigation" took four minutes. I felt pretty good. It was a small matter, hardly make-or-break for the company, but important nonetheless. Think about the messages being sent through the organization.

To the sales manager: "The president really cares about what I do. I call with a problem and four minutes later I'm hearing from someone with an answer."

To the engineer: "Senior management really cares about customers. Thirty samples are a few days late and the president is calling to find out what's wrong!"

To everyone who hears about what happened: "I feel good about working here. We get things done. We don't let problems fester."

I no longer monitor sample-czar reports. It is up to the vice presidents running our seven different product lines (some of which are bigger than Cypress was in 1985) to stay on top of their operations, including "small" details like shipping samples on time. What if that same marketing manager were to call today with a similar problem? I'd telephone the appropriate vice president, ask him to deal with it, and expect that he would fix the problem in four minutes.

VALUES, PRINCIPLES, SYSTEMS

As you might suspect, we don't spend lots of time thinking about management philosophy and corporate culture. We're too busy trying to get the job done. At the same time, Cypress is not an accident. In the early days, the six founders had long discussions, often late into the night, about what this company should stand for. How should we treat our customers? How should we treat our people? How should we hold ourselves accountable for performance? In short, what are our corporate values?

We've never been much for broadcasting those values through elaborate video presentations, formal "indoctrination" sessions, or weekend retreats. People absorb a culture by living it every day and seeing the people around them live it. Our values are imbedded in how we operate.

Two years ago, however, we took an opportunity to make some of our corporate values more explicit. We had just acquired a big, shiny, gold-plated semiconductor factory in Bloomington, Minnesota. Control Data, one of the pioneer companies of the computer industry, had built a showcase wafer-fabrication plant to make chips for its electronic equipment. But the company had hit some hard times and offered to sell us the plant for one-fifth what it had cost to build—a deal too good to pass up. The deal meant that for the first time, Cypress would be signing on a large group of people who had spent years in a different corporate culture. Indeed, it's hard to think of a sharper contrast between companies than the one between the tough, scrappy startup, Cypress, and the paternalistic Control Data Corporation.

So I flew to Bloomington, called together everyone who would be working with us, and made a presentation about the values that inspire our company. I kept it simple. In fact, I kept it to one slide.

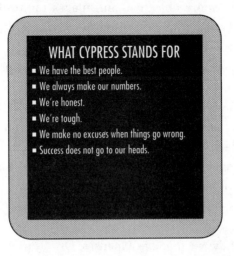

WHAT CYPRESS STANDS FOR
- We have the best people.
- We always make our numbers.
- We're honest.
- We're tough.
- We make no excuses when things go wrong.
- Success does not go to our heads.

These are the simple beliefs behind everything we do at Cypress. They describe how we evaluate our business performance, how we behave toward one another, what we think is important, where I spend my time as CEO. Ask a circuit designer, a test operator, a secretary, or a vice president if that slide describes the organization in which they work—I guarantee they will nod vigorously.

The role of our management systems is to translate these simple values into everyday practice. Which is, of course, precisely where things begin to get complicated. The bridge between our values and our systems is a handful of back-to-basics management principles. Taken together, these principles constitute what we mean by No-Excuses Management.

No Secrets. Everyone in the organization, from top to bottom, shares information openly and is held publicly accountable when problems or opportunities arise. People at Cypress disagree vigorously on many things, but no one can use selective control of information to get their way. We are a virtually transparent organization.

Our goals system is a case in point. Every week our people enter into a computer the action items (goals) they plan to work on. This electronic database allows our people to catalog, prioritize, and sort what needs to be achieved for us to move forward. People like and use the system because it makes them more productive, makes their job evaluations more objective, and makes the tradeoffs and work priorities of the entire organization more visible. It also allows top management to track projects, balance potential overloads, and identify bottlenecks before they become breakdowns.

No Surprises. We collect information in such detail, and share it so widely, that no manager, regardless of rank, can plausibly claim to be in the dark about critical problems or opportunities. Our systems give managers the capacity to monitor what's happening at all levels of the organization, to anticipate problems, and to identify best practices—without creating layers of bureaucracy that bog down decisions and sap morale.

Consider how we manage expenses. Our "Purchase-Order Commit" system gives us ironclad control over spending with no room for surprise overruns. The system creates a quarterly spending meter, and the meter determines how fast money flows out of the corporate pipeline each week. The system also allows me (or our CFO), through one two-hour meeting every week, to scan *every* purchase order in the company, probe for extravagance, and identify good ideas that deserve to be shared more widely. It's no accident that we have never—never—exceeded a quarterly budget by more than 1 percent. Our system simply will not allow it.

No Politics. The way to make tough decisions is to get the right people in one room, require them to look at the same information, and insist that they make difficult tradeoffs on the spot. This approach can make for noisy negotiations; many of our meetings are not for the faint of heart. But it eliminates the behind-the-scenes maneuvering, second-guessing, and backbiting that weakens so many organizations.

How many companies squabble endlessly and divisively over "money" issues like hiring and capital spending? Not Cypress. Every quarter, based on our revenue projections, we establish total corporate allowances for new people and capital investment. Then we allocate the overall targets by departments: how many new people for marketing, how much new equipment for quality control? I don't impose these allocations. Instead, the vice presidents and middle managers running the departments impose the allocations on themselves. We get them in a room, conduct real-time negotiations, use a computer to evaluate decisions as they unfold, and cut the deals that would otherwise lead to memo wars and special pleading—in a word, politics.

Identifying and eliminating corporate politics—as distinct from legitimate, substantive disagreements among managers—is one of my most important and difficult jobs as CEO. Two years ago, after a particularly bitter and divisive meeting, I wrote a blistering memo to one of my top managers. The memo was titled "Politics Is Forbidden at Cypress." It made my position very clear.

"I thought you would have picked up this fundamental feature of our culture by now," I wrote. "We do not undercut each other. We do not plot against each other. We do not tell stories about other people when they are not there to defend themselves.

"Certainly there is a lot of conflict at Cypress," the memo continued. "Even people who are trying to work together run into conflicts. The way we resolve those conflicts is to bring them out (sometimes scream and holler and pound on the table) and resolve them. We do not maneuver for position at Cypress. That is a tactic used in big companies where people have very little power and need to connive to get what they want."

No Distractions. We practice management by exception in the truest sense. Nearly all of our systems are automatic, operate largely in the background, and demand attention only when things go wrong.

Consider a portfolio of applications that our computer specialists have dubbed "killer software." These applications monitor performance without requiring layers of bureaucratic monitors. There are certain things in our business that we simply don't want to have happen. We don't want products sitting for weeks in manufacturing areas. We don't want new orders sitting unattended. Killer software constantly sorts through the company's databases to detect whether these and other key rules have been violated. After a warning, the software shuts down the routine computer operations of that department until the violations are corrected. Think of it as the electronic equivalent of the big red lever that allows Japanese autoworkers to shut down the assembly line for simple quality defects. Only in this case, the system shuts itself down.

Killer software may sound severe, and it is. In fact, some of the original computer-triggered responses were so severe that we have modified them. But the basic principle holds: Killer software should be invisible until invoked but, once invoked, impossible to ignore. The applications have inspired dramatic improvements in factory cycle times, order-entry speed and accuracy, and customer service.

No Confusion. The men and women of Cypress understand what we have to do to succeed, track the same indicators of success, know what the indicators mean, and know what to do when the indicators suggest we are off course. We have a common vocabulary and a shared understanding of the world.

One important vehicle for eliminating confusion and building shared understanding is the company meeting. Twice a quarter (at the very beginning, and close to the end) we gather everyone in the company to review our performance and agree on what we have to do to make our plan. These are not pep rallies. We review operating results, financials, and quality levels for each of our product lines. We track progress on new products, patents, and other technology trends. At the quarter-end meeting, we review where we stand relative to forecasts and identify what specific steps will help us meet or exceed the plan. Everyone (senior managers, junior engineers, shipping clerks, equipment operators) leaves those meetings with a detailed understanding of the state of the company and our prospects.

*   *   *

No Waste. Lots of companies say they're lean and mean. We *are* lean and mean. The seeds of business failure are sown in good times, not hard times. Growth masks waste, excess, inefficiency.

ACTION REQUEST   AR #   7013

FOR (ACTION):   TOM   START: February 18, 1992

CC (INFORMATION):   BOB, JOE   DUE: February 24, 1992

FROM: T.J. RODGERS

TITLE: FAB 1 BILLING

CONTENTS: In a recent poll of your product-line customers, I asked about the accuracy of billing. Everyone rated test as the best group at billing with accurate and timely bills. Each product-line manager rated the assembly area second, also with accurate and timely bills. Recently, assembly has even started to give discounts for late material penalties without being prodded. The billing in Fab 2 was labeled less accurate, but one product-line manager said, "I haven't seen an error from Fab 2 in a couple of months."

Guess why you are getting this AR. The accuracy of Fab 1 billing was ranked last. Everybody agreed that the bills were almost always in error and the errors almost always favored Fab 1.

You know the principles: If you are going to run a quality organization it should exude quality at every level. Obviously, the financial interactions between Fab 1 and its customers should be perfect. Your customers should be able to have total faith in your billing and pay without even reconciling. I have mentioned this to some people before and heard some bullshit excuse about "resources." The fact is you have 200 people in your organization, <u>very</u> <u>few</u> line items to bill (just think about the much more difficult problems faced by assembly and test), and should <u>never</u> have an error in your billing for any reason—in particular, "resources."

TO COMPLETE AR: Please get your act together on billing. It wastes my time going through the reconciliation rain dance every week. I do not view the solution to this problem as a "program" in which you use "kaizen" to reduce the defect level over a period of time. I view this problem as a "slam-dunk, kick-some-ass, get-it-done-now problem." The next billing should be perfect. Thank you in advance for your cooperation.

An example of how we identify and resolve small problems—No Excuses.

That's why all of our performance measures control for the illusions prosperity creates. Sure we want aggressive revenue growth. But we evaluate our corporate performance based on a set of metrics that include ever-increasing revenue per employee, ever-higher capital productivity, ever-lower expense ratios. We don't just want to do more. We want to do more with less, every quarter. And we constantly benchmark our performance against that of our most efficient competitors.

This book reflects our back-to-basics culture and principles. It is, quite simply, a book about what works. A book about the real-life management systems that we use every day of every week—and that we think other managers can use or at least learn from. This is also a warts-and-all book. It is full of memos (Action Requests, in Cypress language), computer printouts, and other items from my "in box"—many of which speak to the shortcomings and dark corners of the systems, and some of our frustrations with them.

Finally, like our management systems themselves, this is an *interactive* book. The computer diskette is designed to provide a "hands-on" feel for how we do things. For our focal-review process, which we describe in Chapter 2, the diskette allows readers to participate in an on-line demonstration—in effect, to "test-drive" our approach for granting raises. The demonstration of the goals system, which we describe in Chapters 4 and 5, walks readers through a series of screens that illustrate its "look and feel" and basic functionality. The demos are quick and easy to understand. They are meant to enhance the reading experience—but the book stands fully on its own.

SMALL IS POWERFUL

It's natural to ask whether the values, principles, and systems I have described can operate in companies much bigger than Cypress. I don't know. But if they can't, then these big companies may well be unmanageable. Let's be clear: This is not a book about how to run General Motors or IBM or AT&T. We'd like to think there are plenty of managers in those and other giant organizations—people running divisions or departments, managers heading subsidiaries or business units—who will find our principles and practices relevant. But when it comes to managing vast, multi-billion-dollar empires— well, that's just not something we have much experience with.

We respect the limitations of size. I am absolutely convinced that any small group of smart, dedicated, hardworking professionals can beat any large group of average professionals with superior resources. There comes a point in any company's growth when adding more people, more buildings, and more equipment *reduces* overall productivity. That is the point at which "big-company disease" takes hold.

I believe that point is somewhere in the neighborhood of $100 million in annual revenues for a semiconductor company. Which is why Cypress today is not one company with total revenues of more than $250 million, but a federation of seven companies linked by a common strategy, vision, and management systems. We want Cypress to grow, and grow fast. We hope to be a billion-dollar company by the end of the decade. But we also expect to be a different kind of billion-dollar company—one that achieves scale without sclerosis.

We fund our growth by seeding new companies under the Cypress umbrella rather than by controlling everything from headquarters. Our first startup, Cypress Semiconductor (Texas) Inc., was founded in 1986. It is now our largest source of manufacturing capacity. Aspen Semiconductor, formed in 1987, develops ultrafast chips using specialized process technologies. Multichip Technology was founded in 1988 to combine multiple chips into modular subsystems. Ross Technology, our fourth startup, designs some of the world's fastest RISC microprocessors.

These companies are startups in the true sense of the word. They have their own shares, their own presidents, their own boards of directors. They receive capital through venture-style funding from Cypress San Jose. If, over time, they need more money, they must sell us more stock. Which creates powerful incentives for them to run every bit as lean and frugal as we did in our early days: Why would the people of Ross or Aspen want me to own more of their equity?

The subsidiaries can also raise capital in other ways. Three years ago, for example, our Texas manufacturing company cut a deal with another Silicon Valley chip company, Altera. The 190 people of Cypress Texas sold their employee-owned shares to Altera for $7.4 million. As a minority owner, Altera received preferential access to the plant's current output and next-generation manufacturing technology. It was a great investment for Altera (which is also, by the way, a Cypress competitor), a great source of financing for Cypress Texas, and a big financial boost for the subsidiary's people. The first president of Cypress Texas made nearly $2 million on the deal and chose to retire. Altera has since invested another $7.6 million and now owns 17 percent of Cypress Texas.

So our subsidiaries have true autonomy. But we do expect two major commitments. First, every subsidiary must use the management systems that have served Cypress so well. Second, they must send high-level managers to a few key corporate meetings in which we track and coordinate activities across the subsidiaries. The result is a "federation of entrepreneurs" that gives us scale and diversity without sloth and bureaucracy. Our startups now account for one third of Cypress's total revenues.

BE REALISTIC — DEMAND THE IMPOSSIBLE

Much of what you have read so far may sound brash, even cocky. That's why our final management principle may well be the most important: *No Illusions.* Every major semiconductor manufacturer in the world has lost money at some point in its life as a public company. That's true for much-celebrated giants like Intel, long-troubled pioneers like National Semiconductor, even world-beating Asian conglomerates like Toshiba and Samsung. It's even true for us. We posted two money-losing quarters for the first time in our history last year.

Indeed, not one quarter goes by at this company when something doesn't go wrong, that one of our "foolproof" management systems doesn't stop working, that a process we took for granted doesn't melt down before our eyes. We are constantly modifying, improving, re-designing, starting over. Sometimes we're slow to recognize the need for change, sometimes we don't make change happen quickly enough. Those are the times we run into trouble.

Over the last year or so we've suffered two big disappointments that reminded us that we are completely capable of screwing up—and just how treacherous our business can be. On January 20, 1992, a few days before we agreed to write this book, we reported our financial results for 1991. The news for the year was good: record revenues, record profits, record bookings, record year-end backlog. But to Wall Street, our fourth-quarter results were "disappointing." And they were. Profits for the quarter fell 28 percent compared with the year-ago quarter, our first quarterly decline in four years.

This was big news. As we've said, we are absolute sticklers about making our numbers. Unfortunately, in the fourth quarter of 1991, we didn't get the job done.

Wall Street's reaction was fast and furious. Trading in our stock was suspended at about one P.M. New York time while we made our earnings announcement. Trading resumed at two P.M. Within two hours Cypress lost 20 percent of its market value—about $135 million. Our average daily trading volume is about 200,000 shares. That day 3.3 million shares changed hands. By the end of the week nearly 11 million shares had changed hands—remarkable turnover, since we had only 40 million shares outstanding! Years of hard work and unassailable performance were quickly forgotten in the frenzy of selling. It was certainly hard to tell, based on Wall Street's punishing reaction, that Cypress was the fourth most profitable semiconductor company in America that quarter—behind giants Intel, Motorola, and AMD.

I recount this story for two reasons. First, I don't want anyone to think Cypress never makes mistakes. This book is based on an arrogant premise: that our business experiences have value to other managers. I suppose we're arrogant enough to accept that premise. But we are not so arrogant—or so misguided—to think we never make mistakes. We *constantly* make mistakes—hundreds of small ones, a few big ones.

But we are quick to recognize our mistakes and to deal with them honestly. Did we endorse Wall Street's response to our fourth-quarter results? No. But we didn't blame the analysts and money managers. We rolled up our sleeves and got to work.

ACTION REQUEST   AR # __3080__

FOR (ACTION):   LT2/TN2/JN2/BV2/AREA
                     SALES MANAGERS   START: June 6, 1989

CC (INFORMATION):   DUE: June 13, 1989

FROM: T.J. RODGERS

TITLE: BRUTALITY IN THE MARKETPLACE

CONTENTS: Perhaps you noticed what happened to 3Com yesterday. The analysts had forecast that they would do $115M–$120M for the quarter. They ended up at $112M. Seems like a small miss, except their stock dropped from $27 to $19!

The investment world is brutal right now; let's not give them a whack at us this quarter.

TO COMPLETE AR: FYI only.

We made our end-of-June target in 1989. We weren't so lucky in the fourth quarter of 1991—and the investment world took a big whack at us.

What did we do? Within a matter of days top management had submitted an in-depth report to the board of directors. The root cause of the poor quarter was obvious: We generated $4.7 million less revenue than we had forecast, which meant our profits were lower than expected. The report explained in excruciating detail what portion of that $4.7 million "revenue miss" was beyond our factory's control (expected orders that did not materialize) and what portion was based on shoddy execution (solid orders that didn't get out the door). We determined that $2.2 million of missed revenue was within our control.

Next, the report assigned responsibility for the $2.2 million miss by departments and product lines. What percentage could be traced to manufacturing? What percentage could be traced to marketing? What percentage could be traced to the SRAM group? What percentage to the logic group? And so on down the line. The idea was not to point fingers, but to paint a vivid picture of why things went wrong and what needed to be fixed. There's nothing like precise accountability to spark decisive action. Within weeks, we implemented a series of big organizational changes.

Third, we communicated our analysis and recommendations to everyone at Cypress. We convened a special companywide meeting and reviewed the report we had delivered to the board of directors. (Remember, *No Secrets*.) We showed unflattering excerpts from the latest Wall Street reports on Cypress. We unveiled a set of additional measures to get the company back on track.

Fourth, over the weeks that followed, as I met with analysts, investors, and the press, I accepted personal responsibility for the disappointment. A reporter from *USA Today* attended one of my presentations to investors soon after the quarter-end results. The next morning the newspaper's headline declared "Cypress Chief Takes Blame for Troubles." I asked my secretary to post the clipping on every bulletin board in the company. I was determined to keep the focus of scrutiny and criticism where it belonged—on the CEO.

Our disappointing fourth quarter turned out to be the first in a series of tough quarters—a real challenge to the record of uninterrupted growth in revenues and profits that we had established over six years. That challenge forced us to make a tough decision that qualified as our second big disappointment of last year. When we formed Cypress in 1983, we vowed that our company would be 100 percent American. In particular, we declared that we would not join Silicon Valley's exodus to assemble in foreign countries computer chips designed in the United States. For lots of solid business reasons (quicker turnaround, higher quality, shorter design-to-manufacturing cycles) as well as for just plain patriotism, we vowed to assemble our chips at home.

We held our ground on that pledge for nine years—until our financial performance could no longer justify it. The economics had simply become overwhelming. On one product alone our America-only policy was costing us $6 million per year. Across the company we were losing as much as $17 million per year by assembling at home. This for a company whose total (record) profits in 1991 were $34.2 million!

On May 13, 1992, we announced that we would transfer part of our chip assembly to a highly automated plant in Thailand and eliminate several hundred American jobs—the first layoffs in our history. Even after this decision, 90 percent of Cypress's people live and work in the United States. No other chip company of our size, and certainly none of the giants, can make that claim. Still, our decision closed the last computer-chip assembly line in Silicon Valley.

Which may be an instructive way to end the introduction to a book about doing things right in business. Championship boxers lose a round every once in a while. Championship companies lose rounds too: markets shift, people stumble, things change. The test of a company is not whether it never loses a round. The test is how quickly it dusts itself off and climbs back in the ring.

We don't claim to have definitive answers to the hard questions of management. What we have are management systems that work for us and that we believe can work for other companies, big and small, in lots of other industries. Plenty we do can be improved on. And there are plenty of ways to use what you read here without doing things just as we do them.

There is, however, one nonnegotiable prerequisite: an unshakable belief that your organization can win, and an insatiable desire to make it happen. People and companies are capable of a remarkably wide range of performance. What they achieve is almost always a function of the standards to which they are held. A sign above my desk reads BE REALISTIC—DEMAND THE IMPOSSIBLE. That's a pretty good theory of corporate success. Expect miracles and you will get them. Expect mediocrity and you will get it too.

Setting high standards sometimes means pounding a desk or firing someone who's just not doing the job. But consider the alternatives. My first job in the semiconductor business was with a company called American Microsystems (AMI). I signed on in 1973 and became chief memory-chip designer responsible for a new chip-making process I had invented at Stanford. AMI was a relaxed, supportive, nurturing environment. People seldom raised their voices, managers seldom held their people accountable. No one would mistake it for Cypress.

Over the next five years my operation lost $20 million. The technology just never really worked out. Right through to the day I left, I got pats on the back and words of encouragement. I deserved tough questions, but I never got them.

Today AMI is a Silicon Valley memory. The building where I worked has been dismantled, the land returned to orchards. It's like evolution in reverse. And that, to me, is the ultimate hypocrisy of warm-and-fuzzy cultures that don't deliver. Life is cordial right up to the day the company dies. Winning is what matters. And if winning means being tough, demanding, impatient, then that's what you have to be.

Too many American managers seem to prefer whining over winning. As a nation, we have been mesmerized and demoralized by some of the disastrous economic events of the past decade: the orgy of government debts and deficits, the huge trade gap, the painful humbling of the American auto industry. Everywhere we turn, we read chronicles of doom, especially when it comes to competing with Japan.

America has plenty of problems. But we also have plenty of strengths. And in terms of the economic and technological forces reshaping the world of competition, our strengths can carry the day. The era of the corporate juggernaut has passed. There is a new logic to competition: Think specialized, think flexible, think change. Small is not just beautiful, it is powerful.

What does this new, smaller-is-better logic have to do with management? *Everything.* Flexibility and creativity are not silver bullets shot from the guns of cowboy entrepreneurs. They are the result of tough-minded management. The way to win is to determine what your company has to do and to do it—all the time, every time, accepting no excuses along the way.

It's that simple. And that hard.

*　*　*

Our statement of values makes it plain: Success does not go to our heads. Inside Cypress we rarely talk about what's going right. How does that help us get ready for the next test? We focus on what's going wrong, where we can improve, how we can anticipate and react to emerging problems. Indeed, if an archivist combed through the thousands of memos and reports written over the past decade, he or she might conclude that Cypress has been on the verge of bankruptcy since the day it was founded.

In fact, by any objective measure we have been one of the fastest-growing companies in the semiconductor industry. We just don't talk about it very much—at least not internally.

This memo is one small illustration of how tough we can be on ourselves. We've disguised the names of Cypress people, but nothing else has been edited.

ACTION REQUEST　　　AR # ___5960___

FOR (ACTION):　　　VICE PRESIDENTS　　START: December 16, 1991

CC (INFORMATION):　　　　　　　　　DUE: December 24, 1991

FROM:　　T.J. RODGERS

TITLE:　　THE EMPLOYEE MEETING: A DISASTER OF MANAGEMENT
RESPONSE

CONTENTS:　　We all should be embarrassed to be part of "management" after our Thursday direct-labor employee meeting. We demonstrated collectively both by our past actions and by our current attitude that we really don't care about our direct-labor employees.

There are two old pieces of conventional wisdom that we certainly proved again in that meeting. The first is that you show how you feel by what you do, not by what you say. The second is that your employees are really smart, perhaps smarter than you are.

Consider how the meeting went from the perspective of our employees.

At first no one is willing to ask a question. They are afraid of being criticized for complaining. After a while, one woman asks another time about her group's proposal (which they have brought up to us many times) to have the shifts split

---

between Saturday and Sunday. In the prior meeting, on the third or fourth time the question was asked, I committed publicly to getting out a written, posted response. It was a big deal to them; they have been asking about it for quarters, and they <u>deserve</u> an answer—even if the answer is not favorable. But we again give no answer; we have "forgotten" again. I take a poll of the employees; most of them feel we have not responded to the issue. After the meeting, I discovered that we have written a policy memo on the issue, but the document has been put into a spec book and not distributed to employees; that's why the employees do not feel they have been answered. This story is a clear example of management ignoring its employees. It's a clear example of how our actions speak about our feelings more strongly than our words. Maybe our collective management asses were covered legalistically by some memo stuffed in a book somewhere. But if we had been dealing with <u>revenue</u>—something <u>really</u> important— we would have checked up to make sure that the desired result had happened. If we had been dealing with <u>wafers</u> <u>out</u>—something <u>really</u> important—we would have not tolerated the "I think I wrote a memo" answer from a supervisor who would have had his ass reamed out for such poor follow-up. Yet when it comes to an important request from our employees, we write a memo, forget about it, and never follow up to see if our employee-customers have been satisfied.

The next person asks a question about probation and warnings. She is clearly very concerned. I am amazed that she is brave enough to discuss her problems in a large meeting, because she is worried that we have a policy that could cause her to get fired for any infraction in the next six months. She clearly wants to stay at Cypress. She asks if our policy isn't a bit too strict, if it doesn't allow enough room for normal human behavior. Rich Clark knows the details of the policy. He states that the policy is that for one warning, there is a six-month probation; for a second warning, a second 60-day probationary period; for a third warning, possible termination. I reiterate that policy to the employee, who is visibly relieved and surprised. Just to check to see if our manufacturing management communication has failed again, I poll the employees. About two-thirds of them say they were unaware of the policy as described by Rich Clark. I check back again with Rich to make sure that I have heard him correctly and have not misstated the policy. Rich reconfirms the fact that the policy as stated is correct. Another employee asks why the policy wasn't posted. I tell the employee that I have discovered in my staff meeting that the way we handle policies is to create them in personnel, send them to policy books around the company, and forget them. There is no formal mechanism for communicating the company's policies to employees. I tell her that we have agreed to fix that problem. (Frankly, it is somewhat embarrassing for the president of a company to stand in front of employees and admit that the company—after eight years—still does not have a working system for communicating personnel policies to its employees.) The employee asks a follow-up question about personnel policies, which clearly implies that she feels that our policies are not distributed, so that management can make arbitrary ad hoc decisions on personnel issues. About 50% of the heads in the room nod approval. They don't trust us. They view us as classic "management." We are quite willing to be unfair. We don't

continued

want policies to be distributed because that would limit our flexibility to exercise our own discretion with employees.

Another employee asks for the obvious. She asks whether or not we could put together a small book of policies that relate to direct labor employees. The book would include policies on attendance, warnings, etc. It is an embarrassingly simple and obvious idea (this is one example of why they complain about management salaries). Sensing a chance to demonstrate to the employees that we do care, I ask the vice president of Human Resources (remember, he's the one who is supposed to care about people) to get the book out ASAP. His answer is that he can "get something out sometime in the middle of the first quarter." He might as well have said, "I'm real busy and helping these direct labor people understand the rules that could cause them to be fired really isn't too important."

A guy in the front holds up a set of Allen wrenches. In the last meeting—two full months ago—he came up to me after the meeting (he was embarrassed to talk in public) and asked me if it was Cypress's policy to ask people to buy tools to do their job as his supervisor told him. I said that it was not. I took him to John Jones, our test director, to make sure that the problem was corrected. John is supposed to be one of our most people-oriented managers. I figured that John would sense the opportunity to do something for one of the employees, clean up a problem; therefore, I didn't track the issue in my typical error-tight manner. The guy again holds up the Allen wrenches and says that he still has to buy his own tools, that he wonders if we have done anything yet. We then proceed to have a discussion about the PO system. Did the mean old PO system cause us not to order his Allen wrenches? Those tight systems are great excuses for "arbitrary meanness in management." However, in this case, we determine that the tools have been ordered; at least, somebody thinks that a PO has been signed. But did we close the loop? Did we show any care whether or not the employee's problem was solved? Did we seize this opportunity to show that we cared? No, we dropped the purchase order into "the system" and forgot it. Of course, if it had been something important—like test outs—we would have checked and double-checked to ensure the result. We would have used our Day-Timers (of which I bought hundreds last week) to close the loop. But his is just a chicken-shit problem which doesn't deserve real follow-up.

Fran Stuart, a valued employee who has been with us for almost seven years, then asks about her safety glasses. The company has directed that all employees have safety prescription glasses. She wants to know if her glasses have arrived yet, since she ordered them over a month ago. They are another victim of the Cypress PO system; no one knows the status. Too bad her glasses are not something important-like spare parts for a down piece of fab equipment. In that case, we would have been hammering on the source for late delivery, perhaps even expediting their president, as we have found effective.

A new employee says that she cannot figure out the information printed on her check. Mark Allen, who apparently has better instincts than the other members of the management team this day, scores some points by saying that he has never been able to figure out his check either. There are gales of laughter. Mark has managed to build a small bridge between "us" and "them" on an otherwise disastrous day. Before getting slapped over the head with it, I asked the obvious question, "Why isn't there a form for new employees to explain the information on their check?" The response is that we have a system, and that by filling out a card people are given information about what is on their checks. The new employee indicates that she <u>has</u> filled out the card, about a month ago. . . .

TO COMPLETE AR: People, our employees are smart—they can see right through our platitudes and can study our hollow actions. If Cypress is ever to become a great company, we on the management team must change the way we treat them.

People

how to hire the best

Great people alone don't guarantee corporate success—but no company can succeed without great people. This may sound like a truism, but few companies are as committed to and scientific about hiring as they are about perfecting the latest market-research techniques or financial maneuvers. Hiring is one of the most bureaucratic, arbitrary, and passive parts of corporate life. In part this is because great hiring is such hard work, harder than many other things a manager is asked to do. But it is also because many companies, despite their good intentions, are neither disciplined nor imaginative enough to make it happen right.

We have no choice but to make it happen. Finding, recruiting, and keeping great people is a struggle anywhere. But in Silicon Valley it is like guerrilla war. The vast majority of our recruits do not come directly out of universities or graduate schools. They must be pried away from our competitors or from companies in related businesses—companies that are eager to hang on to their best people. If we are looking to take a really top performer, someone, say, in the top 20 percent of a competitor's talent pool, guerrilla war turns into hand-to-hand combat.

This intense competition for people has forced us to develop a rigorously structured approach to hiring. At Cypress, hiring is a *process*, not an event. There are only eighteen people in the company—me, the twelve vice presidents, and the five subsidiary presidents—who are authorized to extend job offers. An offer comes at the end of a demanding evaluation process that takes place only after we prescreen a huge number of candidates. When we make an offer, the offer comes in person, in writing, and ready for the candidate's signature *on the spot.* Before the candidate goes home, we want a signed letter or absolute certainty that we have identified and removed all barriers to signing.

Our hiring system represents a decade's worth of thinking, revising, and improving. It works because it *must* work for this company to win—and it has had to work from the first day we started Cypress. Four of the company's six founders, including me, came from Advanced Micro Devices, one of the giant players in our business. Naturally, we expected that we would staff Cypress with some of the best and brightest from our alma mater. Just as naturally. AMD threatened us with a lawsuit. We reluctantly agreed not to hire AMD people for six months.

We immediately confronted a daunting challenge: how to stock up on top-flight people without hiring from a major source. Our solution was the raiding party, a technique we used to hire most of the first 300 people at Cypress. The process of creating the raiding party, perfecting it after several awkward starts, and then rolling it out across the country led to all of the procedures in our current hiring system.

The idea behind the raiding party was simple. In military terms, hiring is a small-unit tactic. In the early days of a startup, you need a handful of people to evaluate talent, sell the company, and deal with the worries and fears of recruits who are about to jump ship for a new venture. The raiding party's goal was to land in a city, scout out the top few hundred engineers and managers at a particular company, and leave with the ten very best people—the absolute cream of the crop. We started out in Texas. We hit Mostek in Dallas. We hit Texas Instruments in Dallas and then in Houston. We hit Motorola in Austin. Then we branched out. We hit Inmos and United Technologies in Colorado Springs, Intel in Phoenix and Portland. All told, over two years we dispatched more than a dozen raiding parties across the country.

We kept records (we still do) on how many people we were able to recruit from which companies. We reported regularly to the board of directors on our successes. (At that time our directors were venture capitalists eager to see us hire excellent people.) Different companies tended to be excellent in specific areas: AMD at marketing, National Semiconductor at low-cost manufacturing, Intel at product development.

Raiding parties became well-planned commando assaults. Let's say that our objective was to grab ten great people from a big chip company in Texas. We came to expect a "distillation factor" of 3 percent. In other words, if we wanted ten people we had to begin the screening with 300 people. We would hire a top headhunter to pass the word over the headhunter network: Cypress will be in town one month from today looking for good people. We never—*never*—used newspaper advertising, and to this day we don't allow it. We were looking for the hotshots, the stars, the people who are guaranteed to hear the jungle drums once they start beating. If someone was not "in the loop" enough to know we were coming to town, he or she was, by definition, not our kind of person.

The headhunters would collect 300 résumés over the course of a month and screen for "fatal flaws:" people who expected big housing allowances to move to Silicon Valley (we didn't offer them), people who absolutely would not leave their job without a big raise (we wouldn't pay it), people who expected us to find jobs for their spouses. A few of us would work from San Jose to help filter the résumés down to 60 or 75 real prospects. Then it was time to move. A team would fly out on a Monday morning: me, three Cypress vice presidents, two or three senior technical people, a secretary. On average, over the course of two or three days, we would conduct between five and nine interviews with each of the 60 or 75 candidates, extend formal job offers to the 11 we wanted, and come home with 10 new members of the team.

SWAT-team precision really mattered in these raids. You can imagine the logistics challenge: how to interview at the same time, in the same place, without anyone knowing who else was there, a vice president, a manager who works for that vice president, and two engineers who work for that manager. We would occupy rooms on six floors in a hotel. The candidates would arrive every fifteen minutes. Representatives from our headhunter would meet them at the door, whisk them to a holding room, and then escort them up a "safe" stairway or elevator to the appropriate floor.

(This delicate choreography caused a few problems during the early raids. So many of the recruiters were women and so many of the candidates were men that hotel security got suspicious about all the rendezvous in the lobby and all the rides up the elevator. The Dallas Marriott actually called the police on suspicion that we were running a prostitution ring. We quickly learned to notify security in advance about what was taking place.)

Then began an intense round of interviews. During the course of a day we'd shuttle candidates between floors as they went from technical interviews to sessions with the vice presidents. The pressures of time forced us to make precise, quick, sharp evaluations. As the day wore on, we would report to one another on what we were finding. It was virtually impossible to be alone in the room (there was always a candidate within earshot), so we developed code words that we would innocently drop into our conversations. If we discovered fatal problems with a candidate, we'd use the code to indicate that he wasn't to continue.

Likewise, when we found a real star, we had to let others know what we thought it would take to close the deal. For these communications we used "fish" codes: trout, bass, and catfish.

Fish codes? When a trout grabs a fly, the hook just barely penetrates its very thin lips. It often jumps out of the water and can flip the hook off its mouth. Translation: "A trophy: Real tough to catch, but I'm working on it."

Then there were bass. A bass is a big strong white fish. It always hooks itself right in the palate and gives you a good fight, but unless you do something stupid, you can always reel him in. Translation:

"We have to be careful with this one, but the odds are very good we've got him."

Then there were catfish. You catch catfish by putting a hook with a big glob of worms on the bottom of a pond. Catfish literally swallow the hook. Translation: "This one's in the bag."

It's a bit awkward to slip a fish reference into an otherwise serious conversation with a colleague, but we managed.

After three days of evaluations and late-night dinners to debate the merits of particular candidates, we would make our decisions, print out formal offer letters with salary, stock options, and start date, and get signatures. The net result: With the investment of three intense days from six to ten Cypress people, we walked away with the company's ten best entrepreneurs—a colossal catastrophe for them and a fabulous coup for us.

Raiding parties helped us hone a set of corporate skills that remain valuable today. It's like working on big Wall Street deals; once you perfect the techniques and understand how to manage through the manic atmosphere, the skills never leave. In fact, we used those skills two years ago when we bought that semiconductor plant in Minnesota from Control Data. It was our biggest acquisition ever, and we faced the prospect of evaluating hundreds of former Control Data people before we could get the plant up and running.

The answer? Re-create the raiding party, this time on a grander scale. We put 26 Cypress people on airplanes, including me and all of our vice presidents, and interviewed 109 candidates over several days of marathon sessions. We made 65 offers, received 65 acceptances, and opened for business quicker than anyone expected.

More important, our early raiding parties became a laboratory in which to experiment with and perfect the hiring strategies and tactics we are about to describe. We used to marvel at the big companies from whom we were taking people with impunity. They screwed up all the time, and better yet for us, they screwed up *predictably*, each company with its own bad habits and patterns.

Today, ten years later, Cypress employs nearly 1,500 people. But our philosophy of hiring, and the system that puts the philosophy into practice, is a direct outcome of what we learned on our trips to

Dallas, Austin, Phoenix, and other cities. We have developed carefully documented, ironclad rules about how to screen candidates, evaluate them, check references, and close the deal.

I know the entire organization is implementing the system because no one can bring in a new employee, no matter the rank, without submitting a "hiring book" that documents the entire process. The first page of every hiring book is a checklist of thirty-five specific steps and procedures (see the hiring checklist below). The book itself includes detailed results of interviews, reference checks, and career prospects.

Until we reached one thousand employees, I read a synopsis of every one of those books before we made a job offer. I now share that task with thirteen other senior managers. But our commitment to compliance still holds. In no more than fifteen minutes, with no verbal communication whatsoever, any one of us can determine whether or not a hiring manager has followed our procedures, guaranteeing that a good job has been done. If not, the hire becomes an "exception."

HIRING CHECKLIST

CANDIDATE NAME: _____

☐ OPEN REQUISITION   HIRING MANAGER: _____

☐ TELEPHONE INTERVIEW (especially for out-of-town people)

☐ FIRST INTERVIEW: Date: _____

    ☐ Prepare Interview Folder With All Forms (Dept. Secretary)
    ☐ Employment Application
    ☐ Resume (Handwritten OK) in Folder
    ☐ Cypress Slide Presentation—Initials of person delivering slide presentation _____
                  (initial)
    ☐ Cypress Information Package Given Out
    ☐ Technical Interview #1, Evaluation Sheet
    ☐ Technical Interview #2, Evaluation Sheet
    ☐ Hiring VP Interview (fatal problems, technical, personality, career path, referral), Evaluation Sheet, Career Path Sheet

- [ ] Second VP Interview (fatal problems, technical, personality), Evaluation Sheet
- [ ] Group Interview (see Matrix for required classifications)
- [ ] Applicant Declared to Have Passed or Failed Technical Interviews [ ] Pass [ ] Fail
- [ ] Verified Referral Award Entitlement with Applicant

- [ ] Non-disclosure Agreement [ ] Waived
- [ ] Career Path Questionnaire [ ] Exempt
                                 [ ] Non Exempt

- [ ] REFERENCE CHECKS (Absolute minimum of two)

- [ ] PREPARATION FOR SECOND INTERVIEW (VP reports to TJR)

  - [ ] Interview Strategy Defined Prior to Interview (career path, relocation, sensitivities)
  - [ ] Offer Approval Form Filled Out
  - [ ] New Hire: Equity Evaluation Form
  - [ ] Paperwork Quality Verification (Department Secretary) _____
  - [ ] Paperwork Quality Verification (TJR Secretary) _____
  - [ ] Offer Letter Typed, Signed Through VP, Put in Folder
  - [ ] Offer Letter Quality Verification (TJR Secretary) _____

- [ ] SECOND INTERVIEW

  - [ ] Schedule Second Interview
  - [ ] TJR Interview

  - [ ] Offer   [ ] Reject   Date: _____

  Total Number of Interviews: _____

- [ ] FACILITY REQUIREMENTS

  - [ ] Phone   Location   [ ] San Jose
  - [ ] Office   [ ] Other
  - [ ] Cubicle Office

Not so long ago, for example, one of our vice presidents submitted a hiring book that violated one of our cardinal rules: We don't offer big raises for people who join the company. The hiring book was sent to me as an exception. His explanation was one I've heard dozens of times before: "At my old company, we had to give people big raises to convince them to sign on." My response was unequivocal: "We've been in business for eight years, and we've hired thousands of people with this system. Is there any reason we can't hire the next person the same way?" The vice president then resubmitted the hiring book two weeks later, and it still contained an out-of-policy raise. To emphasize my point, I tracked down a big pair of scissors, cut the book neatly in half, and mailed it back to him. He now does it right the first time. (And his secretary helps him do it right, to avoid the reconstruction hassle.)

The hiring book also serves as an important tool for learning. We give no raises to about 3 percent of our employees every year, a sign that they are low performers. This company would die if 3 percent of the products we shipped were defective. We strive for 100 percent quality in manufacturing; we have the same goal for hiring. In many cases, when an employee leaves because of poor performance, we send his or her manager the hiring book, ask how we might have spotted the problem prior to hiring, and use the departure as an opportunity to improve our procedures. (For example, a lesson we learned early on is that a few in-depth reference checks are much more valuable than lots of superficial reference checks.)

Many of our managers, especially those who aren't as good at hiring as they should be, complain about the system and criticize it as bureaucratic. After all, what can be more rigid than a binder full of forms and checklists? In fact, our system, and the hiring book, is a vaccine *against* bureaucracy. It is an enabling tool that energizes and disciplines the process—a tool that documents to everyone who needs to know that the evaluation has been thorough, crisp, and smart.

RECRUITING: MANAGERS AS TALENT SCOUTS

Good hiring may be tough, but it's not complicated. Three guiding principles are at the core of our system.

First, we believe that the only way to hire outstanding talent is for managers themselves to find and attract the talent they need. As

I've said, the only people with final hiring authority at Cypress are me and our thirteen vice presidents. But all managers at Cypress have hiring *responsibility*. If one of these managers gets the authorization to add an individual contributor, it is up to *that manager*, not the human resource staff, to locate candidates, prescreen them before they enter the formal evaluation process, and monitor the process as it unfolds. Human resources maintains a database of résumés and plays a modest role in suggesting candidates. But it plays almost no role in evaluating them. Indeed, prospective employees don't see anyone in HR until they report to work and fill out their insurance applications.

Most companies—especially big companies—do just the opposite. Managers sit behind their desks and wait for personnel to begin the parade of candidates. Of course, personnel is never as motivated as the hiring manager is to fill an open slot. As the hiring schedule falls behind, the manager grows increasingly desperate and makes an offer to the first warm body that meets rudimentary requirements. This approach guarantees that the quality of the company's workforce will nicely (and disastrously) mirror the quality of the available labor pool. The organization inexorably drifts toward average.

What's more, this passive approach to hiring virtually guarantees that executives will lose touch with the job market. In semiconductors, as in most industries, there are multiple, complex markets for the different types of people who make up a company. Product engineers, process engineers, technicians, and sales and marketing people have different skills, run in different professional circles, value different career opportunities. Regular interaction with the outside world generates valuable intelligence on the unique dynamics of these markets.

Not every manager is comfortable with hiring responsibility. Many junior managers see hiring as a burden rather than an opportunity to staff their own team. So they hang back. Or they try to delegate hiring vertically ("maybe my boss will worry about filling the slot") or horizontally to personnel. Or they make "downward-spiral" excuses: "I'm so busy, I don't have time to hire anybody to help me out."

ACTION REQUEST   AR #   4395

FOR (ACTION):   John S.   START: May 17, 1990
CC (INFORMATION):   DUE: May 22, 1990
FROM: T.J. RODGERS
TITLE: ADVERTISING AS A BARRIER TO HIRING

CONTENTS: Yesterday, I noted your comments that not advertising was a barrier to hiring. All of the empirical data at Cypress over seven years says that opinion is wrong. We have put together the entire company without formal, paid advertising and, therefore, you certainly have no barrier in hiring people to work for you. On the four occasions in seven years when I was reconvinced to give advertising another try, we spent thousands of dollars in the *San Jose Mercury News* and hired zero people in the last three tries. The first try netted one thousand resumes (back when we were a hot startup) and only one hire. Every time we form a subsidiary, the president of that subsidiary comes up with a wonderful "new" idea to advertise. Each time, he wastes money and nets no new hires.

With regard to your opinion that Cypress has to be known via advertising, do you really believe that burying yet another ad in the many pages of ads in the *San Jose Mercury News* will cause Cypress to be known better than it already is? We are a very well-known company with only the older, larger companies being more well-known than us. In order to get known, a company needs to be in the news. We are in the news a lot—a lot more than AMD or National and probably second only to Intel. We are in the news in a positive way, and that free advertising is very much more effective than some blurb about "advancing your career" buried on page 29.

If you take a look at Tony Alvarez's organization, you will see that Cypress has built one of the strongest technical organizations in the world without any advertising whatsoever. I think it's time for you to re-read a memo I wrote some years back when complaints about lack of advertising and other imagined barriers to hiring were running around Cypress. It tells why advertising and buying people with high raises is counter-productive to good hiring. I have attached a copy of that memo to this AR.

TO COMPLETE AR: FYI only.

Managers who fail to scout for talent (and thus have trouble finding good recruits) often object to our prohibition against advertising as a vehicle to attract people. Here's a typical reaction to such objections.

The power of our system is that it doesn't allow middle managers to defeat themselves. Managers understand that not filling open slots is one of the quickest ways to fail as a manager in our company.

Hiring, like most everything else in business, is an acquired skill. The more people you interview, evaluate, and select, the better you get at interviewing, evaluating, and selecting. We've developed a good feel for the employment "hit rate." It takes ten prescreen telephone interviews, each lasting fifteen minutes or so, to find one person good enough to enter the formal evaluation process. Of those who start the formal process, 25 percent receive offers, and about 85 percent of them accept. The bottom line: Managers will need to make about 100 telephone calls to wind up with two great people they can hire. By the way—and this is important—the system imposes a "time clock" that starts ticking the moment a requisition is approved. If a manager doesn't fill an open slot by the end of the quarter in which it was approved, he loses the requisition and has to justify the position again.

So even the most reluctant middle manager quickly understands the importance of scouting. It's not all that different from assembling a professional sports team. A good manager is always nosing around for talent, always collecting business cards, always calling people on the phone. "How's it going? Word is there was a bit of a shakeup in your department." No promises, no offers, at most a few hints of opportunities at Cypress. But lots of questions, genuine interest, and plenty of continuing, collegial contact.

The savvy manager who is always scouting has an inventory of good prospects once a slot does open up. If she learns in mid-January that she has authorization to bring on two new people, she leaps into action. The poor manager, who hasn't been scouting, panics. "How do I make 100 phone calls in ten weeks?" Then he complains about the "bureaucratic" system. "Why doesn't personnel give me more résumés? Why can't I get money to hire a headhunter?"

Maintaining a commitment to scouting is a real challenge for us. All our managers are under the gun, and it takes genuine long-term thinking to invest time to find people we may not be able to hire for six or nine months. My sense is that all our vice presidents and subsidiary presidents know what it takes to do a good job of scouting and are committed to it. Probably half the people who report to vice presidents know what it takes, and probably very few people below that. We are constantly preaching, cajoling, training, and trying to lead by example. As we get bigger, and hiring responsibility flows to more and more managers, it is critical that we drive the commitment to scouting further down the organization.

INTERVIEWING: BIG GUNS AND THE PACK OF WOLVES

Scouting creates a stable of prospects. Once a requisition opens up, these prospects must be thoroughly and rigorously evaluated—our second principle of hiring. Quality interviewing may be the most difficult part of the hiring process, something most managers are terrible at. We've developed a set of techniques and procedures to keep interview sessions useful and productive. The hiring book documents that these techniques are used and used effectively.

Just as the key to effective scouting is to keep things loose and informal, the key to successful interviewing and evaluation is to keep things substantive and rigorous. A candidate should perceive the start of the evaluation process as a watershed date: "Last Monday I went to Cypress. When I arrived I was met immediately in the lobby and given an agenda. That agenda contained the names and titles of all the people I would interview with and the topics of our interviews. The sessions were tough—grueling, even—but I survived. And every day since, the manager who brought me in has been in contact by phone and kept me posted on the process."

How do we create that kind of mindset in our candidates? First, we use the big guns. If a company wants its job candidates to know that it is serious, high-ranking executives *must* get involved in the interview process. No one, including the direct labor force, gets into Cypress without a minimum of four interviews. All candidates for exempt positions, whether or not they are senior enough to report to vice presidents, must go through at least six interviews, including an interview with a vice president. I interview all candidates who would report to vice presidents as well as many important individual contributors who report to managers.

I learned the importance of the "big-guns" technique from Jerry Sanders at Advanced Micro Devices. When I was considering joining AMD, the first day I walked in the door the receptionist in a building of several thousand people smiled and said, "Oh, yes, Dr. Rodgers, Jerry is waiting for you." She took me right upstairs—no waiting in the lobby—and our sessions began. That's the way to communicate to job prospects how valuable they are.

Second, we make interviews tough and technically demanding, even for people we know we want. We are a hard-charging company in a tough business and we have a no-nonsense way of communicating. All too often, a slam-dunk candidate—the education is right, the résumé is right, the personality is right—walks through the door and gets an eight-hour sales pitch. That demeans the company and the candidate. The quickest way to lose a top-flight prospect is the no-substance backslap interview. Who wants to be part of an organization that grovels to have you as a member?

The best way to sell your company is to make it as tough as hell to get in. When a candidate, no matter how outstanding, walks into Cypress, the first message he or she hears is "We're Cypress, we work hard, and you're not going to get a raise to join up. Should we continue?"

Third, we structure a series of interviews to probe for technical capabilities and work ethic. On the day he reports to Cypress for the evaluation, a candidate receives what we call the "Cypress Welcomes" form that communicates several important messages. It lists the technical skills the job requires, information taken directly from the detailed requirements of the personnel requisition, so there is no misunderstanding about qualifications. It lists the managers with whom the candidate will be interviewing, complete with titles, to communicate the importance we attach to these sessions. It also lists the basic questions for each session, to focus the interviews and alert the candidates to how rigorous they will be.

After several technically oriented interviews and sessions with a vice president, candidates go through what we call the "pack-of-wolves" session. The tone is aggressive but not abusive. The applicant sits in a conference room with several senior technical people. They pepper him with difficult questions while he's standing at a blackboard. When the candidate makes a mistake, they point out that it *was* a mistake and why. We will sweat a candidate for forty-five minutes in this pressurized environment. Answers we hate: B.S. Answers we love: "I don't know, but here's how I would think through solving the problem."

Tough as it sounds, the pack-of-wolves session has been an excellent tool to weed out otherwise qualified managers and engineers who can't take the rigors of our business.

Fourth, we insist that interviews generate detailed written assessments of strengths and weaknesses, not vague oral impressions. Interviews are only as valuable as their impact on the formal evaluation process. All our interview evaluation forms, which are part of the hiring book, include numerical rankings (on a scale of zero to five) that directly mirror the technical qualifications on the requisition.

Our people are tough graders, especially since they were graded tough when they came aboard. I call it the "Cal Tech effect." New students who arrive at Cal Tech experience culture shock. At home they were superstars: valedictorians, physics geniuses, chess champions. At Cal Tech they are one of many; the bar has been raised. Nearly everyone adjusts to the new height of the bar, and most thrive. Our people believe the same goes for Cypress. They don't mind delivering that message.

For candidates whom I see, I require that the hiring vice president (remember, only vice presidents are authorized to extend offers) write an interview strategy before my session. That strategy highlights the specific strengths and weaknesses of the candidate, particular concerns he or she has expressed about the job or the company, and other critical issues. I always share the numerical evaluations from earlier interviews with the candidate, especially one who has been assessed as weak in a particular area. Good people know their weaknesses, appreciate companies that understand them, and are eager to work for companies that can improve on them.

Fifth, we probe carefully for cultural mismatches. Most companies claim to do this, but few are very systematic. The vice presidents emphasize work attitudes and career goals in their interview sessions. But we also use another tool: a questionnaire that requires brief but direct answers to open-ended questions about motivation, character, and aspirations. I wrote the "career-path questionnaire" myself in fall 1985 after we had to fire five of our fifty assembly operators—the first and only time we've taken such a step—when they refused to work overtime at the end of a quarter we were struggling to make. They were young, immature, and this was the first time anyone had asked them to do anything hard. Rather than rise to the occasion, they buckled under the pressure and hurt the organization.

We wanted to avoid a repeat situation. So we went back and carefully reviewed all five hiring books. The books read like gold; there was no hint that this kind of problem might arise. Obviously we needed to improve the system. I created an instrument to help us anticipate these cultural problems.

The career-path questionnaire plays two roles. It is a reality check on a candidate's expectations and aspirations, and it alerts us to "bad apples." It forces the candidate to be as specific as possible about hard-to-quantify issues that are addressed only obliquely, if at all, in most evaluation processes. Among the questions are: How is the morale in your company or department? Why? What would your boss say is your best attribute? What would the "needs improvement" section of your performance review address? Can you describe your personal experience with a difficult boss, peer, or subordinate?

This questionnaire has been effective at raising warning flags. I once interviewed a candidate after he gave an odd answer to the question "What are you most proud of?" During the interview I kicked back and asked him to elaborate on what he had said in the questionnaire. He then proceeded to regale me for twenty minutes about his skills as a political infighter: "I took on the head of my department, wound up with half his responsibilities and half his people, and my boss was very happy because this guy was a jerk and he deserved it."

I thanked him very much for considering Cypress and told him we'd get back to him. Then I scribbled a short note to the hiring vice president and attached it to the hiring book: "How did this guy *ever* make it to my office?"

Sixth, we take reference checks very seriously. Reference checks are one of the most universal, and most universally ignored, parts of hiring. Our system requires at least two reference checks, and we expect the checks to be candid and thorough. As with interviews, reference checks must lead to detailed written evaluations that become part of the hiring book.

Reference checks are a critical part of the evaluation process, not just (or even primarily) for what they reveal about the candidate, but for their role as a feedback loop. This point is important and almost always overlooked. Reference checks are a powerful way to manage a candidate's expectations as the process unfolds. More than 80 percent of the time, the minute you hang up the phone with a reference, that person will call the candidate and debrief them. Even with people you know you want, the key is to use the reference check to keep them anxious and interested, to maintain "share of mind" as the days pass, and to impress upon them Cypress's thoroughness and attention to detail.

Finally, we expect speed. No matter how tough and thorough the evaluation process, it must also be done quickly. There's no reason that a manager, having prescreened someone by telephone, can't bring him in for two rounds of interviews and make a hire/no-hire decision within one week—two weeks at the outside. We don't meet this goal as consistently as we should, and as we have grown, delays have become more of a problem. But the entire organization knows that our target time frame is one week, that we expect it to be met, and that the founders did it time and again during the raiding parties.

We have another inviolate principle of hiring: We don't buy employees. This is uncommon in Silicon Valley, but at Cypress it serves as an excellent Darwinian screen. Someone who will join Cypress for a few percentage points more in salary or a better dental plan is not the kind of career-oriented person we want. Good people want to be paid fairly, in a way that reflects the organization's success over the long term (i.e., stock options). They are rarely concerned with earning an excessive amount of money relative to their peers. What drives them is the desire to win.

Until 1986, therefore, we had a very simple policy: A candidate who received a raise from a previous employer within the last four months came to Cypress without a raise. Period. We now offer a non-negotiable 8 percent prorated increase, but the basic premise holds. We do not bid for great talent; people with great talent come to Cypress because they want to win. Members of our team are rewarded with stock options and the highest-percentage raises in the industry. We know money matters. But we have no interest in being a temporary stop for a "Silicon Valley Gypsy" who travels from company to company, spending a year at each one, bumping up his salary by 15 percent each time.

We are serious about this, and our people communicate it from the very beginning: "If you come to Cypress, be prepared to come over flat." We don't allow people to play games. Indeed, at the bottom of our employment application form is a legal authorization that allows Cypress to verify the applicant's salary history. Managers have told me that candidates for high-ranking positions, people making over $100,000 per year, will voluntarily hand them pay stubs to document their salaries! We don't want or expect people to do that, but it certainly is a sign that they get the message.

CLOSING THE DEAL: IF PAPER FLOWS, THE BODY SHOWS

Hiring is not just about policies and procedures, interviews and offers. It is also about mindset. In Silicon Valley, and I suspect in all kinds of industries, getting the right person to sign an offer letter is often the beginning of the hiring process and not the end. Remember, joining Cypress means *leaving* another company, often a respected and successful company like Intel or Motorola. Hiring can become an intense battle for the hearts and minds of talented recruits. Our goal is simple: "If paper flows, the body shows."

The way to win this battle is to be prepared to fight it from the start. In our evaluation process, the executive with hiring authority always has a completed offer letter ready for a signature when he meets the candidate for the final session. If the candidate makes the grade, the hiring manager unveils the letter and presents it to the candidate. If we've done everything right, that little ceremony touches off a flood of emotions. One emotion is relief: "These guys are really tough; I'm glad it's over." Another is excitement: "These guys are winners, I'm glad I made the grade." These emotions create an important psychological break from the old company. But the key step, right at the time of the offer, is to prepare the candidate for the three emotions immortalized by IBM in a different context: fear, uncertainty, and doubt.

At the best companies, a valued employee's decision to join a rival triggers an intense campaign to win a reversal. So we go through an entire process to alert our recruit about what to expect. "Sure you're coming over here," I'll say. "But let me tell you what's going to happen. You're going to tell your boss and he is going to flip. He is going to put you in a room and isolate you. Then he's going to bring in his boss, and his boss's boss—hell, he'll even bring in the CEO. You're going to be in a room all day, and they're going to turn you into Jell-O. Eventually you're going to whine and whimper and say, 'I give up. I'll stay here.' "

Of course, someone who has just decided to sign up with Cypress and charge into the future is going to be indignant at that challenge. They'll bang their fist on the table and assure me, "When I quit, I quit. I'm a person of integrity."

"It's nothing personal," I'll say gently and a bit condescendingly. "But I've seen a lot of people turned into Jell-O. Those guys are very good at mind games."

Then I coach the recruit on how to quit. Many recruits, especially after being warned about the counterattack, want to take the chicken's way out and slip a note into the boss's in basket at five P.M. on a Friday. We can't let people do that. We fight tough but we fight fair. We respect our competition and we don't want people sneaking out under cover of darkness.

Our instructions are clear: "You quit at eight A.M. on a Monday. You give them the whole week to talk you out of it. Listen politely to what they have to say. We know you've made the right decision, and that you'll end up here. But you can't screw a great company, and you've got to respect your boss. You've got to play by the rules."

These warnings and instructions do two things. First, they persuade the employee to act properly, which is not only right but to our advantage. A corporate rival will fight harder to keep someone who tried to sneak out because they think you've put them up to it; never underestimate the power of competitive anger. Second, and this is more important, our actions put Cypress above the fray. "*We're* not responsible for the extraordinary pressure you're about to experience; your old company is responsible. *They're* the ones who will turn your next week into a living hell."

Here, too, the agility of a small company proves to be a real strength. We treat these matchups like judo: We know our opponents, we know how they are going to react, and we turn their reaction to our advantage.

For example, in the 1980s, National Semiconductor always reacted in one of two contradictory ways: Either they threw the guy out on the street or they tried to bribe him. Both reactions were counterproductive. Let's say we're romancing some hot recruit and he's agonizing over the decision to leave. National finds out, stuffs his belongings in a box, and calls in a Neanderthal guard to walk him out. Not much of a question as to where he winds up! But even the other extreme—a huge raise—is offensive. In fact, it is a classic argument for why a person should leave. I've made this speech a hundred times: "If you are worth 20 percent more than what you get, why didn't your company do right by you *before* you quit?"

Every so often we have more of a challenge. If we really want somebody, and we know the other side is going to fight like hell, we turn big-company predictability to our advantage. Let's say (hypothetically) that the company is Intel, which is famous in Silicon Valley for its methodical system for retaining valued employees who decide to leave. In fact, we have borrowed some of Intel's techniques in creating our own system for reversing resignations.

On a few occasions I have added nuances to my resignation coaching. "You know, after they turn you to Jell-O, you *are* going to cave in," I'll predict.

"Why?" the recruit will ask.

"Well, you're making sixty thousand right now. We've offered you sixty thousand and a stock-option chance to make a lot of upside money. What if Intel offers you a big raise and *a lot* of extra stock? I'm not saying they will, but what if they do? You know we can't change our offer. So you're going to be sitting there, looking at more stock and more money. And then you're going to have to decide: Do you love your principles or do you love money? What are you going to do then?"

Of course, I know in advance that Intel has an ironclad policy against such counteroffers, which is, by the way, exactly the right policy. All Intel does is put him in a room, beat the stuffing out of him (which is *their* fault since I told him it was going to happen), and then come back and beat him up some more. Guess where he winds up!

It all comes back to judo. The fatal problem with a big company, especially in these hand-to-hand battles, is that it is easily outmaneuvered by a small company. On one side sits a team of savvy senior managers tailoring their arguments to the hopes and fears of a real live person. On the other side is a bureaucracy on automatic pilot. Even a benevolent and efficient bureaucracy is still a bureaucracy. It's no surprise who wins.

We learned early on about the importance of creativity and fast response. Lothar Maier, president of our Minnesota subsidiary, wears badge number 10 at Cypress. Lothar was our first manager of process engineering, a critical job for a semiconductor manufacturer. He was a vital addition to the management team—and we almost didn't get him.

Failure would have meant disaster. For one thing, we needed Lothar's talent. But there was an ever bigger issue at stake. When it comes to hiring, a startup can't ever lose. This was our first run at Intel, a giant from whom we planned to take other top performers. If a new company recruits someone from a big-company rival, and that big company convinces the employee to stay, that big company becomes highly immune to recruiting. It's like having an organizational antibody. The other side has demonstrated that you can be beaten, has a living witness to testify to the defeat, and all the "good" reasons for it.

Our point man on Lothar was Dr. Mike Starnes, one of our founders, an Intel veteran and Cypress's resident guru on hiring. We made Lothar a good offer, and he accepted and gave Intel notice. Then came an eerie silence. Mike would call Lothar every day (an important element of our system), and Lothar would assure him that things were fine, that he'd be reporting as scheduled.

It all seemed too easy—and it was. Intel was putting the squeeze on Lothar, and like many recruits he was keeping the pressures bottled up. Mike called Lothar late in the afternoon of his last day at Intel, and he gave us the disastrous news: "Sorry, I just can't make the move."

Mike's response was immediate: "We're not going to let you do that. T.J. and I are coming to see you." We jumped in a car, turned onto Route 237 (a parking lot sometimes incorrectly described as a freeway), and slowly made our way to Lothar's house.

That trip inaugurated Cypress's tradition of the home visit. On a home visit, two senior managers descend on a wavering recruit's house and talk to him, his wife, his neighbors—whoever's there. We're insistent, persistent, but we don't pressure too much. Over and over again we make the objective case for joining Cypress: more responsibility, more impact on the organization, more exciting projects. We don't leave until we've got a renewed commitment to signing on. Our success rate with home visits is 50 percent—a remarkable track record given that we're going after people who are otherwise lost. In effect, people who need to be raised from the dead.

We also did this visit in style. Perhaps because he sensed problems, or perhaps just to prepare for Lothar's arrival at Cypress, Mike had ordered a batch of new business cards for Lothar. As it looked like we were winning Lothar back, coming close to reaffirming our original deal, Mike ceremoniously broke out the business cards and presented one to the newest member of the team: "Lothar Maier, Process Engineering Manager, Cypress Semiconductor." It was a nice personal touch that meant a lot at the time; we still joke about it as a "sleazy-but-just-acceptable" recruiting technique.

I'll put our hiring system up against any other system I know. But I'm not blind to our problems and shortcomings in execution. As Cypress has grown, we have fallen away from the system in countless small ways. Hiring today is not nearly as crisp as it was in the days of the raiding party. Too many people follow the system but don't understand or embrace its animating spirit. Too many people believe Cypress is big and successful enough that we can "afford" a slipup or two in hiring; some of the pressure is off.

This is unacceptable. I expect this organization to be even *more* effective at hiring than when we started. After all, we have a ten-year record of growth, an organization with more products, more factories, more opportunities. Still, I worry about maintaining the sense of urgency about hiring that was so palpable in the early days.

One way to guard against slippage is to track it. Every quarter we measure the "hit rate" on job offers, that is, what percentage of candidates to whom we make offers come to Cypress. I receive a quarterly report with the overall corporate average, the average by vice president, the average by location (San Jose, Texas, Minnesota), and the average in manufacturing by department. The report tracks every quarter since the day Cypress was founded. Our quarterly hit-rate performance has been remarkably consistent over the years—almost always within a few points of 85 percent.

Equally important, we track how good we are at meeting our goals for the mechanics of the system. We conduct a written survey on *every* job candidate who comes through, whether hired or not. The survey is neither random nor anonymous. If an applicant was left cooling his heels in the lobby for twenty minutes, we want to know. If he had a vague and unproductive interview, we want to know. We use that data, which we also analyze quarterly, to identify managers who need to improve their hiring skills and vice presidents whose organizations are slipping.

We are always searching for ways to improve execution in the hiring system. Recently, for example, I got a letter from a candidate who was very upset. The letter was polite, but the basic message was clear: "Let me tell you how screwed up your company is and how furious I am." He offered a series of minor (but perfectly legitimate) complaints about sitting in the lobby too long and having appointments jerked around at the last minute.

I immediately checked out the letter; it turned out to be unfortunately accurate. I read the letter out loud at my staff meeting; the vice presidents winced as they heard the particulars (especially as they guessed which of them "owned" the abomination). Then I announced the name of the hiring manager at fault. He was, it turns out, an inexperienced manager, so it was hard to pin the rap for this episode on his vice president. But I did.

The outcome: That vice president now runs a companywide program to improve training for the hiring system. After all, there's no commitment like the commitment of a convert.

reviews and raises: how to sustain outstanding performance

Most great people don't work just for money. And no amount of money on its own can inspire and sustain great performance. Yet money *does* matter. Everyone wants feedback on performance, and most feedback, directly or indirectly, involves money.

The most common source of financial feedback is the annual raise. Raises have a direct and universal impact on an organization. Done right, they allow managers to energize their best people and send constructive messages to their weak performers. All too often, though, raises generate confusion and discontent for everyone.

There are at least three classic problems that keep managers from granting raises effectively. For one thing, most managers aren't very scientific about evaluating their people. They may be able to identify their real stars and their weakest links, but the vast majority of people get lost somewhere in the middle. Moreover, even if they're good at evaluating people, managers can lack the courage of their convictions. They try to spread raises around evenly in a misguided effort to keep everyone happy. This damaging tendency—succumbing to the "mediocrity of the mean"—saps the morale of standouts and sends the wrong signals to people who need to improve.

Finally, and most widespread, managers often fail to distinguish between raises based on merit and those given for equity. Merit refers to that portion of a raise awarded for the quality of last year's contribution; the basic goal is to reward outstanding contributors regardless of current salaries. Equity refers to that portion of a raise awarded to smooth out salary disparities among peers; the basic goal is to promote equal pay for equal performance. Merit and equity each have their place, but confusing the two makes for mushy logic, counterproductive results, and dissatisfied people.

Cypress managers are not immune to these problems. I'd say that one-third of our vice presidents still don't have a good gut feel for how to review performance and award raises. But I'm not too concerned about that. Our "focal-review" process, one of the most efficient systems we've ever developed, guards against unscientific ranking, the mediocrity of the mean, and confusion over merit and equity. It can't substitute for good judgment, but it can flag bad habits.

The power of our system is its simplicity and consistency. An easy-to-use software application (it runs on Lotus 1-2-3) guides managers on a step-by-step journey through the evaluation and reward process. It helps us apply our pay-for-performance principles *without usurping managerial discretion.* This is important. New Cypress managers sometimes react to the system with suspicion and apprehension: Does the computer give my people raises? Is some corporate Big Brother looking over my shoulder? Will top management second-guess my decisions? The answer to all three questions is no. The computer processes information, organizes it, displays it, and helps managers reach decisions sensibly, accurately, and consistently. It alerts them to big and obvious mistakes (for example, giving someone a negative raise or exceeding their budget) and to decisions that violate basic company guidelines (for example, giving a top performer an average raise). Beyond that, all power resides in the hands of the manager.

The system also creates a paper trail that managers can use to explain their decisions. This feature is one of its biggest benefits. Our philosophy compels managers to think long and hard about how they allocate their precious raise dollars. That sometimes means having to deliver bad news (in other words, a low raise) to people who deserve it so they can afford to deliver good news (a high raise) to people who earn it. Most people will accept and learn from a raise they are unhappy with so long as they understand the logic behind it. Our system requires managers to think through that logic on a person-by-person basis.

Inside Cypress we sometimes hear complaints about how "tough" the focal-review system and software are, how they force managers to make uncomfortable decisions. That's wrong—there is an important distinction between the *software* and the *philosophy* of raises behind it. There is nothing in our focal-review software to prevent different companies from building wildly different philosophies into it. By revising a handful of key assumptions, I can use the same software to generate a pattern of raises that ranges from communism to laissez-faire capitalism and anything in between. Needless to say, our assumptions are closer to those of Adam Smith than to Karl Marx. And it is our basic principles, not the software, that sometimes compel managers to make decisions that make them uncomfortable.

Four simple principles are at the core of our approach to evaluations and raises:

Every group of peers in the company, no matter the organizational level, receives the same average percentage raise. Every year senior management and the board of directors settle on a total corporate allowance for raises. We review our revenue and profit forecasts, survey compensation trends among our competitors, and settle on a budget that lets us live within our means, but typically still lets us pay the highest average raise in the industry.

In a great year like 1984, the corporate raise budget was 12 percent. In a tougher year like 1990, the raise budget was 7.5 percent. This raise budget is not negotiable, and it drives salary increases throughout the company. If the corporate allowance is 7.5 percent, then every group within the company must meet a weighted-average salary increase of 7.5 percent—whether that "group" is R&D technicians, process engineers, test operators, or corporate vice presidents. The challenge for managers is to live within the budget and distribute their raise pool effectively, which is where the discipline of the review process takes hold.

Outstanding performers deserve outstanding raises. Great people won't leave a company merely because someone else offers them a 10 percent raise. But great people know the value of the contribution they're making and expect to be rewarded for it. The moment it appears that you have been unfair, that you have sacrificed their compensation to throw a bone to someone less deserving, you have launched a process that demotivates them and makes them vulnerable to recruitment.

That's why, when it comes to raises, we expect a big spread between the highest raise and the lowest raise in every focal group. Each year, along with the corporate average raise, we announce the minimum top-to-bottom spread we will allow. Not everyone at Cypress can be a standout, and we understand that. Still, we can't allow managers to subsidize low performers at the expense of high performers.

Merit and equity must remain distinct. One more time, let's talk definitions. The concept of merit is straightforward: great raises for great performance, bigger raises for good performance than for average or below-average performance. The concept of equity is a little more involved. Here is our shorthand description of salary equity: Salaries should be distributed so that the top-ranked performer in any group of peers is paid 50 percent more than the lowest-ranked performer, and people with more or less comparable performance receive more or less comparable salaries. In other words, in a ten-person design unit where the best designer makes $75,000, the lowest-ranked designer should make $50,000 and the remaining eight designers should be distributed evenly between the two extremes.

Of course, such ideal distributions seldom exist in the real world. A top-ranked designer who joined Cypress right out of graduate school might make less than an average designer who joined Cypress after working for a company that threw money around.

Any sensible process smooths out such "accidents of history." But these equity adjustments must always be made independent of raises granted for merit. You can't give an outstanding performer a small merit raise simply because she already gets a big salary. You can't give a poor performer a big merit raise because he is a junior member of the group and makes even less than he "deserves." We sharply distinguish between merit and equity and don't allow managers to mix the two.

Precision matters. Raises are as much about messages as they are about money. If, say, the average corporate raise is 7 percent, the difference between a raise of 6.5 percent and one of 7.5 percent is not just 1 percent. It's the difference between being below average and above average—that's an important message.

Our system is designed to communicate clear and customized messages to everyone in the company. We want no ambiguity in how we rank people. We don't evaluate performance with fuzzy categories like "acceptable" or "above average." Instead, we divide our people into groups of peers and rate them one by one within each group, from top to bottom, in rank order. These rankings are used to determine merit and equity raises. (Don't worry, we do not pass along rankings James Bond style: "Congratulations Number 4, your raise is 7.2 percent.")

But when it comes to granting raises, we do emphasize clarity. At the end of the process, everyone in the company learns what they received for merit and what they received as an equity adjustment as well as their final percentage raise. These three numbers become the basis for productive discussions about what the raise means and how it can be improved on next year.

The concept of focal reviews is hardly unique to Cypress; focals have become a way of life in Silicon Valley. What *is* unique is the attention we pay to the logic and rules of the process and the role of the computer as an enabler and learning device.

A word of caution: On first pass, the focal-review process can seem a bit complicated. In fact, inside the company it is simple and straightforward. That's its main virtue. New managers typically need an hour or so of training before they become comfortable with the system. But once they understand the philosophy and mechanics, making it work is simple—even if working within it, and making the kinds of tough-minded decisions we expect, can be anything but simple.

We divide the process of awarding annual raises into distinct phases: **selecting focal groups, ranking, granting merit raises, granting equity raises, conducting an overall corporate review.** Each phase stands on its own, each involves commonsense, well-documented rules, and each has built-in "quality checks" that identify discrepancies between individual decisions and corporate policies. The goal in each phase is to make the logic as clear and transparent as possible, and to require managers to think sensibly and carefully about every decision they make.

RANKING: WHY NOT IDENTIFY THE BEST?

The process begins by defining the focal groups. Each year we divide all the people at Cypress into "focal groups" of between five and twenty-five members. Essentially, focal groups represent peers with comparable skills and responsibilities: people with the same or similar jobs, usually at the same organizational level, within a specific department or product line. All weekend night-shift factory operators are in one focal group. All memory-chip circuit designers are in another. All vice presidents who report to me are in a third. There are roughly 120 focal groups in the company, and these groups are the building blocks of the ranking process that follows.

Each focal group gets assigned a ranking committee. If there are 120 focal groups, there are 120 ranking committees. The job of the ranking committee is what the name implies. It evaluates the performance of the focal-group members and establishes, from top to bottom for that group, numerical rankings for annual contribution. In other words, if a focal group contains eight members, the ranking committee must identify which member deserves to be number one, who should be number two, and so on down the line.

We take great care in defining the focal groups and selecting the ranking committees. The easiest way to blow up the process is to make mistakes in this initial phase. Thus, at least ten days before evaluations take place, we post rosters of focal groups and ranking committees to allow people to question their assignments.

Ranking committees typically have at least three members, and they each play different roles. The chairman, called the focal-group leader, is the lowest-level supervisor common to every member of the focal group—the person in the best position to judge day-to-day performance. In the simplest (and most typical) case, the focal-group leader is everyone's boss, the person they report to and who writes their quarterly and annual performance reviews. (These reviews, qualitative evaluations of achievements and areas for improvement, play an important role in the ranking committee's deliberations. We'll explore them in our chapters on the goals system.)

The second member of the ranking committee represents "internal customers" of the focal group. For example, the ranking committee for production-control planners, the people who set and revise factory schedules, might include the customer-service manager for a product line. This representative broadens the perspective of the focal-group leader: "Joe may not have done an exceptional job on your criteria, but every quarter he saves our neck when we have to get last-minute orders out the door." That kind of help-the-company contribution should count, and internal customers are in the best position to identify and measure it.

The third member of the ranking committee is someone in a position to judge the *quality* of each person's output. In the case of an R&D team, it might be a senior manufacturing engineer. This representative brings yet another critical perspective to the deliberations: "Tom may not be the most productive designer in the group, but his code always has the fewest bugs." If we're serious about quality—and we are—any legitimate performance evaluation must incorporate and measure it.

We also take great care in specifying how the ranking committees should do their job. Their deliberations focus exclusively on one question: *How much did each person contribute to the company last year?* We don't allow evaluations like "Ann isn't the best engineer in the group, but in a couple of years she's going to be a real hotshot." That kind of evaluation is about potential, and we use stock options to reward high-potential people. (Our Evergreen stock-option system works much like focal reviews.) Or, "Tom is the best person in the department, but he's been here for eight years. He's basically an overpaid old-timer." That statement represents a classic confusion of equity and merit, and it is inappropriate. The only criterion for the ranking committee is merit, which we define as total contribution to Cypress.

Finally, and of greatest importance, we insist that the ranking committee conduct its comparisons in a structured way that is simple and accurate. The point of this procedure is to control for a common problem that undermines so many performance reviews — especially in a ranking process like ours. I call it the mayonnaise effect.

Suppose you're running a food company that wants to enter the mayonnaise market. You can make your mayonnaise with olive oil, sunflower oil, or corn oil. You can use vinegar, lemon, both, or neither. You can emulsify with egg yolks, dried eggs, or whole eggs. You can use lots of salt or not much salt.

Let's say you wind up with ten different mayonnaise recipes and hire a taster to evaluate them. How do you proceed? One method is to ask the taster to sample each of the ten recipes and record the ratings. A simple approach, to be sure, but one that is bound to generate big errors. The taster will probably recall his two favorites and the recipe that made him ill. But what about all the recipes in the middle? Are you confident the taster will correctly rank recipes three through seven — none of which made a dramatic impression but each of which has its unique qualities?

Now consider a different approach, called pair-wise comparisons. The taster samples recipe one and recipe two and records which he prefers. Then he samples recipe one and recipe three and records his preference. After comparing recipe one with each of the nine other recipes, he proceeds to recipe two. He compares recipe two and recipe three (he's already compared it with recipe one) and records his preference. And so on down the line . . . for all forty-five possible head-to-head comparisons of the ten recipes. At the end of the process, by adding up the forty-five head-to-head winners and losers, the taster generates a top-to-bottom ranking that is totally accurate.

Ranking committees at Cypress use the pair-wise technique in focal reviews. For a ten-person focal group, the committee's job is to consider every possible two-employee pairing and determine who was the superior performer for the prior year: Has Joe made a bigger contribution than Tom? Has Joe made a bigger contribution than Bob? Has Bob made a bigger contribution than Sue? The software records the outcome of each comparison and calculates, based on the forty-five results, the overall rankings. No confusion, no mistakes, no mayonnaise effect.

Our head-to-head approach is bound to raise some eyebrows. To the outside world it can sound tough, even divisive. Some big companies have moved away from ranking altogether in favor of "pass/fail" or "peer review" systems that basically give all employees the same raise. Last year, for example, the *New York Times* praised peer-review systems at General Motors and Kodak. Executives at these companies, the *Times* said, "are gradually being won over to the notion that rewarding a handful of 'winners' and holding them up as the keys to corporate innovation and success brands the majority of employees as losers, hurting morale and cooperation."

There are plenty of legitimate concerns about ranking, and our system deals with them. But let's be clear: We *must* rank people in order to keep them. Our business, like so many fast-changing, highly competitive businesses, is filled with tough, aggressive, sharp-elbowed people. Silicon Valley's "culture of meritocracy" is not all that unlike the culture at high-powered law firms or investment banks. People don't shy away from tough scrutiny and evaluation. Quite the opposite. They are eager to know where they stand, how they stack up against their peers, whether they are meeting the company's expectations for them, whether it's time to move on.

In the semiconductor business, and I suspect in most vigorously competitive businesses, peer reviews or pass/fail approaches would be a prescription for disaster. Indeed, any company in Silicon Valley that used a pass/fail system would likely get its bones picked clean within a year. There are always more open slots at companies than there are great people to fill them. And when, as the cliché goes, changing jobs in Silicon Valley means pulling into a different parking lot on Monday morning, the exodus from a company that shied away from telling its people where they stood would be quick and devastating.

It all comes back to rewarding outstanding performers. Great people expect to be rewarded. You can't reward great people unless you identify them fairly and accurately. Pair-wise comparisons are the most sensible and logical technique we know to identify great performers and develop accurate rankings for everyone else in the organization.

That said, ranking *is* a contentious process. There is a potentially dangerous contradiction in the psychology of ranking: all people want to know where they stand, but most everyone thinks he or she is above average. But it is an arithmetic tautology that half of all people fall *below* average. So ranking, if done mechanically, can make lots of people feel like "losers."

We want as many people as possible to feel like winners who have contributed to the company—because they have. Our ideal outcome is for two-thirds of our people to hear good news, that is, to receive above-average raises. So we build a budget reserve into the focal-review software to make that outcome possible. We think of it as "Cypress math"—two-thirds of our people can be above average.

We also smooth the rough edges for the bottom one-third. If we hire as carefully as we say we do, relatively low performers at Cypress would be reasonable performers elsewhere. That's why we don't punish good people who rank below average, even those who rank well below average. Far from it. The solid-citizen raise—the minimum increase we allow each year—is designed to reassure people even as it motivates them to do better.

The solid-citizen increase goes to about 10 percent of our workforce in a typical year. It communicates a positive message: "We like you and you do good work. You may not be a standout performer, at least when it comes to people at Cypress, but you know the quality of people we have here. Not everyone can be above average. We value your contribution. We want you to stay."

TOP RAISES FOR TOP PEOPLE — NO EXCEPTIONS

Pair-wise comparisons create as accurate a picture as we can of who did what last year. They generate precise numerical rankings, from top to bottom, for every focal group in the company. These rankings then become the basis of the second phase of focal reviews: merit increases.

Here, too, we place a lot of emphasis on process. Two points are especially important. First, raises, unlike rankings, are not done by committee. Granting merit raises is the sole responsibility of the focal-group leader. We don't allow managers to obfuscate or pass the buck. That most hollow of excuses — "I wanted to give you a bigger raise, but 'corporate' made me scale it back" — is simply never uttered at Cypress. Everyone knows who sat in front of the computer and pushed the buttons that generated their increase.

Second, as with ranking, merit means merit only: a good raise for good performance, a low raise for poor performance. That's why, during this phase, *we do not disclose salaries to the focal-group leader.* All calculations are done in percentages. Salaries, what you're paid for what you do, relate to equity, not merit. By keeping salaries invisible, by taking them off the table in this phase, we get managers to focus on contribution rather than on other distracting factors.

The computer plays an important enabling role in the merit phase. The software reviews the ranking committee's individual judgments and recommends a certain percentage raise for a certain ranking. The calculations are pure and uncomplicated — which means they are only a rough approximation of reality. A computer program can read that Joe ranks number one in a focal group and thus deserves the highest percentage merit raise. It can parcel out first-to-last raises while preserving a budget. But it can't possibly know whether Joe is one of the most valuable employees in Cypress history or just a whisker more valuable than Sue, who ranks number two.

These kinds of distinctions require human judgment. So the focal-group leader merely uses the recommendations as a rough starting point. The actual raises he enters reflect his more detailed understanding of who did what last year. Still, we don't allow raises based on hidden agendas (a middling raise for a low-ranked person who is a complainer) or philosophies that are out of step with our basic values.

How do we preserve judgment *and* maintain a commitment to corporate policies? With automatic quality checks that review a manager's recommendations in real time and warn when they violate company policies. A focal-group leader can't advance to the next phase of the review process, equity raises, until he or she has awarded merit increases that trigger no quality checks.

There are 14 quality checks in all, and every year we improve on them. But six of the checks represent the system's basic warning flags:

- *Monotonic Distribution.* This is a fancy mathematical term for a simple rule: Any focal-group member ranked higher than another must receive a higher percentage merit raise — period. Managers who violate this check see an "**M**" in the quality-check section of their computer screen.

- *Minimum Range.* We require a minimum spread between the lowest raise and the highest raise (typically 7 percent) in every focal group. Thus, if the lowest-ranked member of a focal group gets a raise of 4 percent, the highest-ranked member of that group *must* get a raise of at least 11 percent. Managers who violate this check see an "**r**" (range) on their computer screen.

- *The Forbidden Gap.* We've already discussed the solid-citizen raise and the message behind it. There's a corollary to that message: If a manager does not believe someone deserves the solid-citizen minimum (usually 3 percent), he must zero that person out (grant no raise) altogether. Why insult someone with a 1 percent raise? It won't make him happier than no raise at all, and it burns money that could go to top performers. Managers who award raises greater than zero and less than the solid-citizen increase enter the "forbidden gap." They see an **"F"** on their computer screen.

- *Reasonable Raises Relative to Recommendations.* As we've said, the focal-group leader is free to adjust the computer-generated recommendations to reflect the nuances of individual performance. But we do impose limits on discretion. The software can detect a pattern of raises dramatically different from the pattern of computer-recommended raises. This almost always means that the focal-group leader is succumbing to the "mediocrity of the mean" and clustering raises around the average. That's not allowed. Managers who violate this check see an **"R"** on their computer screen.

- *Borders.* This is a modest check but an important one psychologically. It simply declares that no one at Cypress can be exactly average. If the corporate average is 7.5 percent, the computer will not approve a raise of exactly 7.5 percent. Why not send a more positive message with a 7.7 percent raise? Managers who violate this check see a **"B"** on their computer screen.

- *Average Raise.* The weighted-average raise for the group cannot exceed the corporate average. Not only does the software indicate if the raises granted are above or below budget, but it also indicates the amount of the "overdraft" or how much surplus remains. The value of this quality check is more than bean counting. It emphasizes the zero-sum logic of the system: giving big raises to people who deserve low raises forces you to take money away from high performers. Managers who bust the budget or leave money on the table see an **"A"** on their computer screen.

EQUAL PAY FOR EQUAL PERFORMANCE — IT'S THE LAW

The final phase is equity. At this time—and for the first time—the focal-group leader can see individual salaries. The goal of the equity phase is to adjust merit raises so as to move salaries closer to the "ideal" distribution we described earlier. For each focal group, the computer generates a simple graph that compares the salaries of each member (on the vertical axis) with merit rankings (on the horizontal axis). The graph also displays a trend line that describes the "ideal" salary distribution for the group (based on the 50 percent top-to-bottom spread we explained earlier) and how that ideal line compares with the actual salaries.

The equity phase has nearly all the same quality checks as the merit phase: the minimum top-to-bottom spread, no one exactly average, the forbidden gap. But it also imposes a new quality check: "U" for unfair. Essentially, the "U" check detects when, in the name of equity, a focal-group leader tries to undo some of the tough choices required in the merit phase.

The "U" check makes sense only during the equity phase. Awarding merit raises is full of judgment; the software gives managers lots of flexibility to reward annual contribution so long as they conform to the basic rules. Equity adjustments are more mechanical: Focal-group leaders simply adjust merit raises up or down to move their people closer to the ideal trend line.

Some managers are gradualists. They like to make small adjustments to the merit increase and bring their people closer to the ideal line over a period of years. Others, like me, are more aggressive. They like to make big equity changes and straighten out salaries sooner rather than later.

The "U" check will approve either philosophy. But it *won't* approve inconsistency. It won't allow a manager to make big equity adjustments for a few people and small adjustments for the others. That's an important limitation. Most managers who try to play games in our system do it in the equity phase. In the name of "equity" they adjust a merit raise up or down to solve a different problem: "I had to give Nick a 4 percent raise for merit based on his ranking, but I know he is going to scream. If I raise him to 7 percent in equity (it turns out he is a little underpaid relative to the group), he won't be so mad." That's not appropriate, and the **"U"** check will almost always flag it.

FOCALS IN ACTION: AN ON-LINE DEMO

I'll admit a narrative description of our focal-review system can sound pretty complicated. In reality, for a manager sitting in front of a personal computer, the system is anything but complicated. The best way to understand the mechanics of the system is to participate in an on-line demonstration. Throughout this demo I will do my impression of a middle manager tempted to succumb to the mediocrity of the mean—that is, to minimize griping rather than reward his best people, even if that means some bad news at the bottom. We'll see how the system counteracts those instincts and steers the manager toward doing the right thing.[1]

Let's say I must grant raises to a focal group with six members: Ann, Bob, Joe, Lee, Sue, and Tom. The process begins when I receive a computer diskette from human resources. I convene the ranking committee and share my written annual evaluations of each member of the focal group. We then make fifteen head-to-head comparisons. Has Joe made a bigger contribution than Lee? Has Ann made a bigger contribution than Bob? I enter the results of each comparison and the computer does its calculations. The final rankings, in descending order, are: 1) Joe, 2) Sue, 3) Bob, 4) Tom, 5) Ann, 6) Lee. We do a sanity check on the results, I thank the ranking committee for its efforts, and disband it.

Now I'm on my own for the merit phase. Along with everyone else at the company, I learn the basic guidelines for this year's raises. The announced corporate average is 6 percent. The minimum al-

---

[1]Readers who want to use the diskette can turn to the instructions on page 87, install the demo, and follow along on their computer. Other readers can simply follow along in the book. The discussion will include "snapshots" of the computer screen at all critical points.

lowed spread between the top and bottom is 7 percent. The solid-citizen raise is 3 percent.

These are typical Cypress numbers, but the constraints have already made me uncomfortable. My basic goal is to keep all my people happy, including the two at the bottom: Ann, who tries hard but isn't very effective, and Lee, who will be a real pain if he doesn't get an above-average raise.

It's time to start. I enter each person's ranking in **column D,** hit **[Alt] S,** and watch as the computer generates its recommended raises. (That is, I hit the computer's "Alternate" key, hold it down, and hit the "S" key.)

Interestingly, I note to myself, the top-to-bottom spread between Joe and Lee is only 5.8 percent. The computer hasn't met the 7 percent minimum. I'm not surprised. The computer does not do my thinking for me. It simply distributes raises evenly, along a linear curve, to create a starting point and stay within the budget constraint. There is no guarantee that the computer's recommendations will meet all the system's quality checks. (That would feel more like Big Brother than a simple tool.)

Now it's time for judgment. Like most managers at Cypress, I start with my worst and best performers. First I go to Lee. The ranking committee was pretty rough on him. My colleagues believed, and I had to agree, that he did not meet many of the performance standards we set around here. On the other hand, I know Lee's a whiner who's going to give me a hard time if I give him the solid-citizen raise he deserves. I can't justify giving him an average merit raise; he was ranked last and with good reason. But if I give him what the computer recommends, he'll scream. I persuade myself Lee's not so bad and enter a merit raise of 5 percent in **column F.**

Then I go up to Joe. Joe is more than my top performer; he is a real superstar who deserves a big merit increase. So I give him 12 percent, double the corporate average. As a first try I use the computer recommendations for my four remaining people, enter those numbers into **column F,** and hit the **F9** key (the Lotus "calculate" key) to see how I fare when the quality checks are applied.

Two quality checks show up as problems. **"M"** is for monotonic.

FIGURE A

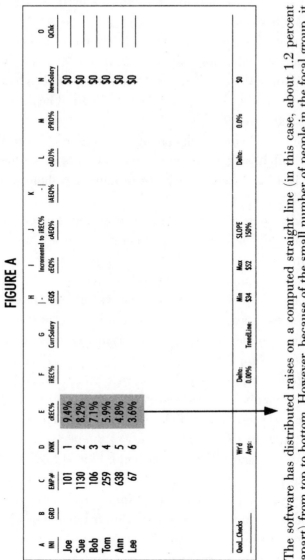

The software has distributed raises on a computed straight line (in this case, about 1.2 percent apart) from top to bottom. However, because of the small number of people in the focal group, it doesn't meet the 7 percent minimum spread. It's up to me to fix that.

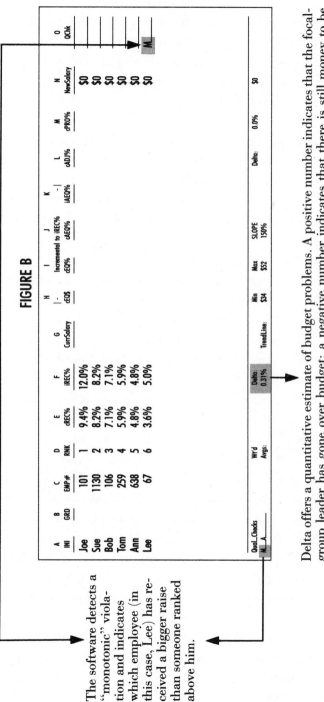

FIGURE B

The software detects a "monotonic" violation and indicates which employee (in this case, Lee) has received a bigger raise than someone ranked above him.

Delta offers a quantitative estimate of budget problems. A positive number indicates that the focal-group leader has gone over budget; a negative number indicates that there is still money to be distributed. In this case, I must take, on average, .31 percent from each person to stay within budget.

Unwittingly, I have given Lee a bigger percentage raise than Ann, even though Ann ranks higher—absolutely not allowed. **"A"** indicates that I've got a budget problem. In this case, I've given away too much money. Under **"Delta"** (displayed in column F on the bottom row of the screen), the computer shows me that I've gone over budget by an average of 0.31 percent (three-tenths of 1 percent) for each person.

This is my first encounter with the system's zero-sum logic. If I give Lee and Joe more money than the computer recommended, I must take money from other people. I haven't.

It's time for some adjustments. First, I eliminate the **"M"** by raising Ann's raise to 5.2 percent, just above Lee's. I hit **F9** and the **"M"** disappears.

Now I turn to the budget constraint. I can't change Lee, whom I've decided must be at 5 percent to avoid problems, and I can't change Ann because of the **"M"** check. Joe deserves what he got, so I have no choice but to take money from Sue, Bob, and Tom. I knock each down by 0.7 percent and enter their new, reduced raises (Sue: 7.5 percent, Bob: 6.4 percent, Tom: 5.2 percent). I press **F9** and my quality checks are gone.

Technically, I've done my job. But if I have any managerial integrity, I realize that *substantively* I haven't done my job. For no good reason, I've forced three of my six people (Tom, Ann, and Lee) to receive merit raises *below* the corporate average. What's more, the distribution of my raises is far from ideal. In effect, I'm taking money from Sue, Bob, and Tom, all of whom are getting a smaller raise than the computer recommendation in order to give more money to Ann and Lee, my lowest-ranked performers. As I look in the mirror, I realize I fit the classic weak-manager pattern—a prescription for disaster that encourages my good people to leave and my weakest links to get the wrong message (good raises despite poor performance).

I decide to start over. Again I go to the bottom, but this time with a little more backbone. The computer recommended a 3.6 percent raise for Lee. I know he will be angry with this, but in reality he doesn't deserve 5 percent. Is it better to make Lee mad or to disap-

FIGURE C

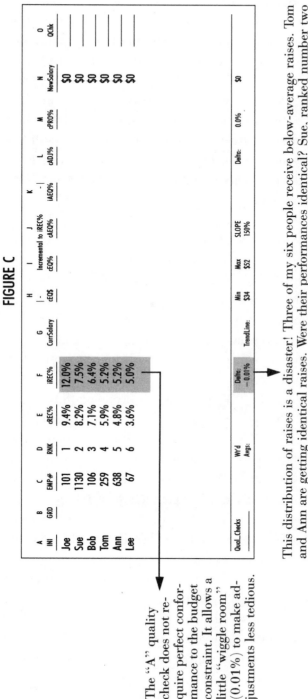

A INI	B GRD	C EMP#	D RNK	E cREC%	F iREC%	G CurrSalary	H - cEO$	I Incremental to iREC% cEO%	J dEO%	K - iAEO%	L dADJ%	M cPRO%	N NewSalary	O QChk
Joe		101	1	9.4%	12.0%								$0	___
Sue		1130	2	8.2%	7.5%								$0	___
Bob		106	3	7.1%	6.4%								$0	___
Tom		259	4	5.9%	5.2%								$0	___
Ann		638	5	4.8%	5.2%								$0	___
Lee		67	6	3.6%	5.0%								$0	___

| Qual.Checks | | | Wt'd
Avg: | | Delta:
−0.01% | | TrendLine: | Min
$34 | Max
$52 | SLOPE
150% | | Delta: | 0.0% | | $0 |

The "A" quality check does not require perfect conformance to the budget constraint. It allows a little "wiggle room" (0.01%) to make adjustments less tedious.

This distribution of raises is a disaster! Three of my six people receive below-average raises. Tom and Ann are getting identical raises. Were their performances identical? Sue, ranked number two on merit, receives a fairly modest raise—only 1.5 percent above the corporate average. What kind of message is that?

point Sue, Bob, and Tom, three of my better performers? Then I go a step further. If Lee is going to be angry with 3.6 percent, why not admit that he's at best a solid citizen and free up that much more money for my other people? I bite the bullet and take Lee down to 3 percent.

Of course, my decision on Lee also affects Ann. I increased Ann to 5.2 percent because of the "M" quality check. By bringing Lee down to 3 percent, I lift that constraint. Ann and I both know she deserves a reasonable but below-average raise. Why give her more money than the reasonable computer recommendation? I bring Ann down to 4.8 percent.

Now for the fun part. By reducing the raises for Lee and Ann, I've freed up money for Sue, Bob, and Tom. I take each of these performers one tick above their computer-recommended raises and feel better (Sue: 8.3 percent, Bob: 7.2 percent, Tom: 6 percent). I hit **F9** and initiate the quality checks.

Unfortunately, my work still isn't over. Tom, at 6 percent, is now dead on the corporate average. That's triggered the "**B**" check. Also, I've been a little too generous with the new money, and once again I've busted the budget.

I could solve the "**B**" problem by dropping Tom to a below-average raise, but that's not the message I want to send. So my first step is to take Tom just above the average to 6.1 percent. I hit **F9** and the "**B**" disappears. Now it's time to take away some money. But from where? I reflect for a moment on the entire focal group. Lee's a solid citizen; the only way to take money from him is to zero him out—which he does not deserve on the basis of merit. Ann's received a reasonable raise, which is all she earned. But why take her down below the computer's recommendation?

That leaves two choices. I can rob a little from Sue, Bob, and Tom, to whom I just gave additional money, or I can scale back on Joe. That decision must reflect who these people are and how they've performed. I decide to take Joe down from 12 percent to 11.6 percent—still a very nice raise and a very positive message. I hit **F9** and all my quality checks have disappeared.

The merit phase is over and I'm pleased with the results. My top

FIGURE D

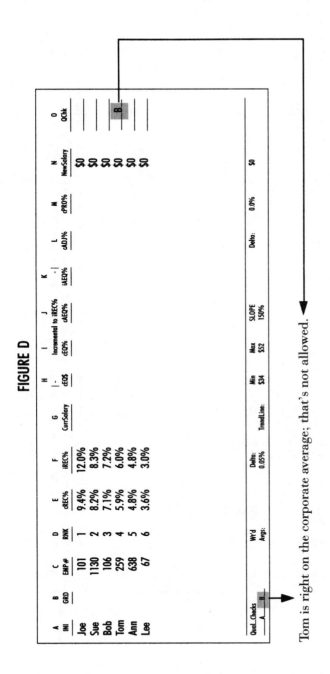

Tom is right on the corporate average; that's not allowed.

FIGURE E

A INI	B GRD	C EMP#	D RNK	E cREC%	F iREC%	G CurrSalary	H - cEQ$	I Incremental to iREC% cEQ%	J dREQ%	K - iAEQ%	L dADJ%	M cPRO%	N NewSalary	O QChk
Joe		101	1	9.4%	11.6%								$0	
Sue		1130	2	8.2%	8.3%								$0		
Bob		106	3	7.1%	7.2%								$0		
Tom		259	4	5.9%	6.1%								$0		
Ann		638	5	4.8%	4.8%								$0		
Lee		67	6	3.6%	3.0%								$0		

Qual._Checks		Wt'd Avg:		Delta: 0.00%		TrendLine:		Min $34	Max $52	SLOPE 150%	Delta: 0.0%		$0	

What a difference from my proposal in Figure C! Joe still gets a big raise (much bigger than the computer recommended). Ann and Lee get the modest raises they deserve. Bob, whose raise was barely above average before, gets a nice bump over the average. This distribution of raises sends precisely the right messages.

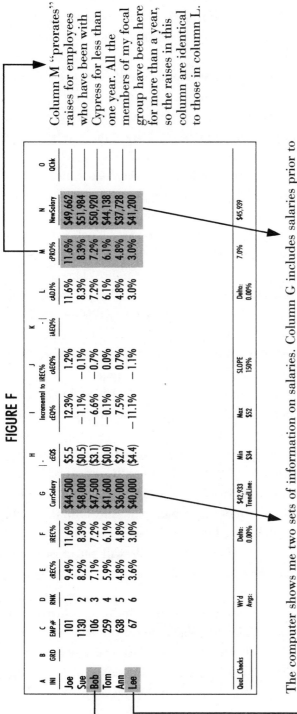

FIGURE F

Column M "prorates" raises for employees who have been with Cypress for less than one year. All the members of my focal group have been here for more than a year, so the raises in this column are identical to those in column L.

A INI	B GRD	C EMP#	D RNK	E cREC%	F iREC%	G CurSalary	H i- cEO$	I Incremental to iREO% cEO%	J cREO%	K - iAEO%	L cAD.J%	M cPRO%	N NewSalary	O QClk
Joe		101	1	9.4%	11.6%	$44,500	$5.5	12.3%	1.2%		11.6%	11.6%	$49,662	———
Sue		1130	2	8.2%	8.3%	$48,000	($0.5)	−1.1%	−0.1%		8.3%	8.3%	$51,984	———
Bob		106	3	7.1%	7.2%	$47,500	($3.1)	−6.6%	−0.7%		7.2%	7.2%	$50,920	———
Tom		259	4	5.9%	6.1%	$41,600	($0.0)	−0.1%	0.0%		6.1%	6.1%	$44,138	———
Ann		638	5	4.8%	4.8%	$36,000	$2.7	7.5%	0.7%		4.8%	4.8%	$37,728	———
Lee		67	6	3.6%	3.0%	$40,000	($4.4)	−11.1%	−1.1%		3.0%	3.0%	$41,200	———
Qual._Checks			Wt'd Avgs:		Delta: 0.00%	$42,933 Trendline:	Min $34	Max $52	SLOPE 150%		Delta: 0.00%	7.0%	$45,939	

The computer shows me two sets of information on salaries. Column G includes salaries prior to this year's focal-review process. Column N includes salaries after merit raises but before equity adjustments. (For each person, it assumes an equity adjustment of 0 percent.)

Lee is a real problem. Because he ranks so low and is paid so much ($41,200 after his 3 percent merit raise), he is "off the charts," he is "off the charts" from an equity perspective. In fact, to achieve an ideal equity distribution, Lee would have to take a pay cut of 8.1 percent!

Bob is also dramatically overpaid, even though he ranks high.

performer gets a healthy raise, almost double the announced corporate average. My next two performers get above-average raises, which tells them how good they are. Tom, ranked number four, still gets a raise just above average; he, too, should feel comfortable. Ann should understand that her performance was below average (although her below-average raise is probably higher than the average raise at most of our competitors). Lee should understand that he's a solid citizen; more important, *I* understand that I have to be honest enough to give him that message.

In classic quality terms, the merit process has taken me through several "cycles of learning." Each time I trigger a quality check, step back, reconsider my decisions, and enter new decisions, I improve the logic behind my raises. When I grant raises (which I do to my vice presidents), I typically go through five to fifteen "cycles of learning" in the course of an hour in the merit phase. These insights simply could not happen (at least not in a reasonable period of time) in a manual system where a focal-group leader grants raises, submits them to HR for approval or disapproval, receives them back as rejects, revises them, resubmits them, and starts the process over. Only automatic quality checks allow for iterative learning.

Now it's time for the equity phase. I hit **[Alt] E** and my screen now displays new information, including, for the first time, the salaries of all six focal-group members.

I scan the salary information, graph it, and notice a few interesting patterns. (To graph, I hit **[Alt] G** and choose **"Current Salary."**)

Sue, who is ranked number two, is the most highly paid member of the focal group. What's more, she gets paid substantially more than my all-star, Joe. Bob and Lee are also substantially overpaid relative to a fair-trend line. These four people will get most of my attention in the equity phase. I hit the **Escape** key, choose **"Quit,"** and return to the focal-review screen.

Next I look at the computer's baseline equity measurements, starting with **column H.** Adjusting each salary up or down by the stated dollar amount in **column H** would move every person right onto the ideal trend line. The highest-ranked member of the group, Joe, would receive 50 percent more than the lowest member, Lee,

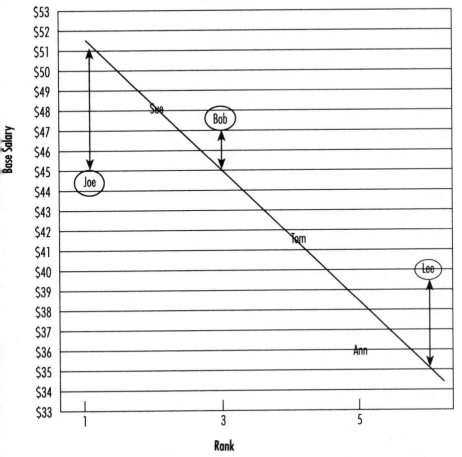

FOCAL REVIEW SYSTEM

Base Salary (y-axis): $53, $52, $51, $50, $49, $48, $47, $46, $45, $44, $43, $42, $41, $40, $39, $38, $37, $36, $35, $34, $33

Rank (x-axis): 1, 3, 5

Sue, Bob, Joe, Tom, Lee, Ann

The line plots an "ideal" equity distribution and shows how the actual salaries of my six people compare. Notice that Joe's "ideal" salary is $51,000—50 percent more than Lee's "ideal" salary of $34,600. Clearly, Joe is dramatically underpaid while Bob and Lee are overpaid.

while everyone else would fall neatly in between. (These dollar adjustments are on top of the merit raises I have already granted.)

The next column merely states those dollar inequity figures in percentage terms. Joe would need an equity adjustment of 12.3 percent on top of his 11.6 percent merit raise (a total increase of 23.9 percent) to achieve ideal fairness. On the other hand, Bob would have to take a negative equity hit of 6.6 percent, off a merit raise of 7.2 percent, for him to be in the ideal salary position.

It's not reasonable to make adjustments that radical. Salary inequities build up over time; they can't be corrected in one year. Would it be fair to Bob, my third best performer, to award him an insignificant final raise simply because he received a big salary at his last company?

That's why **column J** scales down the computer recommendations by a factor of ten. There's no great science here; years of experience have taught us that starting the equity adjustment process with 10 percent of the total gap is about right. Less, and you're doing nothing, more and you cause problems. Unlike merit, where I use the computer recommendations as a rough starting point, I begin the equity phase by simply entering the computer's proposed adjustments from **column J** into **column K.** I hit F9 and, much to my surprise, see an **"F"** quality check.

Once again Lee is a problem. Not only is he just a solid citizen, but it turns out he is overpaid relative to his peers. By accepting the computer's equity adjustment, I have reduced his raise from 3 percent to 1.9 percent and thus placed him in the "forbidden gap" between zero and 3 percent. That leaves me with a stark choice: Either keep him at 3 percent or zero him out (enter a −3 percent equity adjustment for a zero net raise). I'm still worried about Lee's reaction, so I enter an adjustment of 0 percent for Lee in **column K,** keep his final raise at 3 percent, and hit **F9.** The F check disappears.

But I've created a new problem. The computer made its original equity calculations on the assumption that I would take Lee down to 1.9 percent. By returning Lee to 3 percent, I've busted the budget. The computer tells me I must take away an average of 0.16 percent from each of my six people.

How to fix it? I can't touch Lee. Taking Tom down brings him below the corporate average, another bad idea. So I decide to tweak down the four remaining people by 0.2 percent. I adjust Joe's equity raise down to 1 percent, increase Sue's negative adjustment to −0.3 percent, take Bob to −0.9 percent, and Ann to 0.4 percent. I hit **F9** and the quality checks disappear. I breathe a sigh of relief.

But have I done the right thing? Can I live with the messages I'm about to deliver to my people? To gauge my judgment, I look at a

FIGURE G

A INI	B GRD	C EMP#	D RNK	E cREC%	F iREC%	G CurrSalary	H — cEQ$	I cEQ%	Incremental to iREC% cAEQ%	K iAEQ%	L cADJ%	M cPRO%	N NewSalary	O QChk
Joe		101	1	9.4%	11.6%	$44,500	$5.5	12.3%	1.2%	1.2%	12.8%	12.8%	$50,196	
Sue		1130	2	8.2%	8.3%	$48,000	($0.5)	-1.1%	-0.1%	-0.1%	8.2%	8.2%	$51,936	
Bob		106	3	7.1%	7.2%	$47,500	($3.1)	-6.6%	-0.7%	-0.7%	6.5%	6.5%	$50,588	
Tom		259	4	5.9%	6.1%	$41,600	($0.0)	-0.1%	0.0%	0.0%	6.1%	6.1%	$44,138	
Ann		638	5	4.8%	4.8%	$36,000	$2.7	7.5%	0.7%	0.7%	5.5%	5.5%	$37,980	
Lee		67	6	3.6%	3.0%	$40,000	($4.4)	-11.1%	-1.1%	-1.1%	1.9%	1.9%	$40,760	F

| Qual_Checks | | Wt'd Avgs: | | | Delta: 0.00% | TrendLine: $42,933 | Min $34 | Max $52 | SLOPE 150% | | Delta: -0.01% | 7.0% | $45,933 | |

This quality check indicates that I have a problem and which person is in violation.

FIGURE H

A INI	B GRD	C EMP#	D RNK	E cREC%	F iREC%	G CurrSalary	H (-) cEOS	I Incremental to iREC% cEQ%	J dEQ%	K iAEQ%	L cADJ%	M cPRO%	N NewSalary	O QChk
Joe		101	1	9.4%	11.6%	$44,500	$5.5	12.3%	1.2%	1.0%	12.6%	12.6%	$50,107	———
Sue		1130	2	8.2%	8.3%	$48,000	($0.5)	−1.1%	−0.1%	−0.3%	8.0%	8.0%	$51,840	———
Bob		106	3	7.1%	7.2%	$47,500	($3.1)	−6.6%	−0.7%	−0.9%	6.3%	6.3%	$50,493	———
Tom		259	4	5.9%	6.1%	$41,600	($0.0)	−0.1%	0.0%	0.0%	6.1%	6.1%	$44,138	———
Ann		638	5	4.8%	4.8%	$36,000	$2.7	7.5%	0.7%	0.4%	5.2%	5.2%	$37,872	———
Lee		67	6	3.6%	3.0%	$40,000	($4.4)	−11.1%	−1.1%	−0.0%	3.0%	3.0%	$41,200	———

Qual_Checks	Wt'd Avgs:	Delta: 0.00%	TrendLine: $42,933	Min $34	Max $52	SLOPE 150%	Delta: 0.01%	7.0%	$45,942

The quality checks have disappeared. But have I done the right thing?

graphical representation of the final results. I hit **[Alt] G,** select **"Both Salaries,"** and the computer creates "before" and "after" salary graphs.

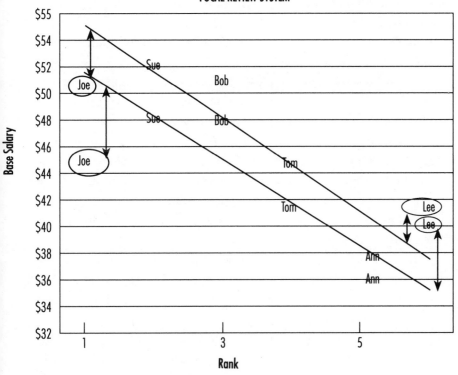

FOCAL REVIEW SYSTEM

These two lines provide "before" and "after" snapshots of equity. The lower line and lower names document salary distributions before the focal-review process. The upper line and upper names show where things stand now.

As a result of his merit and equity raises, Joe has moved substantially closer to the fair-trend line. Before this year's focal-review process, he was nearly $7,000 off the line. Now he's less than $5,000 off the line. But is that enough of an adjustment—especially when Lee remains so overpaid?

I don't like what I see. Joe is getting a nice raise; his salary goes from $44,500 to $50,107. Still, despite being the group's top-rated person, he comes out of the process with a salary well below Sue ($51,840) and even below Bob ($50,493).

That's not a result I can afford. I want to give Joe more money, but I'm back to the budget constraint. To do that, I have to take money from someone else. Who? Obviously, it must come from one, some, or all of my overpaid people: Sue, Bob, and Lee. If I take it from Lee, I'm back to the "forbidden gap" problem. Sue is technically overpaid, but just by a fraction; there's not much wiggle room there. So the money has to come from Bob.

I enter −1.5 percent for Bob, 1.6 percent for Joe, and hit **F9.** I'm through, right? Wrong. The computer signals a new quality check (**"U"**) and assigns it to Bob and Tom.

The software is telling me I've done something unfair. What I've done, in particular, is to be unfair to Bob. I am giving a below-average raise to my number-three person. That makes no sense. Nor, for that matter, does the fact that Bob is now getting a lower raise than Tom, who is ranked below him. So I bring Bob back to the computer's original plan of −0.9 percent, tweak Joe down to 1.4 percent, and hit **F9.** The **"U"** disappears. (Tom gets a **"U"** because I have adjusted everyone else's raise but not his. His **"U"** disappears after I adjust Bob's raise.)

Of course, that doesn't fix my budget problem. I still have to take Joe's new money from someone else. That leaves only one choice: to bite the bullet on Lee and zero him out. I do that, hit **F9,** and still find the **"A"** quality check.

But now the news is good! I just obliterated a 3 percent raise for an overpaid person, which frees up even more money. I leave Ann alone (she is slightly overpaid already) and increase everyone else's equity adjustment by 0.5 percent. I hit F9 and the quality checks disappear.

I hit **[Alt] G,** select **"Both Salaries,"** and look again at the graphs.

I'm pleased with the outcome. By being justifiably tough on my weakest performer (whose silence I originally planned to buy with a 5 percent raise he didn't deserve), I free up money for better performers. Two-thirds of my people receive above-average raises (remember, Cypress math) and all receive the messages they need to hear.

To Joe: "You did a great job and your raise shows it: high merit and also an additional raise for equity. Your final raise is 13.5 per-

FIGURE J

A INI	B GRD	C EMP#	D RNK	E cREC%	F iREC%	G CurrSalary	H cEO$	I Incremental to iREC% cEO%	J cAEO%	K iAEO%	L cADJ%	M cPRO%	N NewSalary	O QChk
Joe		101	1	9.4%	11.6%	$44,500	$5.5	12.3%	1.2%	1.6%	13.2%	13.2%	$50,374	—
Sue		1130	2	8.2%	8.3%	$48,000	($0.5)	−1.1%	−0.1%	−0.3%	8.0%	8.0%	$51,840	u
Bob		106	3	7.1%	7.2%	$47,500	($3.1)	−6.6%	−0.7%	−1.5%	5.7%	5.7%	$50,208	u
Tom		259	4	5.9%	6.1%	$41,600	($0.0)	−0.1%	0.0%	0.0%	6.1%	6.1%	$44,138	—
Ann		638	5	4.8%	4.8%	$36,000	$2.7	7.5%	0.7%	0.4%	5.2%	5.2%	$37,872	—
Lee		67	6	3.6%	3.0%	$40,000	($4.4)	−11.1%	−1.1%	0.0%	3.0%	3.0%	$41,200	—
Qual_Checks			Wt'd Avgs:		Delta: 0.00%	$42,933 TrendLine:	Min $34	Max $52	SLOPE 150%		Delta: 0.00%	7.0%	$45,939	

This quality check indicates I have an "unfairness" problem and who is in violation.

FIGURE K

A INI	B GRD	C EMP#	D RNK	E cREC%	F iREC%	G CurSalary	H cEO$	I cEO%	Incremental to iREC% J cAEO%	K iAEO%	L cADJ%	M cPRO%	N NewSalary	O QChk
Joe		101	1	9.4%	11.6%	$44,500	$5.5	12.3%	1.2%	1.9%	13.5%	13.5%	$50,508	—
Sue		1130	2	8.2%	8.3%	$48,000	($0.5)	−1.1%	−0.1%	0.2%	8.5%	8.5%	$52,080	—
Bob		106	3	7.1%	7.2%	$47,500	($3.1)	−6.6%	−0.7%	−0.2%	7.0%	7.0%	$50,825	—
Tom		259	4	5.9%	6.1%	$41,600	($0.0)	−0.1%	0.0%	0.5%	6.6%	6.6%	$44,346	—
Ann		638	5	4.8%	4.8%	$36,000	$2.7	7.5%	0.7%	0.4%	5.2%	5.2%	$37,872	—
Lee		67	6	3.6%	3.0%	$40,000	($4.4)	−11.1%	−1.1%	−3.0%	0.0%	0.0%	$40,000	—

| Qual_Checks | | Wt'd Avgs: | | | Delta: 0.00% | $42,933 TrendLine: | Min $34 | Max $52 | SLOPE 150% | | Delta: 0.00% | 7.0% | $45,938 | |

A much better distribution! Joe gets a big raise—from $44,500 to $50,508. Bob's salary is only $317 higher than Joe's; next year, if Joe continues to perform, he'll easily pass Bob.

Lee gets no raise at all. A tough message, I know, but he still makes $2,000 more than Ann, who ranks higher! Unless Lee shapes up, he may be looking at zero raise next year as well.

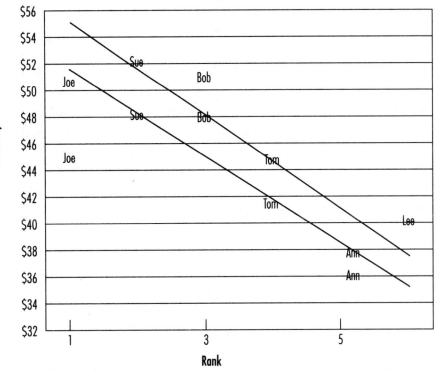

The "before" and "after" salary distribution.

cent, more than double the corporate average. That fairly reflects your accomplishments around here." (I know that Joe hasn't quite caught Bob, but he's gotten much closer. Next year, if Joe keeps it up, he'll pass Bob and perhaps Sue.)

To Sue: "You should be happy. You got a great merit raise and a small positive equity tweak for a final raise of 8.6 percent. Good news on top of good news, all around something to be proud of."

To Bob and Tom: "Your final raises (7 percent and 6.6 percent) are above average. You're doing a good job and you're important members of the team. But, Tom, I have to be honest. Your merit raise was as close to average as you can get; you got a bigger final raise because of an equity bump. If you want to move up next year, there are a few specific things we can talk about."

To Ann: "Your raise is below average. Frankly, it reflects your performance. That's nothing to be depressed about. We have very high performers here and we very much want you around. As you know, in most years a below-average raise at Cypress is at least an average raise at most other companies."

To Lee: "Shape up or ship out. Your performance merited a solid-citizen increase, although even that was a borderline call. But your salary is so high relative to your peers that I had no choice but to zero you out on the final raise. Given the salary you command, we must expect more from you. And if we don't get it, there could be problems down the road. Here's what you need to do . . ."

REWARDING POTENTIAL:
ENDLESS STOCK OPTIONS

That's how simple and quick the focal-review system is in practice. A ranking committee may require an hour or two to complete its pair-wise comparisons. That modest investment of time generates precise, thorough, and well-rounded evaluations based on the standard written reviews as well as inputs from quality advocates and internal customers. A focal-group leader may spend thirty minutes, certainly no more than an hour, granting merit raises, and another thirty minutes on the equity phase. That modest investment of time generates rational, sensible, and meaningful raises that send constructive messages (both positive and negative) throughout the organization.

In fact, we have enough faith in the system that we use a similar computer-aided approach to make annual grants of stock options. Raises reward past performance; options reward long-term potential. Over time, in a fast-growing company like Cypress, the value of stock options can easily translate into tens of thousands of dollars—even for junior managers and individual contributors. Since these options vest over a four-year period, big grants create a strong incentive for our most promising performers to stay with the company.

The mechanics of our "evergreen" system closely mimic focal reviews. Every year the board authorizes a pool of options—usually about one million shares—to be distributed throughout the company. Each focal group receives an allotment from that pool, and each member of the focal group gets a certain share of that allotment. Ranking committees rate their people using pair-wise comparisons, grant stock options from their allotment based on merit, and then make equity adjustments. Only this time the merit criterion isn't "Who contributed most last year?" It is "Whom can we least afford to lose over the next four years?" And the equity adjustment isn't "Is Joe's salary fair relative to his contribution?" It is "Is the number of Joe's unvested stock options fair relative to his ranking on long-term potential?"

None of which suggests the focal-review system is without shortcomings. The biggest problem is delay. Each phase of the process requires modest time commitments from line managers or senior executives. But from beginning to end, focal reviews do take six weeks. We select focal groups at the end of the year for which the reviews apply. We wait until late January to set the guidelines for average raises, required ranges, and solid-citizen increases. (These guidelines require final forecasts for the upcoming year's performance, which aren't available until January.) It then takes several weeks to fully implement the ranking, merit, and equity phases. The "lag factor" is the biggest source of rank-and-file discontent with focal reviews.

We are always trying to make the process quicker. But even with the lags, our computer-based system guarantees that when our managers tell their people "Congratulations, here is your raise for this year," the figure they present will represent the clearest and most consistent logic we are capable of as individuals and as an organization.

For me, focal reviews create a valuable top-down perspective that allows me to practice management by exception. At the end of the process, but before the final raises are announced, I convene a meeting with our vice presidents. Using the computer database, we analyze raise patterns throughout the company. We can compare any person's raise with those granted his or her peers. We can compare raises in one product line with those in another. We can compare this year's pattern of raises in a department with raises in the same department over the past few years. This final review seldom takes more than a few hours, but it lets us detect patterns and problems we would never know about otherwise.

Which helps explain, I think, our low turnover rate. We track employee turnover on a weekly basis and I review it on a quarterly basis. Over the last few years our annual turnover has fluctuated between 6 percent and 12 percent. This is low for Silicon Valley, where average annual turnover is somewhere on the order of 25 percent. Tough as they may sound, focal reviews deliver.

They also deliver one last piece of information—my salary. Our philosophy of CEO compensation, a topic that has inspired much justifiable outrage over the last few years, is simple: I can be paid no more than Cypress's most highly paid vice president and no more than twenty times an entry-level worker. So at the end of the focal-review process, after the final corporate evaluations and quality checks, we find the salary of the most highly paid vice president. That becomes my salary too—which in 1992 was $258,145. The "process" takes about ten seconds.

Focal Reviews: How to Use the Demo Diskette

It's Easy!

The demo software contains extensive instructions under the Help option in the Main Menu. Review those instructions if you wish—*but they are not necessary to run the demo.* In fact, they are so extensive they may confuse you. Everything you need to know is right here. So if you need help, just flip back to these pages.

Please read Chapter 2 before you run the demo. The software only makes sense if you understand the management philosophy behind it. Also, we *strongly recommend* that you begin by re-creating the demo in the book. (It starts on page 64.) Follow it step by step: Enter the same rankings, use the same merit raises, trigger and resolve the same quality checks, complete the equity phase.

Then you can start over. You can enter whatever employee rankings, merit raises, and equity adjustments you choose—as many times as you'd like.

The Basics

The focal-review system uses just a handful of easy-to-understand commands. *(A special note to Lotus buffs: Do not invoke Lotus commands. They may damage the demo.)* Here are all the commands you need to run the system:

[Alt] M: Returns you to the Main Menu from just about anywhere.

[Alt] S: Sorts focal-group members by rank and triggers the computer-recommended raises for the merit phase.

F9: Triggers quality checks in the merit and equity phases.

[Alt] E: Moves you from the merit phase to the equity phase by providing salary information and recommending equity adjustments.

[Alt] G: Graphs salaries in the equity phase.

[Alt] P: Prints your worksheet.

[Alt] C: "Clears" your work and allows you to start over.

Getting Started

1. Place the *No-Excuses Management* diskette in your floppy drive. At the DOS prompt, type "a:" or "b:" to access your floppy drive. Hit "Enter" and type "demos" to display further instructions.

2. Boot Lotus 1-2-3 (version 2.01 or higher).

3. Use the Lotus retrieve function (/ , File, Retrieve) to load the focal-review demo. The demo's file name is focal.wk1. (Be patient: It may take a few minutes to load the demo from your drive.)

4. At the Main Menu, choose Printer Type and make the appropriate printer selection. Your selection automatically returns you to the Main Menu. You only need to choose a printer once. (Most printers are compatible with Epson or the HP Laser Jet. If your printer is not compatible with any choice, the software does not support it. But the demo will still work on your screen.)

5. At the Main Menu, choose Select.

6. At "Select a Focal Group #," type 1 and hit Enter. Now you begin the merit phase.

Merit Phase

1. Enter the appropriate rankings (1 through 6) for each employee in **column D.** Again, we recommend that you start by turning to page 64 and re-creating the demo in the book.

2. Press **[Alt] S** to arrange the employees in rank order and generate the computer-recommended merit raises. The raises will appear in **column E.**

3. In **column F,** enter your decisions on merit raises. *An important reminder on entering raises: To enter a raise of 3 percent, you must enter ".03" rather than "3." To enter a raise of 1.5 percent, you must enter ".015" rather than 1.5.*

This is usually an iterative process. Each time you complete the raises in **column F,** hit the **F9** key to recalculate and verify the quality checks. Continue on, changing numbers and hitting the **F9** key, until you have the raises you want with no quality checks.

4. You're finished with the merit phase! Press **[Alt] E** to move to the equity phase.

Equity Phase

1. Enter the computer's equity recommendations **(column J)** into **column K.** (Do not use the Lotus copy command.)

2. As in the merit phase, change any or all of the equity adjustments in **column K.** Hit the **F9** key to recalculate and verify the quality checks and continue the process until you are satisfied with the outcome.

3. You may wish to graph your results during the equity phase. To do so, press **[Alt] G.** If you select **Current Salary,** the software will show one line that represents the group's salary distribution prior to this focal review. If you select **Both Salaries,** it will graph two lines that represent a "before" and "after" salary distribution based on your pending recommendations. To escape from the graphs and return to the equity phase, hit any key and then select **"Quit."**

4. Continue with the equity phase until you are satisfied with the outcome. To print your final results, press **[Alt] P.**

Starting Over or Exiting the Demo

Once you have completed the equity phase, you can start over. Simply remain in the equity phase and hit **[Alt] C.** This will return you to a "clean slate" in the merit phase and allow you to begin again.

Of course, you may also choose to exit the demo. To do so, hit **[Alt] M** and return to the Main Menu. The menu gives you the option to Store your final worksheet. *We strongly recommend that you do not use the Store option—it makes starting over in the future more difficult.* Instead, hit **Quit** and exit the worksheet without storing your results.

If you do choose to Store your results, however, and then wish to start over, follow these instructions:

1. Choose **Select** from the Main Menu, type **1**, and hit **Enter.** You will not see a "clean slate" for the merit phase. Instead, you will see your previously stored worksheet.

2. Hit **[Alt] C** to clear the worksheet and return to a "clean slate" in the merit phase. You can then run the demo again.

3. After the equity phase, hit **[Alt] M,** choose **Store,** and exit the worksheet. The next time you retrieve it you will see a "clean slate" in the merit phase.

One Last Detail . . .

The Select option in the Main Menu allows you to enter choices **1** through **4**. As we've explained, selecting **1** starts the demo. Selecting **2** displays a completed worksheet for the merit phase based on the demo in the book. Selecting **3** displays a completed worksheet for the equity phase based on the demo in the book. If you're having trouble re-creating the book demo, you may wish to return to the Main Menu **([Alt] M),** select 2 or 3, and review the appropriate worksheet. Selecting **4** merely displays a blank worksheet.

CHAPTER 3

holding on to your best people: two game plans for playing defense

With people, as with most things in business, the best defense is a good offense. A company keeps its most valuable people by treating them fairly, rewarding their performance, and creating opportunities for them to do important work. But there comes a time when every company simply must play defense: A startup is determined to steal one of your top salesmen; a big company is launching a new product and wants three of your best young engineers.

No system can generate the honest and constructive dialogue it takes to persuade someone that he is better off with your company than with the competition. (And if that's not true, if someone *is* better off somewhere else, you should honestly wish him good luck!) But when it's time to play defense, and you have a good case to make, systems can improve your chances of winning.

Two major systems help us guard against raids from the outside. One is designed to seal off the company from headhunters. The other is designed to win reversals when a valued employee decides to leave. Without these systems there's no question we would have lost some of our best people.

In any company the first line of defense against headhunters is the support staff. That's because the first "barrier to entry" for headhunters trying to steal good people is finding out who they are. The names and titles of our vice presidents are public information; they're listed in our annual reports. The names and titles of all other people are company confidential.

Headhunters cleverly manipulate the good intentions of support staff to obtain this valuable information. *Their* job is to say whatever it takes to obtain the roster of a department or the names of the members of a new-product team. *Our* job is to make their job as tough as possible, even impossible.

Our defenses against headhunters begin with something as simple as the telephone book. We treat the Cypress telephone directory as a highly proprietary document. On every page of every company phone book, stamped in bright red, is the following warning:

CONFIDENTIAL. Not to be reproduced. Not to be taken off Cypress premises. This information is proprietary to Cypress. This stamp is in red. If it is in black, return it to your departmental secretary immediately!

Then "headhunter control" takes over. We like to test how good we are at protecting our borders. Twice in the last few years I've asked a "friendly" headhunter to penetrate Cypress. Both times the firm reported back that we were one of the toughest companies it had come up against.

The best way to describe this system is to let it describe itself. After all, inside Cypress it is supposed to be instinctive—to kick into action the moment it should be. Here are slides from the training session we use to teach our people the basics of headhunter control.

Of course, it's impossible to completely seal off any company from raids by the competition. Top-quality employees are always receiving job offers. How you react to those offers—how quickly and effectively you make the case for staying with the company—determines your retention rate, how many people you keep or lose.

Five years ago, after a frustrating week in which I was called in

HEADHUNTER CONTROL

Definition: Headhunter (HH)

One who's job it is to obtain personnel for a client (competitor) company.

HH's Objective:

Obtain the names of Cypress employees and HIRE them away to another company.

Your Objective:

Establish if the person is a HH and obtain a name, company, and phone number for Cypress task force.

TYPICAL HH PLOYS

Scenario #1

HH: Hi, is there a Jerry in your department?
SECRETARY: NO!
HH: I'm sorry! Maybe it was Terry. This phone message is not too clear.

(Now he has you thinking that you are helping a coworker.)

SECRETARY: No, there is no Terry either, but there is a Larry!

HH: Yes, it could be Larry. Let me talk to him.

TYPICAL HH PLOYS

Scenario #2

I'm a student/govt. agency/newspaper columnist, etc., and I am doing a study on how many people there are in your department or how it is organized. I do not want names, because I know that is proprietary, but can you tell me the various departments and their names and roughly how many people are in each department?

This data will then be used with scenario #1, where the HH will get into a specific department and job function that he is looking for, or it will be used with scenario #3.

TYPICAL HH PLOYS

Scenario #3

Hi, I got a call from "somebody" in your (XXX) department who wanted to know about...

By this time the HH is in the right department (because of scenario #2) and the secretary or other individual knows the technical terms and the person in charge of that discipline.

TYPICAL HH PLOYS

Scenario #4 (Looking for middle management)

HH: Is John Smith (VP of XXX) there?

(VP's names are public domain information, or they are known in the industry.)

SC: No. (They never are.)

(By this time the secretary thinks that this person is important!)

HH: Well, whom can I talk to of authority in your department? (HH now gets #2 person.)

SUMMARY

In each case HHs get information from YOU!

They try intimidation (asking for VPs).

They try to act as if they are helping by answering a phone call or request on the part of someone.

They pretend they need help and appeal to your graciousness and courtesy.

WHAT TO DO

NEVER give out a name, title, or phone extension!

YOU ask the questions!

- What is YOUR name?
- Where are YOU calling from?
- What is YOUR phone number?

Always be courteous! This may be a legitimate customer or vendor. HHs depend on the fact that we cannot afford to endanger our business relationships with the real world.

WHOM TO PASS THE INFORMATION TO

When you get the name, company, and telephone number, you should do the following:

1. Call the number back! See if the company the person gave you is a real company. Many HHs use fictitious company names and have their secretaries field the calls for them.

- If the individual you talked to answers, say you were verifying the phone number, as you could not read your own writing, etc.

- If a secretary answers or an answering service answers with a different company name or same name, ask what business this company is in. A real business should have no problem telling you its line of work.

2. If anything at all sounds or feels suspicious, TELL YOUR SUPERVISOR or VP what you have discovered. Document the conversation in detail. List the exact questions that the HH used and what he was looking for, and contact one of the task force members.

HEADHUNTER TRAP PROCEDURES

- Task force will function as the contact point.
- Headhunter should be transferred or information obtained forwarded to a task force member.
- Cypress contact pretends to be interested up to a point.
- Task force will trap HH into revealing real identity, company represented, and phone number.

- Task Force will forward the information to human resources.
- Human resources will check approved HH list.

  If approved, it will forward information to our counsel to handle the legalities.

  If not approved, it will contact HH agency and attempt to convince HH of the long-term benefits that can accrue as the result of working with Cypress.

at the very last minute to save two key people, I wrote a memo that articulated how our managers should fight to retain valued employees who quit. Intel inspired much of our approach; for many years its system for retaining key people was a model for doing it right. We modified and added to the Intel principles and developed a system whose batting average has been about .500. This is an excellent turnaround figure that makes our rivals' recruitment jobs exactly twice as hard as they expected—a great invitation to recruit elsewhere.

Here's the memo. It speaks for itself. Our biggest headache is getting people to follow the procedures. Every year or so we make another set of copies of the memo, distribute them to our vice presidents and top managers, and remind them of how we are supposed to do things.

CYPRESS SEMICONDUCTOR CORPORATION
INTERNAL CORRESPONDENCE

DATE: February 24, 1988   WW: 09
TITLE: WHAT TO DO WHEN A VALUED EMPLOYEE QUITS
TO: VPs, Mgrs
AUTHOR: T.J. Rodgers
AUTHOR FILE #: TJR-211, Rev. A   Security File #:
SUBJECT: Administration
DISTRIBUTION:
CIRCULATION:

I have not been called upon to save a valued employee for quite some time. Last week, I became involved in two such instances, both successful, but my job was made much more difficult by our not following the fundamental principles of what to do when an employee quits.

I realized that I have never formally stated what our policy is concerning resignations. Here it is:

1) React immediately (within five minutes). There is nothing more important to do than to react immediately to an employee who has quit. I repeat: there is <u>nothing</u> that takes priority over working with an employee who has resigned (presuming the employee is one that we are intent upon keeping). The corollary of the basic premise "nothing more important" is that your reaction should happen immediately; the next activity you have scheduled

continued

should be cancelled; any delay (such as "I'll talk to you after our staff meeting") is unacceptable. There are two purposes for reacting with a sense of urgency. First, it demonstrates to the employee that he or she* does take precedence over daily activities, and second, it gives you the greatest chance of changing the employee's mind before an irreversible decision has been made.

2) Keep the resignation secret. To the greatest extent possible, you should prevent the knowledge of a resignation from being publicly disclosed. Keeping the resignation absolutely under wraps is important for both parties. For the employee, it removes a major barrier to changing his mind in staying with the company, that of appearing to be vacillating on a major decision. Once the employee's ego gets attached to a decision, right or wrong, he is very unlikely to change course. If other employees are unaware that a resignation has occurred, the employee who has resigned does not face the embarrassment of a public reversal. The company is also given more latitude when a public announcement has not been made. In one recent resignation, the mistake of public disclosure was made. When I managed to convince that employee to remain at Cypress, there were multiple rumors (all untrue) that the company changed his mind by "buying him back." The company does not negotiate the salaries of employees who have resigned. Sometimes, we may make data known to the employee about upcoming raises, evergreen stock option grants, if the information is available at the time. Another disadvantage of public disclosure is that if an employee publicly resigns and then changes his mind, he may face resentment from other employees who wrongly assume that he has been given an unfair pay raise. In addition to the obvious conclusion that management should never disseminate information about a resignation, management should also do everything possible to prevent the employee from disseminating the information. Usually, the best way to convince an employee not to disseminate resignation information is to state the arguments given above: that the employee limits his own flexibility for the future and may unwittingly damage his reputation if he decides to stay.

3) Tell your boss immediately. When an employee resigns, I expect instantaneous communication all the way up through the chain of command to me. I expect that communication to happen within an hour of the time a resignation is received. I will consider management to have done a poor job if any resignation takes more than that time to get to my attention. I can be interrupted in meetings, called out of meetings in outside locations or called at home (I am listed in the telephone directory). There is no excuse for not informing me (and everyone in the chain of command between the individual and me) immediately when a resignation occurs.

4) Listen carefully to the employee. Once a resignation has occurred and the proper people have been informed, the manager of the individual involved

*For the rest of this memo I will assume the employee in question is male in order to avoid the awkward he/she construction.

and his VP should sit down and talk to the employee, listening very carefully to ascertain the exact reasons the resignation occurred. Any attempt to retain the employee will be severely impaired unless management listens to exactly what the employee has to say and accepts it. The message from the employee should be transmitted up through the chain of command without any changes, even if it is unflattering to the manager involved (for example, "I quit because I do not like working for you." Perhaps the company can find useful employment for a valued employee working in another group.) An exact determination should be made of what the employee's options are at the other company. Is the employee looking at a better job, more money, slower pace, faster pace, or a fundamental change in career? These issues will obviously be key in constructing an argument to change the employee's mind.

5) Construct your arguments. Once accurate data have been gathered, you and your VP should sit down and put together a plan to convince the employee to stay, if that is possible. In some cases, a realistic assessment of the situation will dictate that you will not try to keep the employee. When Russ Winslow quit Cypress to start his own company, the only reaction that made sense was to wish him good luck. Ninety percent of the time, however, a good argument can be made that it is in the employee's best interest to stay at Cypress. The only possible effective argument to retain an employee is an argument which validly claims that the employee's best interests are served by staying at Cypress. Typically, an employee will have quit for two simultaneous reasons: a "push" of some sort having to do with a long-standing frustration at Cypress and a "pull" from another company, at which the "grass appears to be greener." A successful retention argument will attack with reality the unrealistic advantages perceived for the other company, as well as truly offering a solution to some of the problems that caused the employee to consider working for the other company in the first place. Once you and the VP have formulated your first-cut employee retention arguments, I should become involved to help set the overall strategy. This strategy should be defined and refined on the very same day the employee resigns.

6) Use all the horsepower at your disposal to win. With a carefully constructed strategy in place, we can then proceed to win back the employee. The employee first got the message that quitting was a big deal because of your rapid reaction to his resignation. We then reminded the employee that the company was truly interested in him because we listened to what was wrong for as long as it took to hear out the problem. On the second day, the employee should be given the message that his quitting was a mistake, that the company knows it was a mistake and that the company will single-mindedly try to rectify that mistake (Cypress will accept only two answers to our proposal that you stay, "yes" and "we'll talk about it some more"). On the second or third days, during which our position is being presented, the employee should be given the firm impression that we are not continuing business as usual. Schedules are interrupted. If appropriate, we may

continued

meet over meals outside the plant during off hours. If the employee's spouse is a major factor in the resignation, she is involved in the discussions. Any level of management required to get the job done is brought in. If it takes the president to get the job done (and it does in half the cases), then the president has nothing more important to do than to sit down with the employee. One of the greatest mistakes middle managers make when an employee quits is to assume that I am too busy to interrupt my schedule to keep a good person in the company.

7) Win back the employee by solving his problems. If our arguments are constructed in a timely manner and really do correct the problems that caused the employee to start looking around, we will be successful more than 80 percent of the time in causing the employee to change his mind. Most often, resigning employees like Cypress, its benefits, and the people with whom they work. They usually are threatening to leave because they do not like some of the particulars of their job or their direct supervisor. Their resolve to leave is further strengthened because they have found a job (typically) at a company which is a poor second to Cypress, but at a poor company, which at a first glance appears to offer some relative benefits. By alleviating the root problem at Cypress, and stressing the fundamental differences between us and the other company, the employee usually can be made to agree that staying is best.

8) Wipe out the competitor. The next step in the process is to shut down the other company. Two objectives are important here: to shut down the competitor so firmly that no further negotiations occur with our employee and to shut down the competitor in such a manner that they believe that they have wasted their time trying to hire Cypress employees (they believe picking some company other than Cypress would be an easier way to hire). Get the employee to agree that he will call up the competitor and shut down their offer himself. Furthermore, get him to agree that while he is shutting down the offer he will firmly state that counteroffers and continuing negotiation are not desired, that he is going to stay at Cypress and that decision is absolutely final. Since we have just caused a long-time Cypress employee to reaffirm his loyalty to the company, we are working with an ally who can help us convince the other company that they are wasting their time. Ask the employee to present the data to the competitor in such a manner as to discourage them from continuing to try to hire other Cypress employees. ("There was no counteroffer, I just want to stay at Cypress. I think my long-term best interests are served by being here. The same hour that I told my boss at Cypress I was thinking about leaving, I had meetings with my boss, his VP and T.J. Rodgers. When they made the comparisons between my career at Cypress and at your company, it was clear that I made a mistake in thinking about leaving Cypress. I really do not want to take any time to come over to your company to talk to you; my mind is made up. It would not be helpful to change my offer monetarily; I am fairly paid and have a good stock option; the issue is not money.")

9) Prevent the next problem. The last step in the process is really the first step in the process: sit down, think about your people and try to project where you might have a problem in the future.

To repeat the nine basic steps of what to do when an employee resigns:

1) React immediately (within five minutes).
2) Keep the resignation secret.
3) Tell your boss immediately.
4) Listen carefully to the employee.
5) Construct your arguments.
6) Use all the horsepower at your disposal to win.
7) Win back the employee by solving his problems.
8) Wipe out the competitor.
9) Prevent the next problem.

Work

real work: how to set demanding goals and meet them

The Cypress goals system has received more public attention than any other management system at the company. And it is without question the most widely misunderstood. One common reaction is fear: "My God, we're almost to the point where computers are taking over!" Another is dread: "The boss will give electronic orders every week!" Another is skepticism: "What a time-consuming, cumbersome, bureaucratic nightmare!"

In fact, as most Cypress people who use the goals system every day would attest, it is neither Big Brother nor Big Bureaucracy. It helps people identify and collect action items (entries on their "to-do" lists), think about them, set priorities, and make tradeoffs. It helps create fair-minded agreements between managers and their people about what needs to get done. It allows vice presidents and managers to track key projects. It also allows me (or any other manager) to "take the pulse" of any department or project, figure out who might be running into problems, and help them meet their goals—without intervening where we don't belong or trying to be in a hundred places at once.

Most people want to achieve. And most people are capable of extraordinary levels of commitment and performance—much more than their bosses give them credit for. Yet all too often organizations have trouble distinguishing between "real work"—things that make a difference to corporate success—and the "drone work" that gets done because it's always been done or because some boss arbitrarily decides it should be done. People know when what they're doing doesn't matter—and it leaves them demoralized and demotivated.

To win, people need clear and quantifiable goals, the resources to achieve those goals, and confidence that their goals matter to the larger corporate purpose. All of Cypress's people have clear and quantifiable goals. More important, they typically set their own goals, review them with their managers every week, commit to achieving them by a specific date, enter them in a computer, track them, and report on whether or not they completed them on schedule. In short, our people create an electronic database of "real work" that crowds out distractions and keeps everyone moving in the same direction.

Cypress's computerized goals system is a critical part of our managerial infrastructure. It is a detailed guide to the future and an objective record of the past. The system can't guarantee that we always work on the right issues or that we always meet our objectives. (There are no "goals cops" to evaluate judgments or monitor intensity.) But it does create an objective basis for setting priorities and measuring accomplishments on a weekly basis.

On a typical day last spring, the goals database provided a snapshot of the flow of work inside the company. The system had 10,217 active goals, of which 1,364 were due within a week and 8,898 within a month. There were 825 goals related to improving quality and 296 related to designing new products. A total of 669 goals were behind schedule (not in itself a major problem), and 320 of these goals were behind schedule by more than five weeks (a problem). There were 118 people with more than two delinquent goals, and 28 managers with more than 20 percent of their goals delinquent.

The system can also provide close-up details on our business by functional group or project. A few years ago, for example, we introduced the third generation of a computer chip called a 64K PROM. (PROMs are "nonvolatile" memory chips that hold data even after the power to a computer is shut off. They are used to store software code permanently.) The new-product plan for our third-generation PROM was approved in May 1989. The first production chip shipped in October 1990. We now ship six different versions of the third-generation chip, the most recent of which was introduced in the fourth quarter of 1991. It has been a big success for us.

A quick review of the goals database chronicles the story behind that success. The 64K-PROM team of circuit designers, product engineers, and test engineers worked for roughly two years on the six chips, a typical design cycle for a new family of products. From beginning to end they completed 3,278 goals. Some were "big" goals that represented major advances in the design process. Others were "small" goals: Fix a minor design glitch, revise some technical documents, send a memo to an outside contractor.

Of these 3,278 goals, 307 (fewer than 10 percent) were completed late. The team missed only three milestones serious enough to trigger "trouble meetings"—a Cypress euphemism for mandatory reviews with top management whenever a critical new-product milestone slips four weeks behind schedule. If every new-product team performed as crisply as the PROM group did on these six chips, we would be unstoppable.

The goals system is also a source of organizational knowledge. Anyone inside Cypress, no matter the hierarchical level, can review the goals for any project, any manager, any individual contributor— even me. A clerk, say, in our Minnesota plant is free to dial into the computer network, choose the "goals" selection from the main menu, enter my initials, and review my action items for the next few weeks.

Few people bother to inquire about my work; most are too busy tending to their own. (By the way, if I have goals of a company-confidential nature, I still enter them into the system. I just use a cryptic sentence that has meaning only to me.) But this organizational transparency is an important manifestation of our "no secrets" philosophy. It helps cut through the uncertainty and politics that can cripple companies and keeps everyone focused on real work.

Moreover, just as with focal reviews, the goals system is independent of the philosophy behind it. The "Big Brother" critics miss the point. The goals system does not presume any particular style of running the business. Goals can work for nuts-and-berries managers: "No sweat, just write down what you feel like doing this week and let me know when you're finished." Under this philosophy, the system functions like an electronic bulletin board. It can also accommodate authoritarian managers: "Every goal must be completed on time. All goals not completed on time will be treated as exceptions—as defects with 'corrective action' requirements."

We don't embrace either extreme, although both probably exist in the corners of our system. We want people to decide what they are going to do, why it makes sense, how important it is, and when they will complete it. We give people plenty of freedom to use the system in ways they find most helpful. There is no "right" number of goals. Some people like to record their to-do items in great detail; they might log twenty-five or more every week. Others focus on "big events" and leave smaller details (sending out a few letters, preparing a short memo) off the system. No matter—so long as the critical activities on which they will be spending most of their time, and that have an impact on other people in the organization, do get recorded.

Of course, we do want people to push themselves, to stretch, to set goals they can achieve but that represent genuine personal challenge. That's why we don't hold it against people if they fail to achieve 100 percent completion every week. At the same time, managers monitor the goals, look for problems, and expect people who fall behind to ask for help before they lose control of or damage critical projects.

The goals system has lots of fervent advocates inside Cypress—managers who look forward to goals meeting with their people, project leaders who can't imagine working any other way. But it also has its doubters. We have at least two minority subcultures within the company that can't or won't use the system the way it is intended. One group insists on treating it as an electronic report card. They pad their goals by entering dozens and dozens of minute action items they have already completed, or know they'll complete, and shoot for "perfect scores"—even though we remind them no scorekeeper is watching.

Another group believes that the system does represent Big Brother—top management waiting to pounce on each and every late goal. They use the system because we require them to, but they would be thrilled if it disappeared tomorrow. We focus on serving the 80 percent of our people who use the goals as an effective personal work organizer and management tool.

The goals system is like any other computer system: garbage in, garbage out. And no amount of software can eliminate bad manners or boorish behavior. At its most basic, the role of the system is to allow people to codify what they intend to do and to allow their managers to conduct reality checks. It is *not* an instrument through which managers bludgeon their people to do more, to "give them their marching orders." Which is not to say some managers don't use the system to pressure rather than to help. Unfortunately, some of our people then equate such bad behavior with the system itself— which is a little like saying English is a bad language because you can use it to hurt people's feelings.

Despite pockets of misunderstanding and resistance, the goals system has always been an integral part of the fabric of our company. Why do we bother? It's simple. In a semiconductor company, problems and opportunities come at you at one hundred miles an hour from every direction. Without some way to make sense of all these demands, many (if not most) of our people would be overwhelmed.

Think about how many high-technology companies skyrocket to glory and then crash and burn overnight. Failure isn't the problem; *success* is the problem. With success comes growth, with growth comes more work, with more work comes more people, and with more people come more opportunities for the organization to spiral out of control.

Think, too, about how dramatically the nature of work is changing. Everything is faster, tougher, more complex—and the consequences of mistakes more profound. As more and more work becomes "knowledge" work, more and more knowledge resides with those closest to the work itself. People often know better than their bosses the details of what needs to get done. Most work (and certainly the most important work) is done by multidisciplinary teams rather than within old-style functional boundaries. And work is becoming more geographically dispersed—even as people need to work more and more closely together.

The goals system reckons with all of these complex new realities. Yet it also reflects one of our most strongly held beliefs: The only way to handle the intensity and complexity of business is to develop management systems that are clear and simple. The goals system doesn't work because it is a technological or managerial marvel. It works because it is an easy-to-use tool.

One of our vice presidents, who was, shall we say, dismayed when upon joining the company he learned about the goals system, used it for a month or so and changed his tune: "This is really the world's most sophisticated electronic Day-Timer." There's something to that description. The system's most basic contribution is as a personal-productivity organizer. But it is much more than that because it offers a powerful added feature: It creates an overview perspective on work (through its database capabilities) that allows us to collectively manage the company more flexibly and intelligently.

It's important to note that the system has not required major investments in computer hardware and software. We have no staffers or equipment dedicated exclusively to the goals. We use the same network of personal computers and workstations that we use for all of our other computing needs. The original software was written with Lotus 1-2-3 and Paradox, two of the most common PC applications. For much of its history, the system ran on "sneakernet": People passed disks back and forth and copied the information into shared personal computers. For the last few years, the system has run over the worldwide corporate network—which eliminates lots of administrative headaches and disk swapping.

Indeed, I developed the basics of the goals system long before personal computers existed. It has its roots in management-by-objectives techniques I learned in the mid-1970s at American Microsystems (AMI), where I ran the random access memory (RAM) group. Back then AMI was a loosely managed outfit whose "supportive culture" was rife with disorganization and political infighting. Projects were routinely behind schedule and over budget, and the company's grim financial performance showed it.

A few years after I arrived, the company brought in a no-nonsense CEO from the outside. Glenn Penisten, who came to AMI from Texas Instruments, quickly let it be known that things would be different. His approach to planning was simple. At the beginning of the year, product line managers made presentations on new products. We were allowed one sheet of paper per product. One side of the sheet projected schedules and sales: when the product would be available, how many units would ship, how much revenue it would generate. The other side projected costs: expenses, new equipment, headcount. The system's very simplicity cut through a lot of the politics and excuses.

My RAM group had grandiose plans for ten new products. We wondered how such a small development team (twenty-five engineers) could possibly pull it off. We decided to get organized. For each product we wrote down everything that had to be done before it could ship—and I mean *everything*, in lawyerlike detail. Then we attached names and due dates to each task. Our "information technology" was my whiteboard and some Magic Markers. Our "update routine" was an eraser. As we completed tasks, we wiped them off the board. Our work program amounted to doing whatever it took to be able to use that eraser.

When I left AMI for Advanced Micro Devices (AMD), I became responsible for RAM production engineering as well as design. It became even harder to keep score. So I covered all the walls in my office with whiteboards, used masking tape to divide them into project panels, and "ported" the system I had developed at AMI. Once a week my assistant would wheel in her IBM Selectric typewriter, record the goals, and send them out to the troops as the minutes of the goals meeting.

With seventy-five people in my group, I spent six hours a week poring over the goals. But there was no other way for me or my people to do a good, detailed management job. Anyone who wanted information on a project could walk into the war room, look at the boards, and see what was happening. The whiteboards became an essential tool for communication.

The Cypress system is an enhanced electronic version of that simple system. It has been improved and modified to serve Cypress managers at all levels—managers with 75, or 175, or 5 people in their groups. The computer record called a "goal" includes a description of the task, who has agreed to complete it, the manager or project leader to whom that person reports, the vice president to whom the manager reports, when the goal was set, what project the goal supports, when it is due for completion, what priority it is, what generic type of goal it is (quality, new product, strategic, or other), and its on-time status. People who want to know what's going on with a project tap into the network rather than knock on my door— but the basics are the same.

Here is an excerpt from actual records in the Cypress system.

During a typical week last spring, Rick Foreman had thirty goals, twenty of which are shown here. We know these are Rick's goals because his initials ("RF") are in the WHO field. The FROM field records the manager or project leader to whom Rick reports. "PV" is Pat Verderico, our vice president of finance and CFO, and Rick's direct boss. FROM does not mean that Pat ordered Rick to take on the goal, or even that Rick reports to Pat. (Pat could be the manager of a project in which Rick participates.) Rick sets almost all of his own goals, as does almost everyone at Cypress.

The seventh record shows that Rick agreed to evaluate "electronic calendar" software for use by Cypress management. (We've put check marks next to goals we'll discuss here.) He entered the goal in workweek 8 (under B for begin) and expected to complete it by workweek 16 (under E for end). Most goals take only a week or two to complete. However, every quarter, people in the administration group at Cypress establish three longer-term goals or strategic objectives. The "O" under TYPE shows that this software evaluation is one of Rick's three long-term objectives for the quarter.

WEEKLY GOALS: AN EXCERPT

FROM	TYPE	CATEGORY	B	E	D	S	WHO	P	GOAL
PV	Q	ADMN	8	16		C	RF		Q1-2: Establish consistent E-Mail standards
RF		TOPG	10	14	15	C	RF		Official ruling regarding shipments to international customers
PV		ADMN	13	16		D	RF		Next killer software meeting with TJR and task force
PV	O	ADMN	13	16		C	RF		Identify bills paid to banks and law firms
PV		ADMN	8	16		C	RF		Q1-5: Support various lawsuits
PV	O	ADMN	11	14		C	RF		Define DQT quality goals for 1992
PV		ADMN	8	14		C	RF		Q1-4: Evaluate electronic calendar software for Cypress mg't
PV		ADMN	12	14		C	RF		10K: Complete final revision
RF	O	TOPG	11	15		C	RF		Verify that we can receive F/A units from int'l customers
PV		ADMN	8	16		C	RF		Q1-3: Hold legal expenses to quarterly budget
PV		ADMN	13	14		C	RF		Proxy: Complete final revision
PV		ADMN	5	13	16	CD	RF	1	Stock: Analyze administrative errors for quality program
PV		ADMN	9	15	16	ND	RF	2	1991 market-share data available by country?
PV		ADMN	3	16			RF	3	Renegotiate bank contract due for renewal in May '92
ENB	Q	RIMS	10	16			RF	4	Set up 1992 W-2 payroll/stock upload
PV		ADMN	13	16		R	RF	5	Send copy of legal memo and insurance policies to broker
PV		ADMN	13	16		N	RF	6	Send comparative cost banking analysis to JT
PV		ADMN	13	16			RF	7	Review competitor proxy to examine ESPP plan—contributory?
PV		ADMN	15	16		N	RF	8	1Q '92 indies for earnings announcements
PV		ADMN	6	17			RF	9	Evergreen: Exclude restricted stock from employee's unvested shares

This entry was created on the goals database for the Records and Information System (RIMS) quality team. The RIMS project report is fed into the central computer on Monday afternoon, and the computer automatically "copies" the goal into Rick's functional goals report—which allows his boss to see what project assignments he has taken on.

Rick Foreman's schedule for workweek 15 includes thirty completed and pending goals. Twenty are shown in this excerpt. Some goals (e.g., completing final revisions on the company's proxy statement) require only one week to complete. Other goals (such as renegotiating bank contracts) take three months.

The priority (P) field is critical for time management. And it is an important topic of discussion and compromise between managers and their reports. Rick has seventeen pending goals, nine of which are shown here. That means seventeen different activities are vying for his time and attention. How does he decide what to do when? In discussions with his boss, Cypress vice president and CFO Pat Verderico, Rick assigns each task a specific priority and organizes his time accordingly.

(Blank entries in the TYPE field mean the goal is a standard short-term assignment.) The "C" in the S field (for status) shows that he completed the objective on time.

Records on completed goals (the first eleven in this excerpt) do not include one important piece of information that is part of the record for still-pending goals. The P field (for priority) shows how each pending goal ranks among the various activities that need Rick's attention. Rick's full weekly report includes seventeen pending goals. He plans to complete nine by next week, ten by the week after, two in three weeks, one in a month, and one even further into the future. These goals are ranked 1 to 17 based on Rick's estimation (and his boss's) of where he should be spending his time. Essentially, it is Rick's work plan for the upcoming week. This excerpt shows nine of the pending goals.

Notice that Rick's second-priority goal in workweek 15 is behind schedule. The "ND" in the status field means "newly delinquent"—that is, the goal slipped behind schedule for the first time this week. Another goal is marked "CD" in the status field. This means that it is "continuing delinquent"—that is, the goal has been rescheduled more than once. The record shows it was established in workweek 5 and originally due in workweek 13. Rick now expects to complete it by the end of workweek 16.

I've circled a few other interesting bits of information from this goals excerpt. Multiply this report by 1,250 (the number of Cypress people on the goals system), think about the different ways Cypress managers can sort and review the information (by project, by manager, by type of goal, by "lateness" of goals), and you begin to understand how rich and revealing a database it can be.

No matter how good the software, however, this company's performance ultimately comes down to good management. The goals system does not put Cypress on autopilot. It merely provides useful instrumentation. If our people believe in the goals they set for themselves, and if our managers work with them to establish the right priorities among the goals, we move quickly and effectively. If not, we stagnate.

PROJECTS VS. FUNCTIONS — BALANCE,
NOT BARONS

The most visible "output" of the goals system are the computerized records that answer the "3Ws" of management: who, what, when. But you can't understand the importance and uses of the records without understanding the process of communication and negotiation that creates them. The goals system helps resolve one of the most common and debilitating tensions within companies: whether to organize work creatively and dynamically, through project teams, or more cautiously and carefully, through the functional chain of command.

Most startups (like Cypress in 1983) are intensely project-oriented. In the early days they have one big project (the company) and one project leader (the president). The needs of the company take absolute priority. People may have familiar-sounding functional titles—vice president of manufacturing, vice president of marketing— but everyone is focused on a handful of make-or-break projects: finishing the design of the first product, closing the first sale, getting it out the door. People who run departments hurry to pitch in wherever they can. Things just happen.

Then, at around $50–$100 million in sales in our business, things start to change. It's three A.M. one Sunday, an important piece of equipment breaks down, the factory comes grinding to a halt. None of the project missionaries has paid much attention to production basics. The vice president of manufacturing, aroused from a deep sleep, angrily declares: "We need to grow up!" He turns to the plant manager, who hires a director of production control, who jealously guards access to the assembly line.

Two months later a critical shipment fails to arrive at a customer's warehouse. The vice president of marketing gets a call from this irate customer and becomes irate himself: "We need to grow up!" He complains to the vice president of manufacturing, who asks the inventory-control manager to develop a more intricate set of procedures for what orders go out when.

Later that year an important new product fails to launch on

time. A critical mistake in process development, a mistake made eight months earlier, went undetected and fouled up the entire chip. The vice president of R&D can't believe it: "We need to grow up!" He creates a special unit to monitor all similar process technologies and catch problems early.

Pretty soon this project-driven startup has created all kinds of functional "baronies." The basic role of the barons (no matter how well intentioned) is to make their departments run right—even if it means sometimes running roughshod over the projects they are supposed to serve. The factory may operate more smoothly, products may arrive on time, R&D glitches may get caught, but the company's creativity, speed, and capacity for innovation erode.

A company the size of Cypress needs the best of both worlds. We want to be project-driven, which helps emphasize speed and agility, as well as functionally accurate, which guarantees good execution. And we want to avoid cumbersome experiments like matrix management. That's where the goals system helps out. Work at Cypress is explicitly organized along two dimensions: by project and by functional chain of command. Likewise, the goals system is organized by project and function.

Here's how it operates. We divide the year into fifty-two workweeks. Each workweek has a standard set of meetings, decisions, and database updates connected to the goals system. One set of meetings involves projects. There are more than two hundred formal "projects" at Cypress. Members of a project team may be (and usually are) from different parts of the organization. Project managers need not be (and often aren't) the highest-ranking member of the group. Some projects relate to quality, others to worker safety, cost reduction, or new products. Some projects last for years, others for a few months. But every project has a recognized leader, team members, a specific mission—and official standing in the goals database.

Every week, project managers check out their "project disk" or electronically transfer all the goals in the database relating to their projects. Project members sit down with their leaders, review what has been achieved in the prior week, decide what needs to be achieved over the next few weeks, set specific goals, rank them in priority order, and enter them back into the goals system. Most project teams hold their meetings on Wednesdays, Thursdays, or Fridays. All project meetings must be completed by four P.M. the following Monday. At that time, goals are fed into a central database and sorted a different way—by functional manager.

By eight A.M. Tuesday, the company's functional managers receive electronic files from the goals database. The files list the new, pending, and completed goals for all the people who report to each manager, including the goals generated in the latest round of project meetings. Functional managers may see for the first time goals their people took on in project meetings. ("As a member of the manufacturing safety committee, I agreed to . . .") There are about two hundred managers in the company, so the computer generates about two hundred different electronic reports.

Take Pat Verderico, our vice president and CFO. Pat has roughly sixty people working under him, ten of whom are managers. Five of these people report directly to him: his assistant, the director of purchasing, the controller, the treasurer, and the director of administration. Naturally, these people (and the people who report to them) spend much of their time on work directly related to their functional responsibilities under Pat. But they (and the people who report to them) each participate in projects outside Pat's immediate direction.

Pat's Tuesday goals file includes information on his five direct reports' functional goals as well as the project goals they accepted in the prior round of project meetings. The excerpt from Rick Foreman's goals was taken from that Tuesday managers' report. Pat's full report for that week included 110 goals for him and his four people, 90 of which related to functional work, 20 of which related to the six different external projects with which they were associated.

Look again at the excerpt from Rick's weekly report. Under CATEGORY, most of the goals are identified as ADMN (administration), which means they are goals that Rick generated or agreed to take on as part of his direct functional responsibilities. But Rick is also a member of two project teams, and his report includes goals from these projects.

In workweek 10, for example, as part of his membership on the

Records and Information Management System (RIMS) quality project, Rick agreed to make some modifications in payroll and stock procedures by the end of workweek 16. Notice that the goal is not FROM "PV" but FROM "ENB"—Elizabeth Bayez, a human resources rep who manages the RIMS project. (Elizabeth is junior to Rick in the corporate hierarchy, but that doesn't mean she can't lead the project.)

After reviewing the data, managers spend Tuesday mornings in meetings with their people. Some managers use one-on-one sessions, others meet with all their people as a group. This is a critical step. The failure mode in our company (and I suspect in most growing companies) is that people overcommit themselves rather than establish unchallenging goals. The manager's job is to help his or her people sort out problems, not to demand more goals faster. People talk about possible overloads and conflicts, establish priorities, organize work, and make mutual commitments about what is going to get done. They may reschedule some goals, change some priorities, transfer goals between people, delete goals that are no longer relevant. By four P.M. Tuesday, the revised schedule is fed back into the central database.

The nearby flow chart provides a simple overview of how the goals process works. This "two-pass" system generates the work program that coordinates the mostly self-imposed activities of every Cypress employee. By allowing the project meetings to generate the goals "menu," it is responsive to the needs of projects. But by allowing functional managers to have a "last look" every week, it helps the organization remain in control. At least that's the theory. In practice, life in a semiconductor company is so fast-paced that even weekly goals planning can't anticipate everything that needs attention. Crises of the moment can crowd out goals that were decided just a few days earlier.

I don't want to create wrong impressions about how much time all this takes. Individual contributors spend perhaps two hours a week in meetings related to the goals system: an hour or so with their projects, forty-five minutes or so on Tuesday with their manager. Middle managers may spend three or four hours a week in project meetings, a one-on-one with their boss, several one-on-ones

HOW THE GOALS SYSTEM WORKS

Schedule	Who	Activity
Thursday 8 AM through Monday 4 PM	Project Leaders & Team Members	Update and Submit PROJECT Goals from all locations into the central database.
Tuesday 7 AM	Goals Administrator	Merge PROJECT goals with Manager goals and download to each Manager's computer.
Tuesday 8 AM through 4 PM	Managers and Employees	Update and Submit MANAGER Goals from all locations into the central database.
Wednesday 8 AM	Goals Administrator	Create management reports. Distribute reports across the network for all locations.

with their people, some time looking through and thinking about the electronic reports.

Of course, most of the time in meetings involves debating the substance of work. The goals system merely provides a framework for the discussion and a record of what was decided. In return for this investment, we generate fair and precise weekly work plans that intelligently balance the needs of projects and functions. The goals system codifies, classifies, sorts, and stores the kinds of conversations and tradeoffs that take place at any company—and that typically create confusion rather than crisp work plans.

FIVE COMPANIES, FOUR STATES, TEN MONTHS

The "interactive feedback" between projects and functions is one of the central organizing dynamics of our company. It's worth exploring in a bit more detail. I recently ran a project (since completed) dedicated to putting Cypress on the cutting edge of semiconductor assembly: attaching chips directly to computer boards, thus eliminating the need for bulky packages and thick lead wires. This so-called TAB (tape automated bonding) assembly process is a demanding, complex, multidisciplinary challenge. But the benefits are significant: smaller, lighter, more powerful computers.

We acquired some important TAB technology when we bought Control Data's plant in Minnesota. We decided to integrate it with the rest of the Cypress organization and launch a series of TAB-based products. Our TAB project team took shape in January 1991. We shipped our first modules ten months later and began shipping our most powerful TAB-based microprocessor in the middle of 1992. The TAB team drew on virtually every outpost of the Cypress federation. In Texas, our Ross Technology subsidiary worked on microprocessor design and engineering. Our Minnesota factory made wafers and did the TAB work. Cypress San Jose monitored quality, ran marketing, and interacted with customers. Our design center in Starkville, Mississippi, worked on a new memory chip for the module.

All told, the TAB team included as many as twenty people, four layers of management, five different Cypress companies, four states. How did I, as project leader, coordinate these far-flung organizations and people? With the goals system. Every Friday morning at ten I convened a TAB project meeting in my office. A few people attended in person, but most participated through speaker phone. We discussed problems, successes, future milestones. We got results from tests and experiments, and brainstormed ways to break through technical roadblocks. We made lots of technology decisions and scheduling tradeoffs. But all the discussions and decisions led to specific goals entered into the computer system.

Throughout the course of each meeting, which normally lasted about two hours, I acted as the scribe, updating completed goals on the computer screen, entering new goals, revising assignments. We didn't need a recording secretary or administrative assistant. And at the end of the meeting we didn't need minutes, memos, or action plans. The goals system had recorded everything *as we decided it.*

By noon, people scattered across the country had a detailed understanding of who needed to do what by when.

But that was just the beginning. The goals we identified on Friday then got fed into the central database and distributed to the appropriate functional managers across the Cypress federation. Remember, everyone on the TAB project team also played a role in some functional organization—as a manager, a direct report, or both. What we decided on Friday could have big impacts on their other responsibilities.

Those impacts got addressed during the Tuesday functional meetings. Let's say the president of Cypress Minnesota (a member of the TAB project) agreed to solve a problem with chip bonding. He might spend his next Tuesday meeting with his engineering managers identifying the specific actions items required to deliver on his promise. These managers might then hold one-on-ones with their engineers, refining the assignments even more. So this one TAB project goal could translate into ten or fifteen goals spread through several layers of the Minnesota operation.

Sometimes a functional manager would use the Tuesday meeting to revise a project goal. Let's say the TAB team included a process engineer from our Texas plant. On Tuesday he would meet with his manager in Texas. Through the goals file the manager would learn that this engineer had accepted a high-priority TAB goal due in two weeks. The manager might then remind this engineer of all the other goals competing for his time and persuade him to delay: "Look, I know T.J. wants you to get that done in two weeks. But we've promised to solve a yield problem on the 64K PROM, and that's going to take work. Let's push the TAB goal out one week; that won't hurt the project."

In other words, we could decide whatever we wanted during our Friday TAB meeting. But all our decisions were subject to reality checks the following Tuesday. As a project leader, would I have preferred that everything we decide on Friday happened exactly as planned? Sure. But as CEO, I realized that every member of the TAB team faced lots of other urgent demands. The two-pass goals system lets team members and their managers sort through those demands accurately and objectively.

<u>ACTION REQUEST</u>   AR #   5401

FOR (ACTION):   VPs AND SUBSIDIARY
                     PRESIDENTS
                                              START: May 13, 1991
                                              DUE: May 14, 1991
CC (INFORMATION): HC1/JJC1/GK2/TJR STAFF

FROM: T.J. RODGERS

TITLE: ROSS MODULE DREAM

CONTENTS: You may call this my "Martin Luther King" AR. This is a
dream I have that would put us in a clear-cut position of superiority in the
microprocessor business in the United States. The dream, as first conceived,
will undoubtedly need to be modified to succeed. However, the basic concept
and the benefit we would gain from it are very clear to me and will not change,
even if the details of the dream need to be modified.

I would like the Cypress family of companies to manufacture a computer on a
module that is about two inches by two inches. The module would be assembled using a TAB process mounting the Ross chipset onto a multi-layer, FR4-
type substrate. The module would be completely designed and manufactured
by Cypress, eliminating the need for subcontractors and the ability of our competitors to pick away at our products. LSI Logic, for example, which currently
screws up our average selling price on the 7C601, would be eliminated from the
business, because Sun would refuse to buy single 7C601's. Likewise, Logic Devices, which has cut in half the price we can charge for our cache RAM, would
be eliminated from their parasitic effect on our business. Anyone not selling
complete processor systems on a board would not be able to compete with us.
Furthermore, the cost of the TAB assembly materials appears to be about $26,
as opposed to $86 for our current assembly materials. The cost reduction would
drop right to the bottom line and also allow us to move along Sun's demanded
pricing curve without injuring our profits.

The difficult part in executing the dream is that it will require the cooperation
of four different companies: Cypress, Ross, Multichip, and Company X (a company specializing in ultra-high-yield module manufacturing in which Multichip
is about to invest). I will describe the dream by talking about one potential
manufacturing flow (which I think is about right), including the advantages,
disadvantages, and risks that I currently see at each step.

Cypress Semiconductor would have to begin to manufacture what I am going
to call the "T" package or the TAB package. A 7C601 in a TAB package would
be a 7C601 die with hermetic gold bumps, inner-lead bonded to a 35mm poly-
amide/copper tape. The product would either be shipped on reels or with the
frames separated and mounted in plastic TAB holders. The product would be
sort tested before being TABed, but would not be final tested. TAB lead would

provide probe points for class testing by Ross. (For some other products, Cypress would also be required to do class testing in the TAB form, if the products were required to be shipped in a tested form to the end customer, but this feature is not required for Ross.) To accomplish the bumping and TABing, Cypress will purchase VTC's Minnesota facility, which includes several million dollars' worth of equipment. The facility is currently operational with high yields. We should be able to begin shipping bumped, TABed products as quickly as we can get the TAB tape required for each of the chips in the Ross set. The Minnesota facility will report as Assembly II to Joel Camarda who will have responsibility for both the assembly areas. Just as Cypress manufacturing today ships packaged chips to Ross for test, in my plan, Cypress Assembly II would ship TAB chips to Ross for test.

There are challenges to getting a bump facility going in Minnesota. The facility must be managed from a distance. There are opportunities for missed execution. Given that the plant reported to VTC, I am sure that no one has ever looked at manufacturing efficiency and that its current costs are unacceptable. They must be driven down to be competitive with Assembly I. Assembly II must be able to perform a significant engineering activity, the ability to tool-up all TAB frames for the corporation. That engineering capability must include the ability to provide accurate electrical modeling for the packages, because one of the potential major advantages of TAB is to provide low impedance, low inductance wiring to speed up the products. Since the Ross chipset will consume a significant amount of power in a small area, the Minnesota facility must also have the engineering capability of providing models for power dissipation that can be used by the product lines. The challenge: to establish Assembly II in a remote facility while, simultaneously, improving manufacturing efficiencies and creating a significant engineering capability—all without overstaffing a plant which will be a financial burden in the beginning.

The challenges for Ross are significant. We need to procure equipment and learn how to handle TABed products. We also need to learn how to do burn-in. We might even need to do our own burn-in, if there are no external sources available. In addition, Ross will have to give significant engineering help to the other companies with regard to the problems of high frequency performance of the TAB structure and thermal dissipation. Ross will also be challenged to do a better job of testing than they have ever done in the past. Currently, even the reject rate on products we get from Sun would be enough to seriously depress the yield of the modules. The TABed chips that go into the module have to have virtually perfect yield to ensure overall success.

If we can put aside the parochial issues of separate companies and work together as a team, we can be responsible for the actual shipment of the most advanced-technology computer available in the merchant market. That accomplishment would give worldwide recognition to all of us.

Let's go get it done!

ACTION REQUEST   AR #   5536

FOR (ACTION):   VPs AND SUBSIDIARY
                       PRESIDENTS
                                               START: July 24, 1991
                                               DUE: July 30, 1991

CC (INFORMATION):

FROM: T.J. RODGERS

TITLE: I HAVE A NIGHTMARE

CONTENTS: Many of you read my "I HAVE A DREAM" AR. This one is on the other end of the spectrum. It relates to gate arrays and my fear that companies good in gate array design may eventually take over the logic world. The story goes like this:

SiArc, a startup company in gate arrays, called me to review their plan for potential collaboration. They have an advanced gate array technology which threatens all other forms of logic design (including GDT) for performance, die size, and design time.

The basic SiArc cell is a BiCMOS cell with twenty-seven CMOS transistors and one Bipolar transistor. The single Bipolar transistor allows the pull-up transition to be very powerful and the transistors driving that Bipolar transistor to be very weak (small). Thus the cell has very high drive capability and very low input capacitance, making it capable of 80 megahertz clock rates without any special effort. The cell also has a small degree of self-adaptability to customize itself for load size without intervention. Having a lot of transistors, the cell has been carefully designed to be able to create a lot of gates. The cell is not the typical TWO-HAND cell used in gate arrays, but a complex cell with a "large grain size," allowing it to create a lot of logic. Furthermore, the cells are interlaced in such a manner that they share supply and ground as well as allowing logic elements to be automatically allocated from one cell to the next to improve efficiency. There are only a few primitive cells in the technology, so that each cell can be carefully designed by technology for optimum results. Furthermore, the porting of the technology from one process to another is very simple, because only primitive cells need to be ported.

The second step in the design methodology is the use of GTD for routing of macro cells. The cell array is so efficient that macro cells need not be hand-drawn, they can simply be routed like mini-gate arrays. Thus, the creation of several hundred macro cells can be done much more efficiently than in a standard cell technology. The routing of macro cells presents the same problem to this technology as any other technology and the best available tools can be used. SiArc feels that the best available tools are gate array tools, not anything currently used in the custom silicon business.

The main advantage of the technology is that it really is still just a gate array. Therefore, very powerful and quick-to-market gate array tools can be used to bring SiArc gate arrays to market. However, the efficiency of the basic cell and the large library of macro cells allows the density of the SiArc array to be about 1.5 times better than a typical gate array for logic and several times better than a gate array for RAM-type functions such as registers, dual ports, etc. The cell is so efficient for RAM and registers that standard gate array routing is used, rather than the time-consuming effort in dropping in specialty RAM cores. The bottom line is that SiArc feels they can compete on die size and speed with full custom layouts, but blow them away by factors and design cycle time. That is the nightmare. If this company is real, the logic world will become the domain of LSI Logic and we will be pushed out of the logic business.

I have chartered Paul Keswick to evaluate carefully and thoroughly this potentially threatening technology. If it looks good, we will want to work with this company, rather than having it be an enemy. Paul will probably have to work closely with Ross if he chooses the SPARC controller as a vehicle. Dave Pederson in Minnesota apparently has been chosen by Paul to be the person who evaluates the technology. We all need to keep "heads up" on this one.

TO COMPLETE AR: Nothing specific required, but know that it is a company priority and your help is cordially demanded.

A glimpse of the promise and perils of high-technology competition. Some of the language in these memos is technical, many of the details hard to follow. But their tone does suggest the excitement and fear that is such a big part of our business.

The first memo was an attempt to inspire the troops about a new product vision—the creation of a microprocessor module (the "brains" of a computer workstation) about the size of a credit card. Our execution was neither as crisp nor as cooperative as I might have liked. But we did manage to introduce a working prototype by the end of the year.

The dire scenario in my "I Have a Nightmare" memo never quite materialized. Still, in a business where unknown competitors can obsolete products overnight, the price of success is indeed eternal vigilance.

I don't envy the headaches of middle managers. They are the most overwhelmed, overburdened, underappreciated people in an organization. They get heat from all sides: from the top, from their subordinates, from project leaders. But no one is better positioned to help make the detailed, reality-based tradeoffs that keep people from overcommitting and keep the organization from breaking down. That's why the goals system is tuned for their use and puts so much authority in their hands.

At the same time, I have seen parochial middle managers hurt important companywide initiatives. By giving projects official standing in the goals system, and by automatically transferring project goals into the computer-generated reports distributed to managers on Tuesday mornings, we create a "bill of rights" that documents what members of our teams believe need to get done for their projects to succeed. Functional managers retain the power to revise those plans during their Tuesday meetings—but they can't do so arbitrarily or capriciously.

We are always working to increase the organizational clout of projects. For example, Cypress's ten most important new products don't just have a project leader in our traditional sense—someone who runs the meetings, manages the database, sets the priorities. Our Top Ten products also have "godfathers"—vice presidents or officers of the company who intervene if middle managers slow down critical projects, or when they need extra resources to make things happen.

Middle managers think twice before they postpone a goal connected with one of our Top Ten projects. As well they should. We expect these Top Ten projects to generate $100 million of additional revenue next year and $200 million the year after. It's worth disrupting daily routines to make these projects move faster. The goals system, combined with "godfather" oversight, gives these projects special standing throughout the company.

Ultimately, the goals system is only as good as the people who implement it. Databases can't substitute for good judgment and open minds. Smart, savvy, flexible managers make for smart, savvy, flexible companies. The goals system merely creates a factual, objective basis for rational discussion and productive compromise. Like so many of our systems, technology makes people more important than ever.

CHAPTER 5

the goals system in action

The goals system plays a big role in helping our people, managers, and project leaders organize their work and make smart trade-offs among competing demands. It also operates as a real-time monitoring device that allows Cypress managers to identify problems and to intervene quickly before they become crises.

Think of it as an instrument panel that not only indicates how fast the organization is traveling, and in what direction, but that also helps explain what's holding us back. None of us expects that our people will never have delinquent goals: Priorities change, highly motivated people are too ambitious about what they can achieve, day-to-day crises interfere with even the best-laid plans. But the system helps us spot patterns of trouble and overload.

That said, I don't want to give the impression that the goals system is strictly a support mechanism. People at Cypress know we don't tolerate bureaucratic politics—it's one of the items on a very short list of what can get you fired. They also know the goals system gives top management ammunition to cut through bureaucratic obfuscation. No one can accuse me or Cypress's vice presidents of not "knowing the details" of our business. Yet we don't have to meddle or badger to get at those details. The goals system provides warnings when something goes wrong and offers instant access to data in any area that we are concerned about.

The knowledge that we can call on this kind of detail means we seldom have to. One common concern about the goals system is that it creates the potential for "electronic" management. Some people envision me, or other top Cypress managers, huddled in our offices like Captain Kirk on the bridge of the *Enterprise,* scrolling through reports, wandering through databases, and running the company from a computer screen. Instead of barking "Scotty, we need more power!" the instructions are "Marketing, we need more goals!" or "Manufacturing, we need a lower delinquency rate!"

This is ridiculous. It represents a fundamental misunderstanding of the philosophy behind the system. As with so many of our management tools, the role of the goals system has changed as the company has changed. I sometimes do use the system for top-down monitoring—especially when it comes to tracking progress on our most important new products. But I am not nearly as involved with monitoring goals as I once was, just as I am not nearly as involved with the details of our purchasing system, our hiring system, or killer software. Even if I were so inclined—and I'm not—Cypress is simply too big for me to become Silicon Valley's equivalent of Captain Kirk.

In the early days of the company, until we hit about a hundred people, I did in fact use the goals system as a top-down management tool. Indeed, I reviewed everyone's goals every week. That was perfectly appropriate. At the beginning of a startup, attention to detail matters more than anything else. Time is scarce, money is scarce, bodies are scarce. I simply had to know what our people were doing, that everyone was pulling in the same direction, whether we were meeting the timetables we had set for ourselves. The goals system meant that I could know those details, still attend to other business, and not bog down our people with wasteful "fact-gathering" missions.

Soon things changed. In the second phase, which lasted until we hit about five hundred people, I used the system in cooperation with my vice presidents. Our oversight and tracking was nothing like my detailed reviews in the early days. Instead of reviewing actual goals, we reviewed a series of "exception reports" designed to draw attention to worrisome patterns. We weren't trying to second-guess managers or catch people in awkward positions. Rather, we wanted to anticipate problems, sort through conflicts, and pitch in to help.

ACTION REQUEST

AR # 5203

FOR (ACTION):   Bob/Stu

START: March 8, 1991

CC (INFORMATION):

DUE: March 12, 1991

FROM: T.J. RODGERS

TITLE: BULLSHIT DATA ON THE 7C1234

CONTENTS: By the time problems get elevated to my level—especially by vice presidents—I expect the data to be accurate, the conclusions to be well thought out, and politics to be absolutely absent. None of the above criteria were met in your recent skirmish over 7C1234 wafers.

Stu, you declared that your problem was a Fab problem (it is always easier to have your problems be someone else's problem) based on your estimation of what wafers out should be. When I checked into your calculation, you were using a planning number which may or may not have been related to the Fab's original commitment, which you did not know. For the Fab to be delinquent with a plan they may or may not have committed to had they known about it does not make a lot of sense.

Bob, in your response to Stu's complaint, you declared that the Fab was "ahead of plan." Instead of relating the phrase "ahead of plan" to some mutually agreed-upon plan between you and your customer, you created your own "plan" on the spot and declared yourself to be ahead of it. Your "plan" was to take the wafers you started for the quarter, multiply them by the current but terrible fab yield of 62 percent, and declare that actual wafer shipments were ahead of that "plan." Whether or not your plan had anything to do with the commitment of your fab in the beginning of the quarter is currently unknown.

In case you can't tell by the tone of this AR, I will state it explicitly: I do not like being in the wafer-production control business (especially with bad data) or interdepartment squabble-resolving business. As a matter of fact, I pay both of you guys to keep me out of the businesses mentioned above.

My reaction to a classic intramural squabble over problems on a particular chip. Stu, the product-line manager, blames Bob, a factory manager. Bob in turn blames Stu.

Our reviews took place on Wednesday afternoons at my weekly staff meeting. We developed something of a routine: We thumbed through the exception reports and talked about what they told us. The more we talked, the more we learned; the more we learned, the better decisions we made. But even at these meetings the exception reports were never more than an aid to smart discussion and follow-up. They offered early hints of problems we might not have noticed otherwise. They provided confirmation of problems we had heard about through the grapevine.

Let's re-create one of those meetings and give you a sense of how it worked. We'll do it in the present tense to create more of a "you-are-there" feel. Keep in mind, though, that in terms of how top managers use the goals system today, this is a stroll down memory lane. It is now our middle managers, many of whom run operations with thirty or fifty or seventy people, who should work with the goals system along the lines we'll describe.

The first report we look at is "Delinquent Goals by Vice President"—that is, the number of goals and percentage delinquent for all people reporting up the chain of command to the vice president. (We've disguised names other than mine, but all the information is from actual Cypress reports.)

When I scan this table, one humorous point quickly gets my attention. My goals (TJR) are perfect, no delinquencies. Does that mean my performance has been perfect? Hardly. I know I have delinquent goals, and I know which goals are delinquent. My assistant is generously resetting my goals to make me look good—something that doesn't fool me or anyone else. I'll ask her to stop being so kind.

Notice that some vice presidents have substantially more goals than others. That's normal. Most of the differences can be explained by who does what in the company. Consider Dan, whose people have 2,318 goals. Dan runs manufacturing, and manufacturing, by its very nature, is a detail-oriented operation. It always generates more goals than any other function, and it must run with low delinquency rates. Dan's numbers look about right.

Still, the differences do point to some interesting trends. Together my vice presidents and I discuss what they might mean. For exam-

DELINQUENT GOALS BY VICE PRESIDENT

VP	Total Goals	# Delinquent	% Delinquent	# Qual Goals	% Qual Goals	% Qual Delinquent
JIM	491	66	13%	7	1%	43%
SAM	1158	147	13%	62	5%	10%
EVE	716	88	12%	48	7%	19%
NAN	509	61	12%	0	0%	0%
IRA	873	96	11%	74	8%	31%
HAL	376	39	10%	16	4%	25%
ED	679	63	9%	111	16%	14%
DAN	2318	176	8%	247	11%	13%
KAY	595	42	7%	30	5%	20%
AL	716	40	6%	21	3%	0%
TIM	675	37	5%	15	2%	33%
JON	530	28	5%	22	4%	0%
PAT	1639	85	5%	115	7%	14%
STU	365	10	3%	129	35%	5%
TJR	22	0	0%	6	27%	0%
	11,662	978	8%	903	8%	8%

During the workweek this report was generated, the goals database contained 11,662 active entries. Everyone in the company reports up some chain of command to a vice president, a subsidiary president, or the CEO. This report allocates all 11,662 goals to the appropriate top managers.

Notice that the report sorts and lists the vice presidents in descending order of delinquency rates. Jim, whose 13 percent rate leads the group, appears first. My initials appear at the bottom—the computer can't know my assistant has prettied up my numbers. By totaling up the figures, we learn that 978 of the 11,662 goals are delinquent—8 percent.

Based on our experience, that's a solid performance, with no VPs out of control. I like to see VPs "stretch" to the point that 10 to 15 percent of their goals (but no more than 20 percent) are delinquent. The system, of course, can accommodate any style of management—from "zero-defects" drill sergeants to carefree managers who tolerate high levels of delinquency.

ple, the people in the chain of command reporting to Sam, one of our product-line vice presidents, have 1,158 goals. That's a pretty big number. The people reporting to Stu, the vice president of another product line, have a total of only 365 goals. That's a pretty small number. The delinquency rate for Sam is 13 percent; the delinquency rate for Stu is at 3 percent. I've known all along that Sam and his people seem to be running flat out, pushing hard, maybe in need of some additional resources. This report confirms that general impression.

The vice president that worries me is Jim. His group's overall delinquency rate is not only the highest (13 percent), but I'm surprised by the low number of quality goals and their high delinquency rate. We started separately identifying and tracking quality-related goals two years ago. Ask a chip-company manager whether quality is life and he will agree vigorously. It's like asking if he loves his mother. But then look at the actual decisions that same manager makes every day in the trenches—about people, priorities, resources—and quality all too often takes a backseat to more "pressing" concerns.

You know the aphorism: What gets measured gets attention. Identifying specific quality goals, putting them in the database, and reviewing them independently reinforces the importance of quality throughout the company. Quality is not a platitude. It has achieved official standing in a management system used by virtually everyone in the organization. That sends a powerful signal.

Jim runs an important operation, where quality is paramount. Yet only 7 of his people's 491 goals specifically relate to quality. Either he is not paying attention to quality, or he is running "subterranean" quality programs that don't use the system. Neither option makes me very happy. I might begin a discussion by asking Jim to reiterate his basic quality plan and explain how his organization's current goals support that plan. That message will not be lost on the other vice presidents. We might then call up another exception report and take a closer look at the operation—not to put Jim on the hot seat (although he might feel that way) but to better understand what's happening.

Let's say we call up that report, "Delinquent Goals by Vice President and Manager." This excerpt resembles the first, except that it provides greater detail on what's going on beneath each top manager. The full report lists goals data for the 189 managers who report directly to Cypress vice presidents or subsidiary presidents. We focus on Jim and his thirteen managers.

The pattern is obvious. One manager, Ron, accounts for a huge portion of Jim's delinquent goals (36 out of 66). I'm not surprised but I am a little concerned. Ron is the design manager on an important new product. I already know that product is running about four weeks late. (I keep in close touch with progress on big new products.) Once Ron and his people make up some ground, most of his delinquent goals will be wiped out.

Still, there's nothing like seeing the impact of missed schedules in black and white. After the meeting I'll ask Jim to take a closer look—if he hasn't already—to make sure we aren't headed for a brick wall. (I don't want to turn this into a public Jim-bashing session.) I'll be sure to check those numbers for the next few weeks.

A second number surprises me a little more. Joe has only nine goals, but five of them are delinquent. This is a big problem because Joe plays an absolutely critical role on another chip, and we can't afford delays. I ask Jim to send a message to Joe and the rest of the troops: "No more slack. Let's get these goals completed and keep things moving forward." I know I've said we don't count goals, that the system is not a Big Brother watchdog. That's true. But some situations call for healthy pressure—and this may be one of them.

I'm interested enough to keep fishing. So we call up a third standard exception report, "Goals More than Five Weeks Delinquent." Here the detail is even more extensive; it looks more like a traditional goals record than a summary statement.

Not surprisingly, Ron dominates this report. He was responsible for more than half of Jim's delinquent goals. Why shouldn't he also account for the most overdue of the delinquent goals?

For the first time, though, I find something about Ron that genuinely surprises me. It looks like the initial design review for another chip (not the one causing all the delays) is also behind schedule. It

DELINQUENT GOALS BY VICE PRESIDENT AND MANAGER

VP	MGR	Total Goals	# Delinquent	% Delinquent	# Qual Goals	% Qual Goals	% Qual Delinquent
JIM	Sue	10	7	70%	0	0%	0%
JIM	Joe	9	5	56%	0	0%	0%
JIM	Ben	15	6	40%	0	0%	0%
JIM	Ron	134	36	27%	4	3%	50%
JIM	Sam	9	2	22%	0	0%	0%
JIM	Mel	14	2	14%	1	7%	100%
JIM	Tom	52	4	8%	2	4%	0%
JIM	Ike	41	2	5%	0	0%	0%
JIM	Jim	31	1	3%	0	0%	0%
JIM	Bob	124	1	1%	0	0%	0%
JIM	Jan	35	0	0%	0	0%	0%
JIM	Ann	0	0	0%	0	0%	0%
JIM	Mae	6	0	0%	0	0%	0%
JIM	Art	11	0	0%	0	0%	0%
		491	66	13%	7	1%	

The previous report showed that Jim's organization had 491 total goals, 66 of which were delinquent. This report allocates those 491 goals among the thirteen managers who report to Jim (plus, of course, Jim himself). Essentially, it increases the "degree of magnification" of the previous report.

Obviously, Ron is a key player in this group. His 134 goals amount to 27 percent of the group's 491 goals. With 27 percent of Ron's goals delinquent, his VP and I need to worry that programs under Ron's control are running into problems. I ask Jim to take a look, if he hasn't already.

I'm pleased with Bob. He has nearly as many goals (124) as Ron, with only one delinquent. Sometimes that's cause for concern — is Bob padding his goals? But I know Bob runs a tight ship. This report confirms it.

GOALS MORE THAN FIVE WEEKS DELINQUENT

VP	Mgr	Proj	B	E	D	S	Who	P	Goal
JIM	Ron	412	2	5	13	CD	XXX	4	Clean up errors on schematics
JIM	Jan	SOQ	4	7	13	CD	XXX	8	Order eng'ing quantity of pkgs
JIM	Ron	412	6	8	13	CD	XXX	2	Debug vectors for chip
JIM	Ron	412	7	10	13	CD	XXX	1	Update all control schematics
JIM	Ron	412	33	36	14	CD	XXX	7	Prepare for schematic design review
JIM	Ron	TUF	50	51	8	CD	XXX	12	Update spec for mark/test
JIM	Joe	412	38	39	12	CD	XXX	4	Fix existing Level 3 tests
JIM	Tom	TET	32	3	12	CD	XXX	2	Put together procedures for test
JIM	Ron	412	45	47	12	CD	XXX	1	Review FPQ schematics to match std schem
JIM	Ron	412	34	37	12	CD	XXX	9	Review schematics for power conversation
JIM	Ron	X14	8	9	16	CD	XXX	4	Simulation of new speeds with revised th
JIM	Ron	418	7	10	13	CD	XXX	5	Design Review 1
JIM	Ron	415	6	11	13	CD	XXX	8	Design Review 4

There are seven projects in Jim's organization with at least one goal more than five weeks delinquent. As CEO, I'm not in a position to have strong opinions about every item on this list. Some may be trivial, others may be hugely important to the company. But I know enough about the company's highest-priority projects to get nervous when I should. The delay on Design Review 1 for the "418" project makes me nervous.

was due in workweek 7 and rescheduled for workweek 13. This is a problem, and I didn't know about it before looking at this report. The delay shows a troubling lack of discipline and an even more troubling lack of communication. That will attract some personal attention. I might send Ron a note, or give him a call, or ask Jim about what's happening with his group.

Back when Cypress had about five hundred people, this kind of review required less than an hour every week in my staff meeting. We seldom learned anything shocking. As managers, we are all plugged in enough, we all wander around enough, to have a good sense of which operations are running smoothly and which aren't. And yet, in this case, as we called up more and more detail, the sense of urgency about Jim's operation, and especially about a lack of discipline on a new chip, became serious enough to prompt us to do some checking. Maybe there are reasonable explanations; I won't automatically leave the meeting with guns blazing. But I do want to send a strong message about the importance of crisp execution.

Over the years, as we refined the goals system and used it more extensively, I developed some general principles about how to react to news of delinquent goals. First, people are going to have goals they don't achieve on time; the point of reviewing goals reports (at the staff meeting or any other time) is to sense when a vice president or manager is losing control. My rule of thumb is that managers should not have delinquency rates above 20 percent. Again, the point of the system is not the Big Brother totalitarian state. The 20 percent figure is a warning flag, not a death knell.

Second, managers with delinquency problems usually need technical assistance or more resources, not more pressure. In the company's early days, when I saw a manager with a high percentage of delinquent goals, I had a tendency to pounce: "Why is your group running behind? What's wrong?" More often than not, the manager would offer a perfectly reasonable explanation: "When we established our work plan we both knew it was ambitious. Then you decided to expedite a big order. That decision essentially cut off our supply of silicon, and twelve goals went delinquent."

Now when I become aware of problems with delinquent goals, I almost never raise objections. Instead, I intervene with a short note: "Your delinquency rate is running at 25 percent. What can I do to help?" Nine times out of ten I get requests for specific assistance: a temporary assignment of additional personnel, better cooperation from another part of the company, faster decisions by top management. Part of my role is to hold people accountable. But it is also to identify problems and provide help to get them fixed.

With nearly 1,500 people, we no longer review these exception reports in my Wednesday staff meeting. There are simply too many different things happening in too many different places to do a "global" review of much value. We still generate and distribute the reports to top management on a weekly basis. Once in a while, if a critical project is really worrying me, I may review it on my own. But more often than not I don't. I have pushed that oversight responsibility down to the vice presidents, our subsidiary presidents, and their managers. It is up to them, not me, to determine how best to use the exception reports to take the pulse of their own organizations.

Some use them religiously. Others not at all. That's fine—so long as their organizations deliver. The goals system can and does make an important contribution as a high-level tool. But it was never intended to function as an autopilot for top managers. Its real value is down lower in the organization, where middle managers struggle to help individual contributors balance competing demands on their time and energy. Top-level reviews, for all their value, can't begin to substitute for good judgment in the trenches. The goals system is designed to aid in those judgments.

NEW-PRODUCT GUNFIGHT: DRAW FAST AND DON'T FIRE BLANKS

There is one important area where I do maintain tight control over goals—an area where I *can* be accused of functioning as something close to Big Brother. That area is new products.

Who in business doesn't understand that the key to long-term success is successful innovation: getting more and better new products out the door faster than the competition? From the day we founded Cypress, we understood that new products would be our lifeblood. Today, we ship 250 different chips (35 of which were new in 1991) in seven distinct product categories using 33 different process-technology variations.

Our entire competitive strategy has been based on designing and manufacturing a wide variety of high-performance niche products — products for which we can charge a substantial premium over the competition, and thus generate cash we can pour back into R&D to develop the next generation of premium products. We devote 25 percent of our annual revenues to R&D — putting us in the top one percent of all public companies. If we don't leverage that money by getting products out the door faster than our rivals, we lose.

Of course, developing a business strategy based on relentless product development is much easier than developing the products on time and on budget. Five or six years ago you could have set your watch by our product-development timetables. But in recent years, as Cypress has gotten bigger, we have lost some of the crack discipline with which we used to innovate.

That's one of the unacceptable side effects of growth and success. Sure our chips have become more complex and technically demanding. But our resources and computer-aided design capabilities have increased as well. When we went public in 1986, we had 40 circuit designers. Today we have 150. The real problem (and it afflicts most organizations as they grow and prosper) is an eroding visibility of and sense of urgency about the absolute priority of delivering new products on time. When you are a company with three products, everyone understands the importance of meeting your timetables with the fourth. The president probably talks to that project manager on a daily basis. When you already sell 250 products, launching product 251 seems less crucial. And the president is busy attending to loftier matters.

We have reestablished the visibility of and sense of urgency around new products by explicitly identifying new-product goals, entering them into the goals system, tracking them separately (as we do with quality goals), and holding people accountable. Work on a new chip can't begin until I (along with the appropriate product-line vice president and the vice presidents of R&D, manufacturing, and finance) approve a written new product plan (NPP). This "mini business plan" details what the marketplace needs, what the product will do (its performance specs), how much revenue and profit it will generate, what it will cost to build, how long it will take to design, and other critical information. The plan also includes a rigorous development and manufacturing schedule that gets boiled down to forty-eight specific "big-picture" milestones.

To be sure, different chips raise different challenges, different layers of complexity, different technical hurdles—and thus have different development schedules. But the NPP for *every* new chip at Cypress must set precise dates for the same forty-eight basic milestones. Eight of these forty-eight milestones represent truly significant stages of the development process: "NPP" (the official kickoff), "tape out" (when designers send computer tape to begin prototypes), "first silicon" (production of the first working chips), "deliver ten samples to marketing," and so on through to "volume production," which we define as demonstrating product reliability and shipping ten thousand units to customers. We monitor these eight milestones with great diligence. For Top Ten projects we brief the board of directors whenever new chips have passed one of the milestones or fallen significantly behind.

Then comes the critical step: We tie the new product plan into the goals system. The forty-eight NPP milestones require thousands of individual goals (what we call "micromilestones") that must be completed for a chip to become reality. Think back to the third generation of the 64K PROM we discussed early in the chapter. The 3,278 goals completed by the design team weren't pulled from thin air; they represented incremental advances toward meeting each of the forty-eight NPP milestones. The NPP plan and the forty-eight milestones thus create, in advance of actual design work, clear timetables and a frame of reference around which the project team can work and establish its goals.

The milestones also give top management a degree of oversight that is simply not possible in most product-development environments. Every week the goals system automatically generates a series of exception reports for new products. For every new product in the company (and there are about thirty in development at any one time), these reports track the following trends:

- The status—completed, pending, delinquent—of each of the forty-eight NPP milestones (an ongoing check).

- Projects that have missed one of the forty-eight NPP milestones for the first time (products that may start to slip).

- All NPP milestones that are four or more weeks delinquent (products that may be in deep trouble).

This last report is the most important—and the only one I personally review every week. For each new product it is an automatic warning flag that lets me know when a key stage of development has slipped significantly. This slippage then triggers a mandatory review we call a "trouble meeting." This review includes me, other top managers, the relevant product-line manager, the design manager, the product engineering manager, and additional key project players. At this meeting we explore the short-term issue of what caused the delay, figure out how to make up time to keep the project on schedule, explore the root cause of the slippage, and try to eliminate it in the future. We also estimate the "cost of quality" (in terms of lost shipment and revenues) from the delay to make sure everyone understands how expensive late products can be. (The best of our product lines is tens of millions of dollars of revenue away from perfection.)

Things go wrong with new products all the time. If our products were easy to design and build, they would not be part of the high-performance niches in which Cypress specializes—which means we wouldn't make them. The line that separates our products is painted "state of the art" on one side and "edge of disaster" on the other. And lines, in our business, are microscopically thin. So we can't afford to allow managers to deny or ignore these inevitable problems.

Trouble meetings can be tough, sometimes downright unpleasant. There is, however, an easy way to make them less unpleasant: Face the problem squarely, understand what's gone wrong, develop a plan to fix it, and change your approach so the problem doesn't recur.

To be sure, there's more to developing new products than tracking their progress and calling meetings when things go wrong. People need to be energized and inspired, and they need the resources to get the job done. We've already discussed the classic tensions between projects and functions, and the role of "godfathers" in our Top Ten program in giving our most important new products more organizational clout. The Top Ten program involves other innovations as well. For example, we have physically relocated Top Ten team members into special project areas to encourage them to identify with their projects and communicate with each other. Fifty feet of physical separation really does cut communication in half. We believe in team spirit, camaraderie, and collaboration. We want our people to work close to one another.

But we also believe in accountability: What gets measured gets attention. I can't pretend to be on top of all our new-product work. But by linking development schedules with the goals system, and by generating a weekly set of exception reports, I can identify the handful of projects running into serious problems—and intervene before they cause big-buck delays.

THE IMPORTANCE OF BEING POSITIVE

One problem with the goals system is that much of the feedback can be negative. By definition, exception reports highlight problems, not things that are going right. It's like the evening news. People love to complain that the news is always too "negative." To which network executives respond with puzzled looks: "What do you want us to report? It's not 'news' when the economy is doing well, when General Motors isn't laying off workers, when members of Congress are getting things done."

The goals system has the same problem. But life in a company is not like watching the TV news. People need positive feedback. We can't allow negative feedback to become the system's only output. That's why every quarter we issue a completed and pending goals report for every person in the company. The report lists all the goals completed over the past three months as well as those that have yet to come due.

Rick Foreman's goals report for the first quarter of 1992 is a thorough record of his work in January, February, and March. It lists seventy-nine goals, seventy-two of which were completed on time. It lists an additional twenty-nine goals that were begun during the quarter but were not yet due. It is a reminder to Rick, and to everyone in the organization who sees it, just how much he achieved over the last three months. This excerpt lists all of Rick's completed goals for workweeks 3, 4, and 5 of 1992.

The completed goals report is a valuable tool for performance evaluations—and it has a direct role in the focal review process. In Chapter 2 we described the "mayonnaise effect" and the problems it creates with ranking. There's a second classic problem with evaluation and ranking, which I call the "proximity effect." Someone who performs outstandingly for the first ten months of the year but has a subpar two months just before the review is more likely to get a poor evaluation than is a colleague who had a lousy ten months but did a great job in the two months just before the evaluation.

At Cypress, the completed goals report helps combat the proximity effect. Every quarter these goals printouts are the basis of a performance "minireview." Managers read through their people's printouts, hold one-on-one meetings, and prepare brief factual evaluations around a few criteria: three major accomplishments against long-term goals in the quarter; three areas in which the employee could have improved performance; three major goals to be included in next quarter's review. Thus, at the end of the year, managers have at their disposal four reviews to refresh their memories and guard against overvaluing recent performance.

These quarterly reviews revolve around *long-term* goals rather than weekly goals connected with the rush of routine activities. This

INDIVIDUAL QUARTERLY COMPLETED AND PENDING GOALS REPORT

WW	DATE	Mgr	Dp	Proj	B	E	D	S	Who	P	Goal
9203	1/14/92	PV	370	RIMS	2	3		C	RF		PROVIDE VMG WITH STOCK DATA FOR 1991 W-2 PROCESSING
9203	1/14/92	PV	370	ADMN	2	3		C	RF		ANALYST CALL: CALCULATE "% BOOKED," REVENUE/EMP, REV/CAPITAL
9203	1/14/92	PV	370	ADMN	2	3		C	RF		LEGAL: ATTEND SEMICON USERS GROUP MONTHLY MTG., 1/9/92 @ AMD
9203	1/14/92	PV	370	ADMN	50	3		C	RF		LEGAL: SUBMIT PO'S FOR JANUARY BUDGET
9203	1/14/92	PV	370	ADMN	52	3		C	RF		DETERMINE Q192 LEGAL BUDGET
9204	1/21/92	PV	370	ADMN	2	4		C	RF		ANALYST CALL: FACTORY REVENUE SHIPS BY FAB LOCATION
9204	1/21/92	PV	370	ADMN	2	4		C	RF		FOCALS: CREATE DEMO WORKSHEETS FOR FOCAL TRAINING
9204	1/21/92	PV	370	ADMN	2	4		C	RF		FOR MKA: MODIFIED "% BOOKED" FOR NET FACTORY OR BY CHANNEL
9204	1/21/92	PV	370	ADMN	3	4		C	RF		SET UP MEETING FOR SUBSIDIARY CONTRACTS
9204	1/21/92	PV	370	ADMN	3	4		C	RF		BLANKET PO'S FOR LEGAL EXPENSES—WILSON SONSINI AND BROWN & BAIN
9204	1/21/92	PV	370	ADMN	3	4		C	RF		FOCALS: PREPARE DEMO DISK FOR TRAINING SESSION
9204	1/21/92	PV	370	ADMN	3	4		C	RF		SEND LIST OF PATENTS TO JONES: HE'LL GET INFO ON THEM
9204	1/21/92	PV	370	ADMN	3	5		C	RF		PREPARE MINUTES FOR DECEMBER BOARD MEETING
9205	1/29/92	PV	370	ADMN	2	4	5	C	RF		PROXY: FIRST-PASS REVISIONS
9205	1/29/92	PV	370	ADMN	3	6		C	RF		DETERMINE INVENTORY FOR BOTTOM-GATED MATERIAL BY PRODUCT/AGE
9205	1/29/92	PV	370	ADMN	4	5		C	RF		ANALYZE ESPP STOCK HISTORY: # SHARES, % CONTRIBUTING, ETC.
9205	1/29/92	PV	370	ADMN	50	5		C	RF		AR 5936: SIGN UP FOR DIALOG DATABASE (MEMO TO TJR)
9205	1/29/92	PV	370	ADMN	50	6		C	RF		SET UP TJR VISIT TO NEW YORK FOR MEETINGS
9205	1/29/92	PV	370	ADMN	50	6		C	RF		FOCALS: NEW SOFTWARE FOR EQUITY ADJUSTMENTS

is important. The goals system is not a computerized report card in which managers calculate percentages of goals completed on time, numbers of goals set, or anything like that. We focus on long-term performance, long-term achievement, and long-term potential for improvement. And we guard against the proximity effect.

THE GOALS CULTURE: COWBOYS AND CONVERTS

I'm sure the goals system sounds tough—something you couldn't possibly imagine working in your company. It certainly is true that the system has been part of Cypress from day one. We have tended to hire people with the drive, discipline, and self-confidence required to set and meet their own goals. You can't divorce the system from our culture; you can't divorce our culture from our people.

But it's possible to overstate all that. In fact, over the last few years we've had a "controlled experiment" with transplanting the goals system outside Cypress's home-grown environment. The experiment began when we acquired Control Data's semiconductor operation in Minnesota. That acquisition, a big step for us, created cultural as well as technical challenges. Our small, tough, head-strong Silicon Valley company had taken its first step into heartland America—and into an organization famous for big-company paternalism.

The first order of business was getting the plant up to speed—building Cypress quality at Cypress costs. But we also had to take a collection of talented and committed people and introduce them to the Cypress culture. One of the first management systems we introduced was the goals. As a manufacturing site, Minnesota would be interacting with virtually every part of the Cypress federation. It was imperative that the people there understand and work from the goals system.

Lothar Maier, the president of Cypress Minnesota, has been one of our most ardent goals champions. He was eager to install the system as soon as he relocated to Bloomington from San Jose. I asked him to wait a few weeks. I was preparing a major presentation on

Cypress's business systems. I wanted to use that get-acquainted opportunity to explain the goals system, the reasons behind our commitment to them, and win a collective buy-in.

I spent five hours on the flight from San Jose writing a statement of philosophy and execution for the goals. But I didn't complete it, and I didn't want to make a half-baked presentation. So I did the presentation without explaining the goals, and I asked Lothar to wait until my next visit (I travel to Minnesota once a month) so we could "launch it right."

Lothar wasn't willing to wait. He called a week later to inform me that the system was *already* up and running. Technical challenges? A veteran secretary from San Jose transferred to Bloomington and became the "goals administrator"—in addition to her job as Lothar's executive secretary. She ran the training, solved software problems, helped people learn how to enter goals and generate reports.

Organizational challenges? They were tougher than the hardware and software challenges, but not much tougher. Within two months the people of Cypress Minnesota were operating with the same schedule of meetings, database updates, and exception reports as the rest of Cypress. We had synchronized an organization located halfway across the continent and composed of very different people from our crew in San Jose. Our goals transplant was a success.

GOALS: HOW TO USE THE DEMO DISKETTE

Cypress recently formed an alliance with Avantos Performance Systems, an entrepreneurial Silicon Valley software company, to upgrade our home-grown goals software with a high-performance, networked version of its ManagePro software package. ManagePro is a goals-and-productivity application that runs under Microsoft Windows. The high-performance version we are implementing at Cypress operates under Windows and Unix. It will provide all the functionality of the current Cypress system—along with more user-friendly screens and colorful graphics.

The demo is easy to run. Simply place the *No-Excuses Manage-*

ment diskette in your external drive. At the DOS prompt, type "a:" or "b:" to access your floppy drive. Hit "Enter" and type "demos" to display further instructions. Then follow along. The demo provides a tour of ManagePro's "look-and-feel" and key features. It also tells you how to get more information about the system.

Money

CHAPTER 6

People and capital: how to do more with less

The scene unfolds at the beginning of every quarter. Forty or fifty managers crowd into the company boardroom at eight A.M. sharp. A bunch more are "in the room" via speaker phone. There is laughter, some good-natured teasing, a few bets on how long the session will last, predictions about the outcome. The lights go down, the first of many computer-generated slides goes up, the presentations and decision making begin. Cypress's head count and capital meeting is under way.

At the end of the session after much hard bargaining, a little tough language, and a dose of table pounding, these same managers file out. Not many would describe what they have just experienced as fun. A few leave downright angry. But most would agree they had accomplished a critical task — determining exactly how many people the company will hire this quarter, how many people they can hire, why they can hire fewer people than they might have liked, and why their peers compromised to the same pressures. They also know exactly how much money the company will spend on capital equipment this quarter, what equipment they can acquire, and why they can't buy every new computer or oscilloscope they thought they needed when the meeting began.

In short, one of the toughest and potentially most divisive issues for an organization—deciding who gets what resources and why—has been resolved fairly, intelligently, and decisively. No confusion, no secrets, no politics.

Middle managers can be a company's most enduring strength. They are more aware of day-to-day business realities than any other group, and they are earnest, committed, and creative. Middle managers can also cause companies to grow bloated and uncompetitive. Not because they don't do their jobs, but because they think their jobs are the most important in the world. As a result, they lose sight of the broader corporate imperative.

I call this disease middle-management myopia. Organizations that suffer from it (and it afflicts the vast majority of big companies) show classic symptoms. Middle managers clamor for resources while top managers try desperately to hold the line. Almost inevitably, top managers are forced to cave in. How can a senior executive turn down a spending request from a well-respected middle manager who makes a plausible argument that his or her key project will unravel without it?

I am a certified expert on this disease. Until we started Cypress, I had spent my career as a middle manager. No one was a more relentless or effective lobbyist for resources than I. One reason I am such a good CEO goalie, blocking inflated requests for people or capital, is that I took so many shots on goal in my earlier jobs—and scored with great consistency. I know all the moves.

I spun tales of looming disaster that curled the hair of the toughest bosses, who had no chance of putting a dent in my Ph.D.-clad arguments. Such "gun-to-the-head" stories are a staple of corporate life. Any self-respecting middle manager can come up with one on a moment's notice.

Here are two selections from the Cypress arsenal:

- *From a financial manager: "We have $10 million of excess receivables on which we pay $500,000 of interest every year.*

I could get receivables down to $5 million. I just need another clerk to do it. The basic problem is paperwork; sometimes our invoices don't match our customer's records, and we have to work the phones to convince them to pay. If we hire one more clerk at $30,000 a year, we can cut the excess receivables in half, saving us $250,000. It's foolish not to make the hire."

- *From an engineering manager: "We generate annual revenues of $20 million with this particular chip. Our final-test yield is 90 percent, which means we're throwing away $2 million a year. If you let me hire two more engineers (they will cost us less than $150,000 a year combined), we can get yields up to 94 percent—a four-month payback. It's foolish not to make the hires."*

Perfectly reasonable arguments—which, when combined with twenty other such reasonable arguments, often lead to perfectly unreasonable outcomes. The moment senior executives buy into the tunnel vision of their middle managers, they have lost control of their company. And if that happens, it's *not* the middle managers' fault. They're simply doing their jobs as they understand them.

No organization can make sound decisions about resources until it stamps out (or at least controls) middle-management myopia. And I don't mean with high-minded appeals to team spirit or conscience: "I know you think you need that extra clerk, but can't you hold off for the good of the company?" I mean by developing systems that make it impossible for middle managers, however aggressive about the needs of their own departments, to ignore the best interest of the company as a whole when arguing parochial resource issues.

We think we've done that at Cypress. Our resource-allocation systems are designed to push collective thinking down through the ranks. They are a vaccine against middle-management myopia.

This chapter describes how we make decisions on hiring people and buying capital equipment. The next chapter focuses on how we manage expenses and our process for setting, tracking, and meeting budgets. The mechanics of the systems are slightly different, but they all reflect two simple beliefs. First, people and organizations can reach what they think are unreachable levels of performance and productivity—provided they are held to those standards. Second, no matter how high an organization's current levels of performance, it should always be expected to do more with less—and to do so every quarter.

Much of this chapter may sound tough, negative—even adversarial. There is a reason for the tone. For all the talk of teamwork, empowerment, and participation—and those are important values—there remains a basic dividing line inside organizations. Top management sits on one side of that line. The CEO's job—my job at Cypress—is to explain the grim realities of the world and what those realities mean for the organization. There is always some new country getting into the game: Korea, Taiwan, India, Mexico. There is always some company that has found a new competitive weapon, a better way to run a machine, a smarter way to organize people, a more effective approach to quality and customer service.

My job is to gather that data, communicate it, and persuade middle management, the people on the other side of the line, and the people who do the real work, to act on that data as if their competitive lives depended on it. Because their competitive lives *do* depend on it. Even at successful companies—indeed, especially at successful companies—top management must constantly raise the performance bar.

Consider one example from our earliest days as a company. It was 1983. We had just received our first major infusion of venture capital. We issued 11.25 million shares at nearly 67 cents per share and happily put $7.5 million in the bank, which allowed us to borrow another $12.5 million. We were flush with almost $20 million.

It was time to build and equip our flagship plant in San Jose. I received a capital-authorization request for four "steppers"—the intricate, million-dollar step-and-repeat cameras that "print" microscopic circuit images onto silicon wafers. Our manufacturing organization thought this was a perfectly reasonable request. And it *was* reasonable from the perspective of standard big-company practice. After all, steppers are *the* critical piece of equipment for making chips. Didn't we want to meet demand for our first products without any possibility of glitches? Wasn't it worth erring on the side of over-investment?

That's a catastrophically wrong perspective. I wanted to operate the factory with one stepper—provided it was run with maximum efficiency, intelligent scheduling, and virtually no downtime. The gun-to-the-head arguments came fast and furious: What if the stepper breaks down? What about startup bugs? What about flexibility? We debated, we argued, eventually we agreed. We authorized manufacturing to buy two steppers.

A few months later the vice president of manufacturing came back to request a third stepper. "Why?" I wondered. "Our wafers are backing up on the line," came the reply. "The steppers have become a bottleneck."

I asked for a theoretical best-case efficiency study: What was the potential output of the two steppers if they ran 24 hours a day, 365 days a year, at top performance? It turns out each stepper was capable of producing thirty wafers per hour. A finished wafer requires fifteen trips through the stepper. So the finished capacity was 17,400 wafers per year, more product than we knew what to do with back then. The actual output of our two steppers turned out to be only four or five wafers per hour—obviously, well below their theoretical maximum capacity.

To be sure, we were building a wide variety of complex chips that required extensive rework and preventive maintenance. No one, including me, expected the steppers to run at their theoretical maximum. Amid great tumult and wailing, I announced that I would approve a third stepper once our people doubled output on each of the existing machines. It took the San Jose plant one full year to reach that ambitious productivity target—at which time we bought stepper 3.

Now, here's the punch line. In the intervening year Cypress raised a second round of venture capital. We sold 3.2 million shares—this time at $3 per share—and put another $9.7 million in the bank. And we used that second-round money to buy our third stepper. Which meant, in terms of Cypress shares, that stepper 3 was *four and one-half times* cheaper than our first two steppers. What's more, by virtue of all the hard work our operators had done to increase throughput on the existing equipment, stepper 3 came to life *twice* as productive as it would have been just twelve months earlier. From day one it was producing ten wafers per hour. Less than a year later, as our business began to boom, we added a fourth stepper, finally meeting the factory's original request.

An uplifting tale about setting high expectations and meeting them? I suppose. But it's much more than that. Think about the story this way: How different would Cypress look today, ten years later, if we had made one simple mistake and approved the original request for four steppers? How has one decision on capital investment shaped our long-term economic performance?

The answer is—dramatically. In 1983, at $1 million each, steppers 3 and 4 would have cost us a total of 3 million shares. By insisting that our people improve throughput on the machines, waiting a year, and then using second-round capital on the next two steppers, we "spent" only 666,666 shares. Cypress today has about 40 million shares outstanding. In other words, by forcing high productivity on that one piece of equipment, we avoided diluting our *current* shareholders by 2.3 million shares. At today's market values, that translates into $25 million, or a permanent 6 percent increase in earnings per share.

In a very real sense, then, the right 1983 price estimate for steppers 3 and 4 was not $2 million. It was $25 million! It's all a matter of perspective—and productivity.

That's how you hold your own against bigger and better-financed rivals. And we can never relax the standards to which we hold our managers—even those who are genuinely committed to driving productivity as hard as they can. At least once a year I tell my "bricks" joke to underscore how tough our business is—and how productive an organization we have to be. The joke goes like this:

A tour guide in the desert is shuttling an American tourist to the next oasis. There will be no water for 150 miles, so his camel is drinking in advance of the trip.

"How far can a camel go on one drink of water?" asks the tourist as he climbs on the camel's back.

"About one hundred miles," the guide answers.

"Well then, how can we make it 150 miles to the next oasis?"

"I'll show you."

Whereupon the tour guide walks behind the camel, picks up two bricks, spreads his arms as wide as he can, and with one swinging motion cracks the bricks together right on the camel's private parts. The camel grunts and sucks up enough water to make it to the next oasis.

"Doesn't that hurt?" shrieks the tourist, horrified by the spectacle.

"Only if you catch your fingers between the bricks."

Top management carries the bricks. We routinely make demands of our middle managers that we have no business making—demands that hurt. But we have no choice. Trying to compete by outspending Intel or Motorola or the Japanese is a road to corporate suicide. We compete by using less money more creatively than the Japanese or any of our American rivals. At Cypress, no waste is a way of life.

MINDSET, GUTSET, AND THE PROSPERITY ILLUSION

Of all our "money" systems, none is more important than our approach to controlling head count. I consider it one of the three most important systems at Cypress. Why? Because directly and indirectly, people drive virtually all costs in a company.

Adding a new person triggers a chain reaction of spending. First there are salary and benefits, which at Cypress average $50,000 per year. Of course, adding junior people means eventually adding a manager to oversee them, this time at more than $75,000 per year. Adding a new person also means spending $25,000 per year on office space, computers, phone, fax, and other now-standard (and expensive) gadgets. It costs another $4,000 per year to maintain all that equipment.

The bottom line: Approving one personnel requisition, even for a junior member of the organization, adds almost $100,000 to the company's annual cost structure. Multiply that cost by 1,500 people and you get $135 million—almost half of Cypress's annual revenue. Is it any wonder, then, that I expect our managers to treat personnel requisitions like the scarcest of all scarce commodities?

The press loves to lionize "tough bosses" who clean house when business goes south. That's nonsense. Being a "tough boss" is not about unflinchingly sending people to the unemployment line during hard times. It's about maintaining discipline during good times so the organization can weather the inevitable storms.

Economic reversals have a wonderful way of concentrating minds and encouraging people to do what is right. During times of prosperity, danger lurks everywhere. Growth masks waste, extravagance, inefficiency. And the moment growth slows, the accumulated sins of the past are revealed all the way to the bottom line.

That's why the central performance measure that drives this company—and that guides our system for controlling head count— adjusts our thinking to control for the illusions created by prosperity. Sure we want aggressive growth. But we *demand* ever-increasing productivity. For us, the most powerful measure of productivity is also the most basic: revenue per person. When Cypress went public in 1986, we generated annual revenue of $39 million. More important, with 344 people, we generated revenue per person of $113,000—high numbers for our industry back then. Two years later we had grown to annual revenue of $139 million. Meanwhile, our revenue per person was up to $142,000. Today we have revenue of more than $250 million. And we generate revenue per person of about $150,000.

So we're not just bigger than we were six or seven years ago. We're bigger *and* more productive—and that's what counts. Every quarter we benchmark our performance on this critical index against the best of our competition. How do we stack up on revenue per person versus Intel? AMD? The new wave of chip companies in Silicon Valley? The Japanese? Ask one of our vice presidents, or a middle manager who attends our head count meeting, and he will be able to give you an instant history of our track record on this index. It's an important and visible part of how we keep score.

I've met strategy consultants and finance gurus who disagree with our intense focus on revenue per person. They raise a host of reasonable objections. Aren't profits more important than revenues? Shouldn't different kinds of people count differently? (Adding a new vice president, say, imposes vastly different costs than adding a new clerk.) Shouldn't we focus on labor dollars rather than on head count?

All legitimate points. Revenue per person is a crude way to measure productivity. But the flip side of crude is *intuitive*. There are precious few business concepts in whose name middle managers will allow you to make their lives more difficult. This is one of them. A CEO can get middle managers, however committed to their own agendas, to agree with the following proposition: "Here is the revenue we generate today. Here is how many people we have in the company today. Unless, over time, we grow our revenue faster than we grow our head count, the strength of this organization will suffer."

We have achieved what might be called an "actuarial buy-in" on the importance of organizational productivity. Not just a managerial mindset about what is right, but a "gutset" about what has to happen every single quarter. A feeling deep down inside, among all our people, that unless we improve revenue per person, we are going to pay a price. This commitment represents a huge victory for the company—and a big step toward eliminating middle-management myopia.

Which means I can relax, right? Not quite. "Gutset" or not, it is *never* easy to convince individual managers to resist the urge to add individual bodies. For all the rigors of our system, and despite our commitment to ever-increasing productivity, we always struggle to meet our standards.

The summer of 1990 was a case in point. For five years, up to the middle of 1989, Cypress had been on a fabulous high-growth trajectory. Sales were skyrocketing, our productivity was setting records, life was great. Then business began to stall. In the second quarter of 1989 revenues were $50.6 million. By the second quarter of 1990 revenues were forecast to be just $53 million. This in a company accustomed to annual growth rates of 25 percent or more!

Yet despite the slowdown in growth, the number of people at Cypress kept creeping up. A couple of "emergency hires" here, some "key technology" hires there—pretty soon overall productivity was trending in the wrong direction. Revenue per person had actually begun to decline.

This head-count creep required direct action. I wrote a sharply worded memo that was hand-delivered to our vice presidents and subsidiary presidents. The memo initiated a spartan approach to hiring that stayed in place until we got back to the old Cypress discipline. The language in the memo was direct, the limitations severe—but the new policy did the job. Sales growth resumed, productivity started trending back up, hiring was turned back on.

CYPRESS SEMICONDUCTOR CORPORATION
INTERNAL CORRESPONDENCE

HAND CARRIED

DATE: June 28, 1990   WW: 26
TITLE: GOING ON A CONSTANT HEAD-COUNT "ECONOMY" FOR HIRING
TO: VP'S AND SUBSIDIARY PRESIDENTS
AUTHOR: T.J. Rodgers
AUTHOR FILE #: TJR-319   SECURITY FILE #:
SUBJECT: Admin, Personnel
DISTRIBUTION:
CIRCULATION:

Our overall corporation has not grown for over a year. During that time, we have added to our head count in every quarter. In the second quarter of 1989 we shipped $50.6 million and had 1,305 employees. This quarter we will be lucky to ship $53 million (an increase of only 4.7%) with a probable 1,465 employees (an increase of 12.2%). Therefore, our revenue per employee has dropped from $155.1K to $142.8K. This trend must stop. The easiest, quickest and least painful way to stop it is now. The longer we wait, the more drastic the action will be that we will have to take to get it done. Head-count freezes are easier than layoffs. The impact has also reached the bottom line. Our earnings per share were $0.22 last quarter. This quarter we will be stretching to make $0.22. Most of our investors expect us to increase to $0.23. If we do not reverse the revenue-to-expense trends, we will actually be going backward in earnings per share. A reversal in publicly disclosed earnings per share would cause a major change in our stock price and cause our Board of Directors to mandate some changes, probably including management changes in the worst areas. My point: We have a very serious problem and we have to fix it by ourselves now, not in the future.

To this end I am installing a constant-head-count system. The on-board head count as of June 18 (plus whatever people were hired and are on their way to the company) will be the base head count for this system. Hiring will be maintained by using our generous supply of replacement reqs to hire critical people. We should expect to generate 70 requisitions this quarter from turnover. These requisitions will be used to maintain the flow of hiring.

We have to go into a zero-base hiring mentality. We can no longer discuss replacements as though they were a constitutional right; they are not. Obviously, since our productivity has been dropping, we have been adding some people and positions that have not been needed. As people leave the company, we need to ask ourselves how that person's job can be absorbed and to what critical use the replacement req can be put. The system for optimizing hiring and replacement reqs will be outlined in the rest of this memo.

In order to guarantee that we have identified the most critical people to be hired, I have asked each of you to submit to me a list with a number of names on it equal to 3% of the unfilled openings for people that report to you. Both the base head count and the list should exclude direct labor. That critical hiring list should be submitted to Human Resources ASAP; I will not sign replacement reqs until it is in place. The procedure will then be as follows:

1. When a person resigns, the vice president or subsidiary president has the discretion to apply the replacement req to replace the person that has resigned or to hire into the critical hires list of any one of the organizations reporting to him.

2. If the replacement requisition is used to hire someone off the most critical list, my inclination will be to approve it quickly.

3. If the replacement requisition is not from the critical hiring list, I will scrutinize the replacement much more carefully. In particular, I will check the efficacy of hiring that person relative to the top person on the hiring list of any other vice president or subsidiary president. If an effective argument is made that the person being replaced would have been on the critical hiring list and does now belong there or if an effective argument is made that the person being replaced is in a group whose current relative efficiency is 100%, I will still be inclined to sign the replacement req for that group.

4. On the other hand, if the person being replaced does not appear to be a person of high incremental value to the company or if the group in which the person is being replaced has a very low current efficiency rating, I will be inclined to take the req away from that group and give it to a group to make a critical hire. In other words, I reserve the right to move reqs across boundaries in the company for the overall good of Cypress and its subsidi-

continued

aries. For example, I will not replace a clerk in a product line when the same requisition could be used to replace Tom North's critical marketing job.

I believe that this system is the only one that will give us the ability to hold our head count constant—which will be mandated by our board if we do not do it for ourselves now—while still being able to hire critical people and upgrade our organizations. Frankly, I think a couple of months in this mode will cause our organizations to be healthier. In the last few quarters, when promises were made but not delivered, we have been on a hiring binge that has reduced the efficiency of our organization.

The most difficult part of the system will be selling it to middle management. (Here, I presume, your parochial interest will be put aside and each of you will be acting in good faith in the overall best interest of the corporation.) When I was a middle manager, nothing aggravated me more than having my reqs get jerked around. Like most middle managers, I felt that I worked harder than my boss, that he really didn't know what was going on and that I was gravely short of resources. The crowning aggravation was to not only get the ten new people that I needed, but also lose somebody that could not be replaced. The only way around this problem is that you have to make the same speech to your reports that I just made to you; that you are doing what is best for your group by switching a replacement req from manager A to manager B and that you hope they can understand the group will be stronger for it, even if the burden falls on one group disproportionately. Transfers of requisitions out of one vice president's group into another will probably be an easier sell to middle management, "The marketing group really needed the req to replace Tom Jones, I had to give it up for the overall good of the company; I hope you can understand."

Direct labor will be approved as temporaries only, based on a productivity justification. New college graduate hiring will proceed without hindrance.

Please read this memo carefully and completely communicate its contents to your staff.

BLUFFERS, BETTORS, AND REAL-TIME NEGOTIATION

The summer of 1990 was an exception that proves the rule. Most of the time our head-count system guarantees that we meet our productivity goals. Here's how it works. Every quarter, based on our top-line business performance, we establish a corporate "budget" for new hires. We review historical revenue, head count, and revenue per person. We forecast next quarter's revenue, plug in a revenue-per-person target that improves on past performance, and determine the new allowable head count for the current quarter. That target head count determines how many new people we can hire. This is not a negotiable figure. Middle managers usually accept it as a reasonable guideline. It sets the framework for everything that follows.

Naturally, vice presidents and managers always want to hire more people than their piece of the model allows. And there are always "good ideas" behind every proposed new hire. Thanks to the model, however, our people quickly come to understand that the sum total of all their "good ideas" is one very bad idea—declining revenue per person.

That's when we call the head-count meeting described at the beginning of the chapter. In the boardroom are all the company's subsidiary presidents, vice presidents, and most middle managers. Simultaneously and directly, everyone in the room (which means virtually everyone in the company with hiring authority) sees how many new people Cypress can afford to add over the next three months. They also see how many total new hires they have requested (almost always more than twice the target), and thus how many proposed hires we must eliminate to live within our means.

The power of our system is that it allows for real-time tradeoffs among managers. Everyone knows we're playing a zero-sum game. A manager who insists on all of his or her hires understands (as does everyone else) that these slots come at the expense of other requests. Such stark tradeoffs create incentives for everyone else to think imaginatively about solving that manager's overhiring problem. They also create incentives for managers not to "pig out" publicly with wild requests for new hires.

In other words, the classic resource-allocation dynamic in big companies (middle management lobbies for resources, top management tries to hold the line) gets turned on its head. It's no longer me and a few senior colleagues against the world. We enlist a room full of allies in our effort to hold the line.

Over the years, as we have gotten better and better at these meetings, a more or less standard rhythm has developed. I begin with a few slides and a challenge: "Here's how overbudget we are in terms of proposed new hires. Here's how many proposed hires we must eliminate in order to meet the target head count. Let's get to it."

Then comes a series of individual presentations. One by one each manager makes a sales pitch to the group: "Here is the revenue (or units, line items, advertisements) I plan to generate next quarter. Here's how many new people I need. Here's why." More important, each manager presents a justification for *every single proposed hire.* Let's say a manager needs six new people in her design group. She is expected to explain, in detail, why she needs this particular slot for a layout specialist, this particular slot for a circuit designer, and so on through all six positions.

These can be tough, combative sessions. They are not for the faint of heart. People disagree. People raise their voices. People sometimes attack one another: "My department hasn't added new people in six months. We are working an extended amount of overtime. You want to hire three more engineers in a group that hasn't produced a working new product in eighteen months. That's wrong. I think your head count ought to be frozen until you get that new product out the door."

I don't deny that the meetings create the potential for personal conflicts and hard feelings. But bruised egos heal. The value of surfacing conflict in public is that it short-circuits the secret maneuvering, second-guessing, and backbiting that can poison organizations. We argue, but we argue over substance, issues, facts. And we reach decisions quickly, without hallway caucuses or memo wars. More important, we reach decisions *openly.* Everyone affected has the same information. Managers who can't make all the hires they want may feel unhappy. But they understand the logic behind the decision; they don't feel arbitrarily denied. They also see their colleagues sharing the burden equally.

Indeed, our biggest problem with the quarterly meeting is not that people fear conflict or resent "meddling" from their peers. Quite the opposite. Too many managers still try to use the sessions as a way to dump their problems in everyone else's laps. They can't figure out how to convince their own people to resist the urge to add bodies, so they submit new-hire proposals that are wildly out of line and figure

---

ACTION REQUEST   AR #   5822

FOR (ACTION):   VICE PRESIDENTS   START: October 31, 1991

CC (INFORMATION):   DUE: November 5, 1991

FROM: T.J. RODGERS

TITLE: ONE LAST CHANCE TO GET A FREE CAD PERSON FOR YOUR
          DESIGN GROUP

CONTENTS: Six months ago, during a siege of bad CAD problems, I offered
to sign one requisition for each design manager to hire a CAD engineer to report
directly to the design group. I thought having local support and an interface to
the main CAD group would be helpful. Each of the design managers pooh-
poohed the idea (turned a free body down), except for David Hoff. David's NPP
delinquency rate is now 10 percent, a factor of 2 to 7 better than the other
groups. In a recent operations review, he claimed that the CAD person had been
very helpful in preventing those little "airplane crashes" that plague design
groups.

TO COMPLETE AR: You have one last chance to sign up for a free CAD
person for each design manager.

---

*As CEO, it's not always my job to say no. In this case, I am trying to
persuade reluctant vice presidents to hire specialists in computer-aided
design (CAD). It didn't work.*

their colleagues will solve the problem for them. Sure they may take
some abuse, but they can emerge from the meeting, go back to their
people, and blame the "bullies" in the boardroom for denying their
new-hire requests.

I call this phenomenon upward delegation. It is a serious managerial copout. Upward delegation wasn't so big a headache in the
company's early days. Back then we were still a small enough organization for me to know the detailed inner workings of every operation. If managers came in with outlandish requests, I could ask a few
pointed questions, knock down the most absurd proposed hires, and
then throw the meeting open to the wolves. We'd hammer down that
manager in no time.

There came a middle stage in our history, about when we passed through the $100 million annual-revenue mark, when upward delegation became a serious problem. Some people still came in with outlandish requests, but I didn't know the details the way I once did. It became frustrating and tedious to argue people down. We still made our head-count targets, but the meetings were long, tense, and adversarial. Something had to change.

Our answer was the microperformance index, which has become another critical part of the system. Today, as our managers make their head-count presentations, they don't merely announce how many new people they need, for what jobs, and then justify each request. They structure their presentations around specialized indices that track the zero-based operating efficiency of their units over time. These indices become the factual basis for discussion and compromise among departments.

Let's say the inventory-control manager requests an additional clerk. We flash a graph that displays the relevant productivity trend (in this case, line items shipped per week per clerk) and ask the manager to justify the request based on increased productivity. Or say a director of manufacturing wants to hire ten more equipment operators. The group would review a different productivity index (such as wafer output per hour per operator), build in further progress on the index, and weigh the request accordingly. The rule of thumb is simple: Don't even *think* about making a presentation unless you can document improvements in your microperformance index. That rule has gone a long way to reducing upward delegation.

Some managers have done strange things to make their case. A few years ago one of Cypress's founders, who ran manufacturing at the time, wanted to hire a slew of new people. He had all kinds of gun-to-the-head arguments for why the factory would grind to a halt without them. But under the rules of the head-count meeting, he couldn't present his arguments without first presenting his microperformance index.

The trend was horrible. The data (represented by a bunch of dots) were scattered, as it always is, but the basic pattern was clear—a nosedive down at a 45-degree angle. His response? He took a bright red pen, drew a bold line sharply up and to the right at a 45-degree angle, and claimed that was the line that best fit the dots. First people stared at him. Then they looked around at one another. Then they burst into laughter—and almost hooted him out of the room. Needless to say, despite this admirably creative attempt to overthrow a hundred years of statistics theory, our middle managers understood that even a founder would not get his reqs unless the numbers justified it.

This was an important lesson. When it comes to resources, there are two kinds of managers. One kind are the bluffers. Bluffers play the classic game of middle-management myopia. They propose a list of forty new hires when they need only twenty. They hope I will argue them down to twenty-five, get tired, and authorize five more people than they really need. This kind of negotiating ploy is a serious breach of trust—but it happens all the time. It's the kind of brinkmanship our systems are designed to eliminate.

The other kind of manager (the kind we try to cultivate) are the bettors. Bettors make resource requests that are so lean, so well constructed, they dare top management to argue them down. They want me to bet them that they can be more efficient than they think they can. I seldom take that bet. I use all of my creative juices to make sure the manager can achieve what he thinks he can, that he is not overpromising. And I almost always give these managers exactly what they ask for.

Bettors get two important pledges from me. First, I will stay out of their way. I will not microanalyze a request for resources that strikes me as genuinely lean. Second, they will get a sympathetic hearing if they need more resources down the road. Say a manager comes to me and says, "A few months ago I asked for two new people on this project. You thought I needed three. Well, you were right. We are behind, and I need that third person to stay on schedule." The manager will get his third person quickly and without much of an argument.

Recently I encountered both kinds of managers in one new-product group. We had formed a team to design and launch a complex new chip. This group had been "starving" for several quarters. It had fourteen people and was clamoring for more. I agreed to consider a new-hire proposal. I explained that times were tough (they always are), and asked them to submit a solid estimate of how many people it would take to get the chip to market and what each person would do.

The group came back with a plan for thirty-four more people—forty-eight in all. Included in their request was a seven-person marketing group and a three-person administration group, both of which I found wildly extravagant. My response was animated, to say the least: "You are thinking like big-company bureaucrats. I am not going to argue down from this document. This is a bluff. You have one week to submit a new plan in writing. There will be no meeting, no negotiations. I will either accept the proposal outright or reject it outright. So think carefully about what you ask for."

One member of the group, the design manager, was exempt from this harsh reaction. His head-count proposal reflected precisely the kind of middle-management thinking we value—the bettor mentality. First he asked a question: What was the most "productive" chip in Cypress history in terms of how long it took to design with how many engineers? Then he made a calculation: This is how many transistors that chip had, here's how many designers worked on it, here's how long it took. In other words, he created a design-productivity index. Then he extrapolated: He used that index to determine how many designers he needed based on the complexity of his chip and its target delivery date.

That manager was making a bet: "I plan to manage my project as productively as any new-product project in this company's history. If you insist that I hire fewer people, then you are betting that I will set a new record for productivity. That's fine. But if you lose that bet, the design schedule will slip and the launch will be delayed."

I approved his request on the spot, no questions asked.

THE HARD WORK OF DOING MORE WITH LESS

Cypress's approach to allocating head count is designed to extend that hard-headed logic throughout the organization. At the start of each quarterly negotiation our managers know the total number of new hires we can approve, the number of proposed hires we must eliminate to meet our revenue-per-person target, and productivity trends for each department making requests. All we need to do is make the numbers work. What could be more straightforward?

Unfortunately, decisions on head count are never straightforward. There are always exceptions, special cases, legitimate problems that need attention. Reaching a sensible final agreement takes judgment, flexibility, a feel for what's reasonable. We don't want to apply the system so rigidly that we make it impossible for people to do their jobs. We also don't want to "special-case" our way to chaos and inefficiency.

The situation we faced in the third quarter of 1991 underscores how tough it can be to meet people's needs and still live within the rules—and how imperfect even the best possible outcome can be. Most of the time we can make fair decisions and hit our target head count within a person or two. This time we couldn't.

We entered the third quarter of 1991 having posted the best results in Cypress history. In the second quarter, for the first time ever, sales reached an annualized rate of $300 million. Our people were feeling great: record revenues, record profits, a record stock price. And their expectations on head count were clear: Finally, they told themselves, we could fill the slots we had rejected in the past. We had *earned* the right to make our lives a little easier.

The verdict of the head-count-allocation system was something different. We all knew this breakneck expansion couldn't last forever. Our forecasts were telling us that there would be virtually no growth in the third quarter. Sure there would still be plenty of profit. But the glory days were about to end, at least for a while. It is in times like these that the "prosperity illusion" becomes most dangerous.

The basic calculation worked like this. Cypress generated second-quarter revenue at an annual rate of $300 million. We employed 1,904 people. That translates into revenue per person of $157,800. We projected third-quarter revenue at an annual rate of $301.4 million—anemic growth of 0.48 percent. If our goal was just to maintain revenue per person of $157,800, allowable head count at the end of Q3 would be 1,915 people. In other words, although we were forecasting record revenue for the third quarter, we wanted our managers to add only eleven people to the corporate payroll. That's tough!

But the situation was even tougher. The table on page 168, which was the basis of our third-quarter head-count negotiations, tells the story in great detail. It breaks down our projections for revenue, growth rates, and head count by product line, department, and subsidiary. I've annotated the table to highlight some of the most important trends and results.

The numbers show that Cypress was indeed entering a slow-growth period. But several product lines were still expecting to grow at healthy double-digit rates. SRAM memory chips, for example, projected sales growth of nearly 34 percent. Our PROM line projected growth of nearly 31 percent. Multichip Technology, one of our subsidiaries, planned to grow by nearly 11 percent.

The real problem was that one operation, our Ross Technology subsidiary, was in the middle of a major product transition. It planned to *shrink* in revenue by almost 50 percent, from more than $15 million in the second quarter to less than $8 million in the third. Such dramatic reversals come with the territory in a fast-changing business like microprocessors. Ross certainly expected to return to a blazing growth path once the product transition was completed. But its revenue shrinkage—in an operation that accounted for 20 percent of Cypress's second-quarter sales—was a huge drag on the corporate growth rate. Thus it was a huge drag on allowable head count for the third quarter.

You can imagine the objections from the rest of the company. Some managers took issue with the overall corporate forecast. "Sure we are entering a slow-growth quarter," people argued, "but we grew much faster than expected last quarter. So we hired fewer people than we were 'entitled' to. Doesn't that mean we can hire more people than we are entitled to this quarter?"

That argument makes sense—so long as managers are prepared to initiate layoffs every time actual revenues come in below the forecast. Of course, no one is willing to do that.

Another objection involved more parochial concerns. "My division is still growing," some of our managers said. "Why should I be refused new people because an operation somewhere else is shrinking?"

That argument also makes sense—as a definitive statement of middle-management myopia.

The situation was tougher still. The second-quarter head count of 1,904 did not include a group of people whom we call "done deals." These are people who have accepted jobs at Cypress but who are still in transition to the company. They didn't count against Q2 head count; they would count against Q3 head count. Just factoring in our 48 done deals, we forecast an actual third-quarter head count of 1,952—well above the target head count of 1,915.

That left us with several options. We could apply the system rigidly, announce that we were already over the hiring budget for the quarter, impose a companywide hiring freeze, and call off the meeting. That would have allowed us to play by the rules. But it would have been unfair to an organization that had in fact been registering higher than expected gains in revenue and productivity.

Another alternative was to throw up our hands, abandon the system for a quarter, and discuss proposed hires without regard to the corporate allowance. That would have provided welcome flexibility. But it would have violated every management principle we had championed for almost a decade.

Which left the alternative on which we finally settled. We agreed to some flexibility on the hiring allowance. But we also put out the word, as our managers were preparing their new-hire requests, that they should not fool themselves about how much flexibility we were prepared to offer. Record revenues or not, this would be a tough quarter for hiring.

Q3 1991
Head Count And Capital Meeting:
Head-Count Results

	PRELIMINARY CALCULATIONS					PROPOSED CHANGES TO HEAD COUNT				FINAL DECISIONS	
TARGET MODEL	SALES ACTUAL Q291	HEAD COUNT ACTUAL Q291	SALES FCST Q391	SALES GROWTH	TARGET HC Q391	DONE DEALS Q391	ATTRITS Q391	ASK NEW REQS Q391	ASK NET ADD Q391	APPROVED NEW REQS Q391	FINAL HC Q391
Cypress San Jose:											
Finance & Admin	$75,105	63	$75,469	0.48%	63	5	0	1	6	0	68
SJ Manufacturing	$70,647	795	$70,864	0.31%	797	10	(4)	17	23	3	804
Marketing & Sales	$75,105	206	$75,469	0.48%	207	[4] 2	(4)	6	4	2	206
Design Research	$48,920	33	$54,506	11.42%	37	0	0	0	0	0	33
Process Technology	$71,712	64	$71,919	0.29%	64	3	0	3	3	0	67
Quality	$75,105	34	$75,469	0.48%	34	0	0	1	1	0	34
SRAM Direct	$19,545	58	$26,153	33.81%	78	0	0	0	0	0	58
Logic Direct	$6,831	50	$7,403	8.37%	54	2	0	13	15	13	65
Prom Direct	[2] $8,209	34	$10,729	30.70%	44	3	0	0	3	0	37
PLD Direct	$12,009	44	$12,318	2.57%	45	4	(1)	7	10	0	47
Cypress San Jose	$48,920	1381	$54,506	11.42%	1,424	29	(9)	45	65	18	1,417
Cypress Texas	$70,188	256	$70,769	0.83%	258	2	(6)	7	3	4	256
Aspen Semiconductor	$8,222	46	$8,758	6.52%	49	4	0	6	10	2	52
Multichip Technology	$3,791	44	$4,200	10.79%	49	1	(1)	6	6	0	44
Ross Technology	[3] $15,109	89	$7,800	—48.38%	46	3	0	2	5	0	92
Cypress Minnesota	$69,123	88	$69,714	0.85%	89	9	0	19	28	9	106
[1] Cypress Consolidated	$75,105	1904	$75,469	0.48%	1,915	[5] 48	(16)	85	117	33	1,969
Cypress w/o Ross	$59,996	1815	$67,669	12.80%	1,869	45	(16)	83	112	33	1,877

1. Although we projected record revenue for the third quarter ($75.46 million), the forecast represented modest growth over the prior quarter. Which means our head count should grow modestly—from 1,904 to 1,915.

2. Corporate revenue projections and head-count targets are the sum of our projections for product lines, factories, support departments, and subsidiaries. For example, our line of PROM memory chips anticipates healthy growth of 30.7 percent. That means its target head count is allowed to grow by 30.7 percent—from 34 to 44 people.

3. Here's the nub of the dilemma. Revenue at Ross Technology is projected to go backward in the quarter by 48 percent. For the group to maintain its current revenue-per-person index, it would have to reduce head count from 89 to 46 people. That won't happen—which puts all kinds of pressure on the other groups.

4. Marketing and sales ended the second quarter with 206 people and will end the third quarter with 206 people. Here's how. The group hired two people in the second quarter who have yet to join Cypress. These "done deals" count against Q3 head count. Four people in the organization plan to leave over the next thirteen weeks and will not be replaced. These "attrits" reduce Q3 head count. Marketing proposed six new hires for the quarter. The head-count meeting approved only two of the requests—which means the group will maintain its head count of 206.

5. Before the meeting, our managers proposed to increase total Cypress head count by 117 people: 48 done deals minus 16 attrits plus 85 new hires. The meeting approved only 33 of the hires—for a net addition to head count of 54 people.

How did we respond? Did we rise to the occasion and control our appetite for new people? Hardly. Our people asked for the moon. They requested 85 additional hires over and above the 48 "done deals" who were about to arrive. Netting out planned attrition, we were staring at requests for 117 new people—more than ten times what the model allowed!

It came time for the meeting. My first order of business was to introduce some reality therapy: "Based on our revenue forecasts, the model says we should be at 1,915 people. With our done deals alone, we are at 1,952. The managers of this company want to add 85 more. That's crazy. We are going to spend however long it takes to knock down these outlandish requests. We will not leave this room until we agree to eliminate at least 50 of the proposed hires."

The meeting dragged on much longer than usual, late into the night. After lots of hard bargaining we reached a compromise. We approved 33 of the 85 new hires and rejected the other 52. Thus, counting the done deals, we authorized a final third-quarter head count of 1,969. We violated the ideal model by 50 people—or 2.8 percent.

Was this outcome a defeat for the system? Perhaps. On an overall corporate basis we allowed revenue per person to slip from $157,800 in the second quarter to a projected $153,000 in the third quarter. Indeed, we finished 1991 with the first reversal in revenue per person in our history. That certainly looks like a defeat.

But think about the no-win situation we faced. The 50 percent cut in Ross sales made it virtually impossible for Cypress to stay "on budget" in terms of revenue per person. According to the model, Ross's head count should have gone from 89 to 46 as a result of its sales reversal—a massive layoff. But you can't impose layoffs every time one of your operations experiences a temporary revenue setback.

In fact, if you eliminate Ross from the head-count calculations, the outcome looks decidedly less grim. Quarterly Cypress revenue excluding Ross was projected to grow from less than $60 million to nearly $68 million—an increase of 12.8 percent. Based on our final agreement, total head count excluding Ross grew by only 3.4 percent. In that sense, Cypress lived well within its means.

So was the outcome a victory? I think you can make that case. Without imposing unfair penalties, the system forced the entire company to reckon with short-term reversals in one of its subsidiaries. None of our overhead or support functions (finance and administration, quality, R&D) hired a single new person. Our new factory in Minnesota, which was just ramping up to volume production, agreed to add only nine of the 19 people it wanted. Our factory in San Jose requested 17 new slots and got approval for three. Our two fastest-growing products (SRAMs and PROMs) didn't even request new hires despite their bright outlook.

I shudder to think at the number of new people our managers would have requested (and that I might have approved) without the discipline of our hiring system. We emerged from the meeting a stronger company because we controlled the prosperity illusion.

JUST ENOUGH CAPITAL — JUST IN TIME

The organizing logic of our capital system mirrors how we approach head count. And it's just about as important. Computer chips are one of the most "capital-intensive" businesses in the world. Much of our equipment (like the steppers we discussed earlier) comes with price tags in the millions of dollars. And it takes lots of that million-dollar equipment to build a factory that can manufacture the complex chips we design.

Think of the economics of our business this way. The average cost of all the raw materials in one of our chips (silicon, plastic, copper, gold, and so on) is about 28 cents. Our capital costs per chip—the money we borrow to buy our equipment and build our factories—average about 90 cents. In other words, our profits are three times as heavily influenced by the cost of *money* as the cost of *materials*. In our business, having just enough capital just in time is a make-or-break proposition.

The good news is that capital equipment can sometimes be easier to manage than people. All too often decisions about hiring become shrouded in emotion: "How can you not approve the two new clerks I requested? My people are stretched, they need help. I promised I would get these slots." Managers are usually more clear-eyed about machines, although they are also quicker to fall back on gun-to-the-head rebuttals: "Sure I can live without that new wafer etcher. But I can't guarantee that you are going to get all the wafers you need next quarter."

There is, however, one special challenge with respect to capital. In high-tech companies, where I've spent my career, engineers often believe they have a constitutional right to the shiniest new machines, the most powerful new microscopes, the fastest new computers. It's the capital-spending equivalent of keeping up with the Joneses. The role of our capital system is to replace this engineering mindset—newer and bigger is always better—with a business mindset that revolves around a simple question: What is the *least* we can spend to achieve what we think we are capable of achieving?

We instill that business mindset using the same mechanics as our head-count system. We drive capital-spending decisions from top-line revenue projections, evaluate our performance based on an index of capital productivity, insist on continual improvement in that index, approve overall corporate targets that reflect such improvement, and expect managers themselves to make the department-by-department tradeoffs necessary for the organization to live within its means.

Indeed, the two systems are so compatible that we make our decisions on capital spending in the same quarterly meeting that we decide on head count. One at a time managers present their capital requests. As with head count, we expect managers to present a zero-based justification for every new piece of equipment: "Here's why I need this ion implanter, here's why I need this scrubber, here's why I need these computer workstations."

With every manager, and for every piece of equipment, the group poses a long series of tough questions. Can we defer the spending until next quarter? Next year? What business risks will we be assuming (capacity, quality, delivery, reliability) if we do defer it? Does buying this equipment commit us to future purchases of supporting equipment? Are there less costly alternatives? People argue, trade, compromise—and eventually agree to a capital-spending plan that meets each manager's needs as well as our quarterly capital allowance.

Most important (and this is a bit different from the head-count negotiations), people from different operations share expertise. Today we run factories in California, Texas, and Minnesota. We have design centers in California, Colorado, Minnesota, and Mississippi. All these operations make important decisions on capital spending. Many of them make decisions about comparable (if not identical) equipment. Every quarter, by gathering all our managers in the same room, we create a forum in which people swap stories, share experiences, endorse a particular machine or warn their colleagues about it. Thus, decisions on every piece of equipment we buy reflect the combined experience of forty or fifty managers rather than the wish list of one manager and the "just-say-no" skills of the CEO.

The impact of the system is indisputable. It has become routine in our industry to talk about chip factories that cost $500 million and take years to build. We have never understood or lived by that conventional wisdom. Our plant in San Jose, Fab I, opened in 1984. It was completed in seven months, from the time we poured the first concrete to the time we shipped our first revenue wafer. On a total investment of $35 million, Fab I generated $50 million a year in revenue, ran almost sixty different products and over twenty different processes, and does all of Cypress's corporate R&D.

Fab II, in Round Rock, Texas, opened in a used building in 1986. Eight months went by between the time a wrecking ball wiped out the middle of the building (we left the walls up) and the time we shipped our first revenue wafer. Our investment was $40 million. The plant is now generating revenue at an annual rate of $200 million and accounts for two-thirds of our total business.

Much of this remarkable productivity reflects our commitment to "perpetual entrepreneurship" and our system of internal startups. Ultimately, the best way to create a business mindset is to create real businesses that people own and run themselves. (We'll describe our startups in Chapter 8.) But our manufacturing track record also reflects the disciplining powers of our capital system. As a company, and as a group of managers, we have learned how to do more with less: cheaper equipment, older equipment, used equipment, less equipment.

It's not easy, it's not always fun, and it takes constant vigilance. But it works. And it has helped Cypress survive and prosper in an unforgiving competitive game whose rules, at least when it comes to money, are often stacked in favor of our foreign rivals.

CHAPTER 7

lean budgets, tight control

Who hasn't made a cameo appearance in the Great Business Budget Follies? Consider a typical story line from a hypothetical company.

Bob runs a department. Bob wants to spend $1 million next quarter on operating expenses over and above his capital budget. His budget was $800,000 last quarter, and if he and his people stretched, they could probably do the job with the same budget— maybe less. But it's much easier, certainly much more fun, to manage with more money rather than less. Bob's negotiating strategy? Submit a proposed budget of $1.2 million and engage in trench warfare for each dollar of that $200,000 padding factor.

Bob's vice president has a reputation for being tough on costs. After a rough-and-tumble review, Bob diplomatically agrees to a budget of "just" $1.1 million. He is happy—he got more than what he wanted all along. His people are happy—they can buy the materials and supplies they couldn't buy last quarter. His vice president is happy—he knocked $100,000 off Bob's original budget. Everyone is happy—except, of course, the shareholders, who continue to wonder why this division can't make more money.

The curtain rises on Act Two. Bob and his people try to spend their $1.1 million budget. One of his junior managers submits a purchase order for new software to help finalize the design of the division's next big product. The software costs $75,000, which exceeds Bob's signature authority as well as that of his vice president. Bob signs the PO and forwards it to his boss's office, where it sits for ten days. The VP eventually signs the purchase order and kicks it upstairs to the corporate controller for final approval. It sits unattended for another two weeks. Frustrated, Bob complains to the controller's assistant. The assistant digs through a stack of unanswered memos and unsigned POs and puts Bob's paperwork on the controller's desk. At last, nearly a month after submitting the PO, Bob's manager orders the software. (Of course, "order" means send to purchasing, which triggers another delay chain.)

Now it's the end of the quarter—and time for Act Three. Bob is back in his vice president's office. He's more humble than he was thirteen weeks ago. It turns out he just couldn't manage within his budget. Who could have predicted his group would have to pay all that overtime to get its new product out the door? Who expected that $70,000 late billing from the lawyers on his department's patent application? Of course, it could have been worse, Bob explains. Sure he spent $1.2 million. But in this tough quarter, despite all the surprises, he managed to come in right on the budget he had originally requested. Isn't that evidence of dedicated cost control? In the spirit of "realistic" planning, the vice president reluctantly approves a budget of $1.2 million for the next quarter.

Budgets are boring. Budgets are bureaucratic. All too often, budgets are downright bogus. But budgets—or, more precisely, the process of setting, tracking, and meeting them—do matter. Bob, his people, and his vice president all believe they are managing close to the bone. In fact, quarter after quarter, year after year, their negotiating ploys and end-of-the-quarter surprises are making the division more and more uncompetitive.

The most corrosive waste in business is invisible waste—spending that doesn't look like waste because "We've always done it that way." The problem with many budget systems is that they organize and categorize invisible waste rather than identify and eliminate it. Tolerating a "little bit" of waste every quarter is like eating a "little bit" of lead with every meal. You get slower and slower until you finally break down.

We can't afford to participate in the Great Business Budget Follies. Our "PO-Commit" system is a tough and effective approach to managing expenses by eliminating invisible waste. Its logic is so transparent, its disciplining powers so effective, and the problem of runaway expenses so pervasive that it may be the most widely relevant of all the management systems at Cypress.

Our budgets are lean. And we never go over budget—*never*. Yet we meet our spending targets without a cumbersome purchasing bureaucracy or long delays. At Cypress, it takes no more than five working days for a purchase order of any size to be approved or sent back to the sender for cause. The system also allows me, as CEO, to maintain hands-on engagement with how much money we spend and how we spend it.

Meeting budgets at Cypress has become routine—important, to be sure, but routine. At the end of every quarter, we produce a "PO-Commit scorecard" that evaluates our spending discipline. For the company as a whole, and for each of forty reporting units, the scorecard compares actual spending with forecasts and assigns one of four grades. "Sandbag" means a department has come in under budget by 10 percent or more. (Such under-budget performances are not evidence of tight management but of budget padding at the outset.) "Superior" control means a department was under budget by less than 10 percent. "Good" control means a department did not exceed its budget by more than 4 percent. "Needs control" means a department exceeded its forecast spending by 5 percent or more.

The scorecard results for the first quarter of 1992 are absolutely typical. We projected that Cypress would spend $20,653,000 on everything from computer software, to paper for the photocopiers, to silicon wafers, to airfare for our sales force. We actually spent $20,576,000. Thus, as a company, we were under budget by 0.4 percent. Of our forty reporting departments, five posted sandbag results, twenty-five registered superior control, seven posted good control, and only three overspent their budgets by 5 percent or more. Of these three profligate spenders, two were tiny operations, with combined budgets of only $36,000.

I can remember only one quarter in the last few years when Cypress missed its corporate budget by more than 1 percent. That was the fourth quarter of 1991—a brutal period for revenues. Midway through the quarter, we saw our sales projections melt away and clamped down on spending. As a result, we wound up *under* budget by 3 percent. So even when we miss, we tend to miss in the right direction.

THUNDERBOLTS, MICROSCOPES, AND THE SECRETARY'S PRODUCTIVITY CHECK

The PO-Commit system allows no room for budget surprises. But its real value is not that it imposes top-down controls or that it "edicts" compliance. Quite the opposite. Today, 90 percent of our managers operate at or below their already-lean budgets without any top-down interference. Our managers control their own spending. The PO-Commit system is a quantifiable way to delegate that control. It works because it combines the creative powers of decentralization with companywide accountability.

That said, I don't want to diminish the role of the senior team. A culture of extravagance almost always starts at the top. If the boss overspends, or spends unwisely, there is no reason to think the rest of the organization will behave any differently. Likewise, if the boss treats money as the scarce resource it is, and if the boss comes down hard when other people waste money, he or she will generate a culture of efficiency that reinforces even the most rigorous budgeting system.

I learned the value of top-down intervention—and what it meant to run a tight ship on expenses—during my years at Advanced Micro Devices. Back then Jerry Sanders, the CEO, had a well-deserved reputation for being right on top of his managers' budgets and expenses (even though he was lavish with himself). I can still remember the fallout from the dinner celebrating my decision to join AMD. It was an eye-opening introduction to the company's Spartan culture.

The vice president who recruited me to AMD (and ran a $175-million division, half the company's total revenues at the time) took me to Chantilly, a Silicon Valley recruiting spot in Palo Alto. I told him I was studying wine as a hobby, so he asked me to select a couple of good bottles to show off what I knew. I didn't gouge AMD for Lafite-Rothschild, but I ordered some fairly pricey burgundies. A few weeks later I was told the vice president caught a bunch of flak after Jerry signed the expense report for the dinner.

The news made a real impression on me. Imagine: The CEO of a $350 million company, signing the expense report of the vice president running a $175 million division, angrily questioned a $300 dinner tab. Translation: "We don't waste money at AMD. Never spend a dime you don't have to spend." Further translation: "When you do waste money, you may bring down the wrath of the CEO."

From time to time, for all the rigors of our PO-Commit system, I hurl a few thunderbolts of my own. One of my favorite techniques is the secretary's productivity check. I remember back in the mid-1980s, when our manufacturing people decided they desperately needed automated microscopes. These were fancy $30,000 machines, three times more expensive than normal microscopes, but our people insisted they would dramatically improve quality, tolerances, yields—all the "motherhood" virtues invoked to justify gold-plated equipment. (Remember the logic behind that request for four steppers at $1 million each?) I reluctantly approved the POs.

One day the plant manager came into my office with a purchase order for two more microscopes. "What are these for?" I asked. "We're out of capacity," he said. I was flabbergasted. Back then I walked through the plant about ten times a day. We were proud of our state-of-the-art manufacturing operation, and I loved to give tours to investors and potential customers. What's more, we built the production area with big glass windows, so even when I wasn't in the plant, the operation was almost always in view. I hardly ever saw our technicians using the automated microscopes they claimed were so important.

So I refused to sign the POs pending a "capacity study." For two weeks I sent my secretary into the plant at random times to record whether or not the existing microscopes were being used. The results showed the microscopes were used less than 50 percent of the time. I stapled her findings to the back of the unsigned PO, which was returned to the manager. I never heard about automated microscopes again.

(We made the right decision. A few years later I toured our capital-equipment "graveyard." It turns out both automated microscopes had developed defects in their belt-driver wafer transports, the technology that made them automated in the first place. They wound up on the scrap heap. Top-down intervention thus halved the potential damage. It also sent an important message: "If you buy it, use it—twenty-four hours a day, seven days a week.")

I used the same technique with testers, the special computers we use to check our chips for defects. We had grown substantially by this point and owned twenty-five of the $500,000 machines. I kept getting POs for more testers, even though I had a nagging suspicion thta the "capacity" arguments were a cover for machines operating far below their capability. I decided once again to practice a little top-down intervention.

With great fanfare I called our chief test engineer into my office. I asked him to train my secretary in how to read the status lights, how to know whether a tester was being used, whether it was being used to maximum capacity, and so on. Then, again with great fanfare, I accompanied her on a tour of the plant. She carried a clipboard and took notes on the status of each of the twenty-five testers. Finally I announced she would conduct random visits for the next month to help educate me on future POs.

Some days she would not show up at all. Other days she would be in the plant every hour. A few times she made inspections at five A.M. A few times she stayed until midnight and visited the third shift. You can imagine the reaction when the president's secretary walks through the plant with a clipboard and looks at your machine. "My God, she's been here four times in the last three days and the tester has been off-line every time! We're going to get clobbered if we ask for another one."

Suddenly the flow of POs dried up. I am absolutely certain that this show of strength—however hokey—saved us millions of dollars' worth of redundant testers that were never even requested, let alone approved.

QUARTERLY BUDGETS, WEEKLY RECKONING

Ultimately, of course, thunderbolts from the corner office only set a tone. In fact, it's unhealthy to let managers come to expect such top-down controls. It encourages them to dump their problems in the CEO's lap. Real expense-control requires tough budgeting methodologies along with cost-center management and strict accountability. That's how we organize our budgeting system.

As with head count and capital, PO-Commit drives allowable spending from the top line and insists on greater productivity every quarter. But it also goes beyond head count and capital. It creates a *weekly* spending discipline that generates quick, smart decisions on individual purchases and immediate feedback on overall spending patterns.

The easiest way to understand the system is to walk through its main features. Naturally, we begin with departmental budgets. Here we have one basic rule: We expect our people to do more with less every quarter, no exceptions. Product-line vice presidents forecast their revenues (the same projections they use for head count and capital), document improvements in their expense-to-revenue ratios, and submit budgets that reflect these productivity trends. Factory managers base their proposed spending on forecast output and submit budgets that document they are working to build more with less.

Budget reviews are quick, crisp, and highly structured. Unlike head count and capital, there is no companywide meeting. Spending patterns are different enough from group to group that collective "peer pressure" is less valuable. Moreover, the long-term stakes are a little lower. Expenses are here today and gone by the end of the quarter. Capital gets depreciated (and thus affects financial performance) over five years. People are forever.

Budget reviews take place in a single meeting at the beginning of the quarter. I spend three hours in a conference room with a group of staff colleagues: the CFO, controller, director of purchasing, and director of facilities. Every twenty minutes or so, a vice president or subsidiary president presents a budget. We don't allow thick binders or fancy overheads. Presenters get a few pages—no more—to summarize and explain their proposed expenses and relate them to past performance and our current plan.

Each presentation uses the same format. On pp. 184–85 is a sample budget for one of our product lines from the second quarter of 1992. It packs a lot of information onto a single summary page. The figures represent a huge amount of work from a large number of people; it's not easy squeezing waste from an operation every quarter of every year. They also represent all the information I need to make sure our people don't promise more efficiency than they can deliver—or to ask for even more efficiency than what they think they can achieve.

Here's how this budget would be evaluated during a quarterly review. Section 1, total proposed spending, shows the group wants to spend $4.96 million, an increase of 1.6 percent over actual spending in the previous quarter. Is that reasonable? Well, section 2 provides a basic feel for how the budget relates to the top line. It includes quarterly results and projections for revenues, units shipped, average selling price (ASP)—everything needed to size up overall business prospects.

On a first pass, the budget looks troublesome. This group projects net revenues of $10 million, an increase of just 0.3 percent over the previous quarter. Yet spending is up 1.6 percent—not what we expect at Cypress. But it turns out there is more to the story. This product line is planning to make lots of chips this quarter for shipment to distributors. Our conservative accounting policies mean we can't book those chips as "net revenue" until they are sold through to customers. (Essentially, our distributors want to build up their inventories for future sales.) Still, no manager, no matter how creative, can manufacture chips without generating plenty of legitimate expenses.

Thus, a fair quarter-to-quarter analysis would compare net factory revenue, which is a more healthy $10.44 million. Using that metric, this shapes up as a stellar budget: revenues up 18 percent, total expenses up 1.6 percent. We'll take that kind of productivity any day.

In fact, the budget looks too stellar. It calls for a few sanity checks. One relevant check is track record: How good has this group been at meeting its budgets? Section 1 shows that in the first quarter of 1992, the group budgeted $4.98 million and spent only $4.89 million. That's a good sign. It also shows that the group's total spending as a percentage of net revenue has declined over the past two quarters: from 55.1 percent in the fourth quarter of 1991 to 48.8 percent in the first quarter of 1992. The slight projected uptick this quarter (to 49.4 percent) is explained by the projected inventory build.

Overall, comparing the second quarter of 1992 with the second quarter of 1991 shows that the group has made remarkable progress. Revenue (section 2) has increased from $8.2 million to a projected $10.4 million—up 27 percent. Yet absolute dollar spending (section 1) has declined from $5.35 million to a proposed $4.96 million—down 7.3 percent. The bottom line: These people are genuinely dedicated to controlling expenses. Their budget is solid, it hangs together, and it shows a history of good control.

By comparing the track records of comparable groups, this simple process allows us to create tough, demanding, close-to-the-bone budgets. We don't waste time with special pleading or "sky-is-falling" exceptions. Our people know what we expect in terms of overall productivity. Meanwhile, I'm not forced to try to outargue my vice presidents about spending priorities or individual budget items. With their detailed knowledge, I could never win anyway. The PO-Commit system documents what we need to do to get more productive.

After we approve beginning-of-quarter (BOQ) budgets for our product lines and subsidiaries, we divide those budgets by 13 to create weekly limits that govern actual spending. This step is key—and it's what separates our approach to expenses from most other budget systems.

Q2 1992
P.O.-COMMIT BUDGET

CYPRESS SEMICONDUCTOR

DESCRIPTION		Q291 ACT	Q391 ACT	Q491 ACT	Q192 BOQ	Q192 ACT	Q192 DELTA	Q292 BOQ	Q1A-Q2B DELTA
REFERENCE									
NET REVENUE $	RV	$9,856	$9,306	$8,873	$9,475	$10,015	5.7%	$10,048	0.3%
NET FACTORY $	RV	$8,204	$8,559	$8,272	$9,725	$8,848	−9.0%	$10,442	18.0%
ASP $	RV	$10.05	$11.23	$9.96	$10.79	$9.11	−15.6%	$9.75	7.0%
UNITS #	RV	816	762	831	901	971	7.7%	1071	10.3%
EXPENSES—DIRECT									
PROM SUBCON	DM				$145	$137	5.3%	$198	−44.2%
DIRECT MAT.	DM				$0	$0	NA	$75	NA
PROM TEST	DM				$67	$68	−2.0%	$73	−6.8%
PROM BURN IN	DM				$27	$22	15.8%	$23	−2.7%
IND MFG SUPPL'S	DO	$29	$33	$29	$45	$48	−8.7%	$62	−28.9%
BURN IN	DO	$7	$4	$6	$4	$5	−29.1%	$8	−54.9%
TRAVEL	DO	$3	$5	$2	$5	$3	35.4%	$7	−115.5%
TEMP LABOR	DO	$3	$9	$2	$7	$6	15.3%	$7	−20.0%
PROF FEES	DO	$1	$5	$8	$3	$4	−28.4%	$6	−50.6%
OTHER	DO	$5	$3	$7	$6	$7	−20.2%	$6	19.6%
MISC	DO	$7	$6	$5	$3	$2	20.1%	$2	16.6%
EXP EQP/SW	DO	$1	$1	$11	$0	$1	NA	$1	−28.9%
SUPPLIES	DO	$5	$3	$3	$1	$1	14.7%	$0	38.5%
TOTAL DIRECT		$60.1	$69.3	$73.4	$311.6	$305.3	2.0%	$468.0	−53.3%
% OF SALES		0.6%	0.7%	0.8%	3.3%	3.0%		4.7%	

EXPENSES — INTERCOMPANY

	Type	Col 1 ③	Col 2	Col 3	Col 4	Δ%	Col 5 ①	Δ%	Col 6	Δ%
FAB 2	IM	$592	$547	$634	$678	-6.9%	$683	-0.8%		
ASSEMBLY	IM	$1,100	$902	$855	$730	14.6%	$553	24.3%		
FAB 1	IM	$511	$275	$128	$63	50.5%	$225	-255.6%		
MARK	IM	$84	$124	$228	$254	-11.7%	$221	13.1%		
DIRECT MAT.	IM	$0	$0	$0	$0	NA	$175	NA		
TEST	IM	$466	$482	$0	$0	NA	NA	NA		
SUBCON	IM	$96	$87	$274	$0	NA	NA	NA		
BURN IN	IM	$27	$27	$28	$0	NA	NA	NA		
MARKETING	IA	$1,188	$1,045	$1,137	$1,124	1.1%	$1,123	0.1%		
TECHNOLOGY	IA	$647	$695	$653	$1,009	-54.5%	$788	21.9%		
MFG OVERHEAD	IMA		$161	$161	$194	-20.7%	$202	-4.0%		
CAD	IA	$258	$228	$225	$200	11.2%	$200	0.0%		
G & A	IA	$173	$178	$169	$200	-18.3%	$185	7.5%		
QUAL & REL	IA	$151	$135	$173	$127	26.8%	$140	-10.6%		
TOTAL INTERCO		$5,292	$4,925	$4,812	$4,665	1.8%	$4,580	1.8%	$4,495	1.9%
% OF SALES		53.7%	53%	54.3%	47.2%		45.8%		44.7%	

TOTAL EXPENSES — DIRECT & INTERCOMPANY

	Col 1	Col 2	Col 3	Col 4	Δ%	Col 5	Δ%	Col 6 ①	Δ%
TOTAL	$5,352	$4,995	$4,886	$4,977	1.8%	$4,885	1.8%	$4,963	-1.6%
% OF SALES	54.3%	53.7%	55.1%	52.5%		48.8%		49.4%	

SUMMARY

	Col 1	Col 2	Col 3	Col 4	Δ%	Col 5	Δ%	Col 6	Δ%
MFG—DIRECT	$0	$0	$0	$239	4.4%	$228	-61.8%	$369	
MFG—INTERCO	$2,848	$2,418	$2,504	$2,280	15.8%	$1,920	-7.2%	$2,059	
TOTAL MFG	$2,848	$2,418	$2,504	$2,518		$2,148	14.7%	$2,428	-13.0%
% OF SALES	28.9%	26.0%	28.2%	26.6%		21.4%		24.2%	
ALLOCATIONS	$2,293	$2,357	$2,335	$2,373	-14.9%	$2,728		$2,498	8.4%
% OF SALES	23.3%	25.3%	26.3%	25.0%		27.2%		24.9%	

RV = REVENUE, D = DIRECT, I = INTERCOMPANY, M = MFG, O = OVERHEAD, A = ALLOCATION

185

Most managers outside Cypress, like Bob and his vice president in the hypothetical example, control spending *after* the fact: "Here is your budget. Stick to it. We'll meet again in thirteen weeks and see how you did." We control expenses *before* the fact: "This is the budget we've agreed upon. Stick to it on a weekly basis throughout the quarter. If you do, no problem. If you can't, we will work with you as the quarter proceeds to reduce costs. Furthermore, if we fall behind our revenue projections, we will act to preempt costs before they occur."

The logic is simple: If, at the beginning of the quarter, senior management agrees to the total pool of resources available, and if we then establish limits on how fast the spending flows out of the pipeline, we can't be surprised by the results at the end of thirteen weeks. This logic starts at the top and cascades down through the ranks. As CEO, my budget is total corporate spending of about $23 million per quarter ($1.8 million per week). Through the BOQ budget process, my budget gets allocated among my direct reports. I then expect them to allocate their resources among their reports, and so on down the line to literally dozens of Cypress managers. This way, meeting budgets becomes everyone's business.

Consider the manager responsible for maintaining the equipment in one of our factories—an important job. Here's how the system looks from his perspective. His boss, the president of the Cypress subsidiary that runs the fab, might have a quarterly budget of $2.6 million ($200,000 per week). He divides that spending among the five managers who report to him, including the maintenance manager. The quarterly maintenance budget might be $650,000 ($50,000 per week). The maintenance manager in turn allocates that budget among the people who report to him, one of whom maintains thin-film equipment, one of whom maintains photolithography equipment, and so on.

Now it's time to spend the money. During the first week of the quarter, the maintenance manager's people submit POs to him that total up to $55,000. He knows his weekly limit is $50,000. So he approves $48,000 worth of them (the most important) and sends back the rest. The next week they submit POs worth $56,000. He approves the most important $45,000 and rejects the rest.

By the end of the month he is running $15,000 under budget. So he calls a meeting: "Good news, folks. Santa Claus is here. We're $15,000 ahead of budget. We're not going to spend it all, but we'll spend $12,000 of it. Let's review all the POs rejected this month and figure out which ones we need to approve."

This is what we mean by "quantifiable delegation." At all levels of Cypress, managers work to stay ahead of their budgets on a weekly basis and then slowly free up spending as the quarter end draws near. Nearly all of our managers have figured out how to master this discipline, and they do it intelligently and consistently every quarter—which is why we can register such tight control. No amount of oversight from the top can substitute for decentralized spending responsibility from hundreds of managers throughout the organization.

Which is not to suggest that I abdicate such oversight altogether. There is a third step. We don't just establish BOQ budget targets and then set weekly spending caps. We also require that every purchase order in the company—every single PO—passes through one central checkpoint every week. Our managers do control their own spending. But I retain the authority, through one highly efficient meeting every week, to monitor the quality and distribution of our spending.

The spending window at Cypress is open on Thursday's from eight to ten A.M. That's when we hold our weekly PO-Commit meeting. Every ten minutes or so, as with the BOQ reviews, a vice president shows up in my conference room, summarizes his group's planned spending for the week, and gets a guaranteed "yes" or "no" on every PO he submits. These sessions, also like the BOQ reviews, revolve around a highly structured one-page report. This report allows us to probe for extravagance, review big-ticket expenses, and generally stay current with what's happening around the company.

On pp. 190–91 is the weekly PO-Commit log for another Cypress product line. It was submitted at the PO-Commit meeting for workweek 29, the third week of the third quarter of 1992. The log is like a budget microscope that shifts the degree of magnification at will. It identifies nine distinct categories of spending: "regular" expenses, travel-and-entertainment, fixed charges, planned capital purchases, unplanned capital purchases, direct material, temporary labor, bulk purchases, and intercompany allocations. Within each category it gives details (right down to information on individual POs) on how much money the group wants to spend that week and on what. It displays everything from the fact that the group is $94 over budget for the week on temporary labor (see section 4) to the fact that the group is $274,000 *under* budget on manufacturing charges from the factory (see section 6).

The log also displays key overview trends. The upper right-hand corner, marked section 2, is a quick history lesson. It shows how the group has performed over the past six quarters. The lower left-hand corner, section 1, gives weekly and quarter-to-date summaries for this particular quarter.

Every week I start the PO-Commit meeting with section 1. I notice immediately that this group is dramatically under budget for the quarter ($456,237) and for the week ($157,835) and that the biggest reductions are from "intercompany" expenses—charges from the factory ($447, 209). Naturally I ask for an explanation. I hear a good news/bad news answer. The bad news is that the factory scrapped a huge run of defective chips, which meant it couldn't bill the product line for them. The good news is that the group has enough inventory to meet customer demand without the chips. The plant's manufacturing problem should not affect the group's top line for the quarter.

I then use section 3 to scan the report for other details. Obviously, in the course of a ten-minute review, the scan is fleeting and cursory. There are times, though, when individual POs do catch my eye. Say the vice president of marketing wants to buy a new computer workstation—an all-too-popular request. I may have learned at a prior meeting that an engineering group just mothballed three workstations after it reassigned some engineers. Naturally, I "suggest" to my vice president that he use one of the mothballed machines rather than buy a new one. We cross out the line item on the log, pull the purchase order from the stack of POs that accompanies the log, and go on with the meeting. Four or five little catches like that every week, fifty-two weeks a year, and pretty soon you're talking real money.

CEO REVIEWS: STICKING YOUR NOSE INTO THE PO'S

I can hear the objections already: *Why is the CEO of a $250 million company monitoring purchase orders from the marketing department?* A fair question. Here's how I would answer it. First, I don't review purchase orders every single week. The PO-Commit system is so effective and well-enough established that I don't worry about missing the Thursday meeting if I'm traveling. When I do miss a meeting, our CFO attends as my delegate.

Moreover, a few exemplary Cypress managers are exempt from the system. Our vice president for worldwide manufacturing is more of a fanatic about cost control than I am. He routinely spends $1 million per week. But in two years he has never come to a PO-Commit meeting without knowing exactly what was going on with his expenses. The few times he couldn't prepare for the meeting, he called in advance to warn me and ask for a delay. He could have bluffed his way through those meetings; I'm sure I'm not nearly as tough a prober as I think I am. But he never tried. After I began to realize that it was waste of time for me to review his POs (which he always scrutinized much more carefully than I could), I stopped reviewing them, except for big-picture trends and major capital-equipment spending.

Still, I don't skip the weekly PO-Commit meeting if I can help it, and there aren't any managers who have qualified to be exempt. That doesn't mean I use the system to exercise line-item control. I have no interest in that, despite some selective nitpicking. But I am interested in organizational learning. The PO-Commit meeting gives me the opportunity, as CEO, to identify important new ideas on cost reduction, to think hard about them, and then to transfer them quickly across the company. Two hours a week is a modest investment compared with the big returns in better, smarter, more effective spending.

Much of the learning is incremental. A simple question in a Thursday meeting ("Why do you people in Texas need a new telephone switch?") triggers a discussion about long-distance rates,

PURCHASE COMMITMENT LOG
Q3 1992

YEAR: 92 WORK WEEK 29 WEEK OF QTR: 3

		NET		INTERCO	
QTR		BOQ	ACTUAL	BOQ	ACTUAL
					WW 9229
Q2 91		$518	$515	$4,089	$3,094
Q3 91		$471	$445	$4,328	$3,197
Q4 91		$464	$394	$3,903	$2,783
Q1 92		$428	$431	$3,770	$3,820
Q2 92		$480	$443	$5,572	$5,121
Q3 92		$480	$102	$5,572	$410

FIXED ITEMS:

	$ AMOUNT
07/15/92 PREVIOUS FIXED PO's:	
BIN BDS/CONTACTORS	$3,495
MASK AMORTIZATION	$3,125
CONTRACTED EXPENSES	$2,143
PROP TAX/MISC BLDG COST	$1,075
NEW:	

OF ITEMS: 4   FIXED EXPENSE TOTAL: $9,838

EXPENSE PURCHASE ORDERS:

REQ DATE	ROST	VENDOR DESCRIPTION	$ AMOUNT
07/13/92	TMS	VIKI-REPAIR OF 5361 TEST SYSTEM	$300
07/15/92	TJD	FRY'-POWERPOINT UPGRADE	$135
07/14/92	KH	OFFI-FILE CABINET FOR TMS	$107
05/05/92	DDH	PRIN-BUSINESS CARDS	$27
07/08/92	AOB	AMKO-Q3 ASSY ($124K)	$0
07/08/92	AOB	LIBE-Q3 BURN IN ($65K)	$0
07/08/92	AOB	EICO-Q3 BURN IN ($50K)	$0
07/08/92	AOB	BEST-Q3 BURN IN ($11K)	$0

BLANKET PURCHASE ORDERS:

				UN-USED	WW 9229
02/25/92	AOB	AMKOR Q3 BURN IN	PO#	$100,450	$5,755
06/10/92	AOB	LIBERTY Q3 BURN IN	PO#	$41,154	$3,119
02/25/92	AOB	OMEDATA-Q292 ASSY	PO# A920161	$29,901	$2,936
03/03/92	AOB	EICO Q292 BURN IN	PO# A920170	$14,271	$1,493
07/08/92	AOB	EICO Q3 BURN IN	PO#	$50,000	
07/08/92	AOB	BEST Q3 BURN IN	PO#	$5,000	
01/14/92	AOB	LMCO MARK	PO# A920217	$1,539	
				$242,315	$13,302

OF ITEMS: 4

TEMP LABOR:

	NET ACTUAL	INTERCO QTR FC	DELTA
Q392 MTLS CLERK	$368	$462	$94
WW TOTAL:	$368	$462	$94
QTD:	$1,104	$1,385	$281

INTERCO CHARGES/CREDITS:

	NET — WORK WEEK			INTERCO — WORK WEEK		
	ACT	BOQ	DELTA	ACT	BOQ	DELTA
FAB 1-WW28	$135,952	$168,923	$32,971	$135,952	$337,846	$201,895
ASSY P&H-WW28	$30,736	$72,000	$41,264	$74,673	$130,462	$69,327
MARK-WW28	$9,746	$7,154	($2,592)	$11,340	$14,308	$2,968
SUBTOTAL	$176,433	$248,077	$71,644	$221,964	$496,154	$274,189
BLDG LEASE	$4,461	$4,462	$1	$8,922	$8,923	$1
MKTG FEE	$34,980	$65,231	$30,251	$44,990	$130,462	$85,472
ROYALTIES	$1,950	$6,846	$4,896	$1,950	$13,692	$11,742
R&D FEE	$44,231	$82,692	$38,461	$88,462	$165,385	$76,923
CAD FEE	$1,692	$1,692	$0	$3,384	$3,385	$1
G&A FEE	$7,846	$7,846	$0	$15,692	$15,692	$0
MFG ADMIN	$5,538	$5,538	$0	$11,076	$11,077	$1
ORA	$4,154	$4,154	($50)	$8,308	$8,308	($50)
FAB R&D WFRS	$0	$0	$0	$0	$0	$0
OTHER	$2,154	$2,154	$0	$5,427	$4,308	($1,119)

EXPENSE REPORTS:

REQ. DATE	RQSTR	DESCRIPTION	$ AMOUNT
07/08/92	MXA	UNISYS VISIT	$187

			$ AMOUNT
# OF ITEMS:	1	WW 29 EXPENSE TOTAL:	$187

PLANNED CAPITAL PURCHASE ORDERS:

REQ DATE	RQST	DESC/VENDOR	CAP PLAN	$ AMOUNT

			$ AMOUNT
# OF CAPITAL:	0	WW 29 CAPITAL TOTAL:	$0

❶

DIRECT MTL

		$14,295	$14,295	$0	$42,886	$42,886
ASSY BLANKET	$8,691	$1,923	($6,767)	$16,574	$5,769	($10,805)
MARK BLANKET	$0	$1,154	$1,154	$170	$3,462	$3,292
BURN-IN BLNKT	$4,612	$14,462	$9,850	$33,151	$43,385	$10,234
TOTAL	$13,302	$17,538	$4,236	$49,895	$52,615	$2,720

SUBSTITUTED/UNPLANNED CAPITAL PURCHASE ORDERS:

REQ DATE	RQS	DESC/VENDOR	S/UNP	$ AMOUNT

# OF UNPLAN CP	0	WW 29 UNPLAN CAPITAL TOTAL:	$0

SPECIAL CHARGES:

HOLDS WW28	$0	$0	HOLDS QTD	$0
HOT LOTS WW28	$0	$0	HOT LOT QTD	$0
SWR WW28	$1,500	$1,500	SWR QTD	$1,500
SMMALL LOT WW28	$3,500	$3,500	SMALL QTD	$7,375
GROUP B WW28	$0	$0	GROUP B QTD	$0

RED LIGHT ITEM:	WW 28 CR/(DR)	QTD CR/(DR)
FAB	$2,756	$61,053
ASS'Y	$500	$500
TEST	$0	$0
MARK	$0	$0
TOTAL	$3,256	$61,553

PO-COMMIT SUMMARY:

	NET	INTERCO	GROSS
Q3 1992 BOQ	$480,000	$5,572,000	$6,052,000
TOTAL WW 9229 EXPENSES	$24,265	$283,439	$307,703
CUM Q3 1992 EXPENSES	$101,741	$410,175	$511,916
BOQ WW 9229 EXPENSES	$36,923	$428,615	$465,538
BOQ CUM Q3 1992 EXPENSES	$110,769	$857,385	$968,154
WW 9229 DELTA (OVER)	$12,658	$145,177	$157,835
CUM Q3 1992 DELTA (OVER)	$9,028	$447,209	456,237

which triggers a comparison among our phone systems in California, Texas, and Minnesota, which generates three good ideas about slashing phone bills and improving our approach to telecommunications. (Small, lean companies don't want or need a telecommunications department.)

Learning is also about more profound issues. From day one at Cypress, for example, I have been the company's chief environmental watchdog. I take personal and public responsibility for making our operations as environmentally progressive as we can. My direct participation in the PO-Commit system has helped deliver on that commitment.

There are solid business reasons for spending time on the environment. In any company, there are certain things you flat-out don't want to happen. If you are the CEO of Exxon, you don't want your oil on Alaskan birds. If you run a chemical company, you don't want one of your plants to explode and kill people. If you run a semiconductor company, you don't want your factories to spill or dump solvents that contaminate drinking water. Such accidents can cause major environmental damage—and generate lawsuits big enough to put you out of business.

The PO-Commit system gives me in-depth knowledge of what chemicals we use, how they're used, and what containment systems we've installed. Since I do take the time to personally monitor every purchase order for chemicals, and since no one can buy chemicals without a purchase order, I will never discover a barrel of some "mystery" carcinogen in one of our plants.

This monitoring translates into real clout. When we started Cypress, trichloroethylene (TCE) and its supposedly benign replacement, trichloroethane (TCA), were commonly used in chip manufacturing. Both were already on the government's list of known carcinogens. Still, companies were buying TCE and TCA by the thousands of gallons because they were great for cleaning wafers.

These companies then had to struggle with disposing of the chemicals without contaminating groundwater. Some lost that struggle. They chose to use underground gasoline tanks to store their spent solvent. The resulting leaks caused many of the big chip plants in Silicon Valley to become EPA Superfund sites—the targets of messy cleanups and even messier lawsuits.

We took a different approach. We simply announced that not one drop of TCE or TCA would ever enter Cypress. And since either I or our facilities manager (a pollution expert) exercised line-item control over POs for potentially hazardous materials, the policy had real teeth. Many times assembly managers pleaded that they had to have TCE or TCA; there was no other way to "degrease" the units properly. Their persistence about the "need" for carcinogenic solvents eventually earned an ultimatum from me: "Get the job done without TCE or TCA or I will find someone who can."

The result of the ultimatum? We figured out how to apply "plasma oxygen" technology, traditionally used to clean silicon wafers, to the process of cleaning assembled units as well. It was a creative, environmentally benign way to eliminate the need for carcinogens. Containing a seemingly innocuous (but potentially devastating) problem with solvents was just one output of "sticking my nose into the POs" for two hours a week.

The early 1980s already seem like the good old days, when serving as "environmental watchdog" simply meant vetoing the most hazardous chemicals. The challenges today are vastly more complex. Two years ago, for example, the EPA cited us for a violation because the recycled water in our plant contained excess copper. (The maximum acceptable level of copper is 30 parts per million. We were at 37 ppm—a drinkable level, but still over the limit.)

Why were we in violation? The copper lead frames we use to mount our chips must be washed prior to assembly. Minute traces of copper always remain behind in the water. As our business boomed in early 1991, we were in the middle of an aggressive program to conserve water, a critical environmental problem in drought-ridden Silicon Valley. Indeed, we managed to cut our water consumption by a factor of two—an achievement for which we received an award from the mayor of San Jose. Yet because we were cleaning *more* copper leads with *less* water, our recycled water contained a higher concentration of copper effluent. The only solution was to invest several hundred thousand dollars in two small water-purification plants. Today the water leaving our San Jose factory is purer than the water coming in.

Meanwhile, all kinds of "Why don't we?" questions have begun to arise. Why don't we use more recycled materials? Why don't we use manufacturing processes that require less energy? Why don't we try to reduce water consumption even more?

We have bolstered the "learning dimension" of the PO-Commit system to address these new challenges. Mark Beck, our expert on facilities management and environmental compliance, now attends all of our Thursday PO-Commit meetings. Using Mark's expertise, we can review every major purchase to maximize its potential environmental *contribution* and take quick action.

These reviews have led to all kinds of innovations. We replaced the nonbiodegradable Styrofoam "peanuts" used to package our products with peanuts made of water-soluble starch. We eliminated ozone-depleting Freon from all Cypress processes and from most types of equipment long before it became mandatory. We replaced every fluorescent light fixture in our San Jose operation with lights that use half the energy. We print all company reports with soybean ink. The list could go on for pages.

The point is not to boast about our record. It is to show the leadership impact of direct CEO involvement in a purchasing system that transforms platitudes ("We want to be good environmental citizens") into tough-minded decisions about how we spend our money. As more and more managers sit through the weekly PO-Commit meetings, and as they understand the business logic behind our environmental initiatives, they propose their own innovations and propagate the ethos down through their organizations.

There is another big reason for weekly reviews: They make for quicker and smarter reactions when times get tough. Meeting budgets is important as long as revenues roll in as planned. Many companies, including Cypress, go into "crisis mode" when business hits unexpected turbulence: The Gulf War slams the brakes on the economy, a big customer goes bankrupt, a new product doesn't generate as much revenue as expected. The PO-Commit meeting provides real-time visibility of exactly where we stand relative to budgets.

And because I'm familiar with the details behind these spending patterns, we can instantly set new priorities during hard times.

Walk into the office of your CEO or department head and pose the following question: As of today, are our company's (department's) quarterly expenses running over budget or under budget? By how much? Which division is most under budget and why? Which is most over budget and why? If we had to impose immediate spending reductions of 10 percent, what spending would we cut? What would we eliminate altogether?

My bet is that most managers could answer those questions about their own departments without calling in lots of staff people or ordering up a batch of accounting reports. We can answer them instantaneously *for the whole company*—and again on one sheet of paper.

Consider the answers as of June 13, 1992: the end of workweek 24 for the year, the end of workweek 11 for the second quarter. Cypress budgeted quarterly expenses of $23.9 million. Based on the one-thirteenth weekly allocation, we could have spent $20.2 million as of June 13. We actually spent $20.5 million, which means we were running over budget by $300,000. For that particular week, however, we were 6.6 percent under budget. We could have spent $1.8 million (to be precise, $1,839,724). We actually spent $1.7 million (to be precise, $1,739,300).

Not enough detail? Of the forty subsidiaries, product lines, or departments with budget responsibility, thirty-two were running under budget for the quarter, seven had exceeded their budgets, and one was exactly on budget. The biggest line-item overrun for the week ($30,897) was for unplanned subcontract assembly. The biggest under-budget line item for the week was direct materials for our Multichip subsidiary. If disaster struck, as it sometimes does, we would be ready to respond with smart, targeted, effective spending cuts based on up-to-the-minute knowledge of current budget conditions. With the right systems, it doesn't take that much effort to know the details.

LITTLE DETAILS — LIKE $300-PER-HOUR LAWYERS

The logic behind the PO-Commit system is so simple it may seem trivial. And in many respects it is. The system does not represent a major conceptual breakthrough. What it does represent is lots of hard work by lots of smart people on lots of little execution problems that none of us anticipated when we began. Developing PO Commit was easy. Making it work has been much trickier.

When Cypress was a startup, we didn't need a "system" to control expenses. I signed every purchase order, no matter how small. That's not unusual; any sane company founder signs every purchase order for the first few years. Since I was personally familiar with every person and every project in the company, it was easy for me to make quick and accurate judgments about whether or not a particular expense was justified. And since everyone knew that their POs would cross my desk, most of them were perfect.

That approach stopped working once we reached about $25 million in revenues. I couldn't cope competently with the two-inch stack of POs staring at me every night. Worse, I could no longer track the details of every purchase order or, more important, how one PO related to spending patterns on an entire project. I had total authority over spending but little real control. Budgets began slipping, POs started getting bottled up. I faced a lose-lose choice: Sign every purchase order blindly or spend every waking minute getting myself educated on suspect purchase orders.

Joe Hudgins, the first manufacturing manager of our San Jose plant, helped us break through the two-inch-stack problem. I had always admired Joe's ability to meet his budgets. It turns out he was using a system he had developed at Mostek, the Texas-based chip company founded by our original chairman, L. J. Sevin. The system was elegant in its simplicity. At the beginning of every quarter, Joe took his total budget and divided it into equal weekly installments. Then, every week, he collected all his people's POs, put them in priority order, approved them in priority order, and drew the line when he hit one-thirteenth of his quarterly budget. There were always enough discretionary or deferrable expenses to make ends meet.

We decided to apply the Hudgins logic to the entire company. The new approach let me stop worrying about the line-item details of every budget for every department. When departments ran consistently within budget, I gave up line-item scrutiny altogether and spent a few minutes looking at their capital expense and environmentally sensitive POs to learn about what they were doing by what they spent.

This was a major improvement. I was satisfied because I was able to guarantee expense control—which most chaotic young companies can't. Our managers were satisfied because they got their POs approved quickly and fairly. But over time, as we got bigger and our business grew more complex, new problems began to emerge. Big one-time expenses perturbed weekly budgets. We had no way to handle sales between departments at Cypress. And we kept running into "off-budget" expenses that disrupted even our best-laid plans.

We eliminated these problems one by one as we created our current system over a period of several years. We first turned our attention to big expenses. Let's say a manager's weekly budget is $30,000. Among the approved spending for the quarter might be a $40,000 order for silicon wafers. Obviously, no matter when the manager places that order, it will violate the weekly spending cap. That makes no sense.

So we created the purchase-order equivalent of a credit card. The manager can place the order without its full cost counting against that week's cap. Instead, the cost is amortized over an appropriate period of time (in this case, wafer-usage period) with equal installments charged against each week's limit. This small innovation was an important advance. A system to improve spending discipline must be able to accommodate big expenses without blowing up.

Look back to the PO-Commit log for workweek 29. Section 7 lists fixed expenses, one of which is $3,125 for "mask amortization." Masks are the intricate chrome-on-quartz patterns from which submicron circuits are photographically printed onto silicon wafers.

They are an expensive part of the semiconductor production process and come in big, one-time spending "clumps." Every week, then, the group "draws down" $3,125 from the overall price it paid for the masks and charges it against its PO-Commit limit.

Our next challenge was more daunting: how to control internal expenses (say, manufacturing costs) as tightly as we control external expenses (materials and services on which we spend "real money"). Our solution, which we will describe more fully in Chapter 8, was to treat both expenses in precisely the same way.

Three years ago we reorganized Cypress as a self-contained "market economy." Today our factories are not cost centers. They are profit centers in the true sense of the word. Our product lines negotiate manufacturing prices with our factories the same way independent companies negotiate with their manufacturers. If a product line can get a better price from our plant in Minnesota than from Texas, it is free to shift production to Minnesota. Our factories constantly try to steal "market share" from one another. They compete on price, service, delivery schedules—whatever it takes to convince our product-line vice presidents to let them build their chips. Moreover, if a product line can get a better price from a plant in Japan than from any Cypress plant, it can negotiate an outside contract.

This market-based approach has allowed us to budget for and control internal expenses as real money. When one of our factories bills one of our product lines, cash actually changes hands (even though it stays within the Cypress corporate umbrella). Why bother? Because unless internal expenses are treated like "real" expenses, they become what we call "free money." And anything that's free gets used inefficiently—it's a law of nature. Therefore, nothing at Cypress is free.

Look again at the BOQ budget. You'll see that it distinguishes between direct and intercompany expenses. You'll also see that it treats both categories of expenses identically. Each of the "dollar" figures in the intercompany section represents arm's-length negotiated prices between the product lines and other Cypress operations.

Section 3 shows that intercompany assembly charges for this group are going down substantially this quarter (from $730,000 to

$553,000) even though factory output is going up substantially. Why? Because the product line can get a better price from outside contractors and has decided to use them. (Notice the increase in subcontracting charges in section 4.) Likewise, despite big volume increases, charges for Fab 2 are increasing only slightly (0.8 percent) while Fab 1 charges are increasing by 256 percent. Why? Because this group has received a better manufacturing price from Fab 1 and has decided to shift more production there.

The last big challenge in creating a robust cost-control system was "off-budget" expenses: auditors, temporary agencies, headhunters, consultants—the "soft stuff" that always seems to slip through the quarterly planning process and becomes a quarter-end surprise. The classic off-budget expense—and by far the toughest to control—were legal bills. A middle manager can make one innocent call to a lawyer ("We think we've got a neat piece of technology, what are the chances we can get a patent?") and generate a $50,000 bill. Surprises like that can ruin a quarterly budget.

Today no manager at Cypress, including me, can obtain paid legal advice without first submitting a purchase order through the PO-Commit system. In other words, buying a lawyer's time is no different from buying silicon wafers or light bulbs. Our law firms, in turn, have agreed not to accept any business from Cypress until they receive an official PO from the company.

Sounds simple, I'm sure. But it was awfully hard to put into practice. Cypress doesn't have an in-house general counsel or a legal department. When our subsidiary presidents or product-line managers need legal help, they go out and get it. It took a long time for our people, and for our lawyers, to understand that we were serious about treating legal expenses the same way we treat other expenses. We came to agreement in 1986 when, after a series of unexpected legal bills, I sent a letter to all of our outside law firms. I told them that Cypress would honor no legal bills that could not be matched against a purchase order submitted before the legal expenses were incurred—in other words, before the work had gone through the PO-Commit system.

Did the Rodeo Drive lawyers look for greener pastures? No way.

Great law firms realize that their prosperity in an age of spiraling legal costs depends on meeting the needs of cost-conscious clients. Larry Sonsini (of Wilson, Sonsini, Goodrich & Rosati) and Randy Bain (of Brown & Bain) are two of the sharpest and best-known legal minds in high technology. They have been willing to negotiate every dime of their legal work for Cypress. ("Do you want us to spend $20,000 to review Japanese prior art on your patent suit?") And they win.

Too many companies treat lawyers the way people treat doctors—with a mixture of awe, ignorance, and resentment. They turn to them when they have a problem, ask them to solve it, never ask what they plan to do, never discuss price—and then faint when they get the bill. (Who ever asks a doctor whether he or she can get "most everything" checked for less than $100?)

This is absurd for both sides. Good lawyers have more work than they can accept. Good lawyers want to do work that matters, not merely ring up billable hours. Good lawyers don't want to squabble with their clients over bills.

This simple reform has had a powerful effect on our entire approach to lawyers. We no longer just throw money at legal problems. We also throw in our brains and common sense. Say a manager has to defend his operation against an intellectual-property lawsuit from a competitor. He calls a lawyer and gets an estimate for $40,000 for the first response to the complaint. He walks into his vice president's office with a purchase order for $40,000. "Are you crazy?" the VP objects. "We can't afford that. Go find out how well we can be defended for $10,000." (Remember, that vice president eventually has to walk into the weekly PO-Commit meeting and present the purchase order to me.)

So the manager calls the lawyer with a different question: "If you had $10,000, forty lawyer-hours at $250 per hour, what could you do for us?" That's a big change in the client-lawyer dynamic.

Not so long ago a new design engineer came into my office with a puzzled look on his face. "What's wrong?" I asked. His reply: "I applied for a patent on a new piece of technology. It went through the Cypress patent committee and got approved. So I figured I was free to pursue it. I called up our attorney quite excited and said, 'We're ready to go on this patent.'

" 'Fine,' he said, 'What's your PO number?'

" 'What are you talking about?' I asked.

" 'I need a purchase order or I won't do any work.' "

At that moment I knew we had the problem licked.

The end result of all these modifications is the PO-Commit system in place today. That system imposes minimal bureaucracy: one three-hour review meeting per quarter, one two-hour meeting per week. It delivers four important benefits: companywide weekly budget control; weekly quarter-to-date spending feedback; fast, high-quality spending decisions; full budgetary delegation.

Plenty of things keep me awake at night. What are my Silicon Valley competitors up to? Are we holding our own against the Japanese? Are we doing a good enough job serving our customers? One thing that does not keep me awake is whether or not this company is living within its means. The PO-Commit system sees to that.

ACTION REQUEST   AR # ___7029___

FOR (ACTION):   Nick T.   START: March 17, 1992

CC (INFORMATION):   DUE: March 23, 1992
FROM: T.J. RODGERS   3:23 PM
TITLE: FOLLOWING THE RULES—THIS MEANS YOU

CONTENTS: I was very disappointed today to find out that—once again—you deliberately violated a Cypress specification. A few weeks ago, direct orders were given to get rid of all non-essential temporary employees. In addition to that directive, it is a Cypress policy not to hire temporary layout designers. This has caused great morale problems in the past at Cypress and we made a policy decision to avoid temporary layout designers in the future. Later I found out that both directives were being violated by hiring a temporary layout designer in your facility. I further found out that you were quite aware the hiring of that temporary layout designer violated company principles.

Monday morning I signed the new product plan for your next project. Later, in a QIP meeting, I found out that the product is due to tape out in three weeks. Obviously, you cannot do the layout work required on that product in three weeks. Therefore, you must have been violating another Cypress specification

continued

which requires that no layout work be done prior to the signing of an NPP. Again, you indicated that you were aware of the policy, but decided to violate it (apparently with the agreement of your boss). For your information, violating the "no layout before the NPP" rule has been a firing offense at Cypress.

We made that policy in 1983 after interviewing people from your alma mater, Mostek. I had one designer walk into an interview with me (I was about to give him an offer letter) and show me a chip photograph of his project. He had written in the scribe line in 10-micron aluminum letters, "This ram has been made without the knowledge of management." The bootleg project syndrome at Mostek was one of the sicknesses that eventually did the company in. Dealing with the engineers at Mostek (who I thought were a bunch of arrogant prima donnas) is one of the reasons I put the policies in place which have caused Cypress to have a 100 percent record for bringing to the market products which have been started in the wafer fabrication area. It is also that designer's arrogant behavior which caused me to call together Cypress design people and explain to them— in no uncertain terms—that violating this principle would result in immediate dismissal. After having reaffirmed that principle dozens of times over three or four years, the culture got established at Cypress and I stopped beating people over the head with the policy.

Apparently the company has started to backslide on following this policy. I am particularly disappointed that you violated the policy, not from ignorance, but from direct intent. I do not remember if you attended a quality kick-off meeting last year but one of the fundamental quality principles at Cypress is that we follow our specifications or change them. The specifications are not something that can be violated based on the opinions of individuals as to what is good or not good for the corporation. They are policies and specifications because the company wants them done exactly as stated. It is my expectation that you will be a leader in quality in following specifications in the corporation in the future. Will you have any problem in following our rules in the future?

TO COMPLETE AR: Answer my question.

The language in this memo is harsh. But given the time, money, and energy we invest in our management systems, we expect our managers to abide by them. When managers knowingly violate our practices, we call them on it—in no uncertain terms.

ACTION REQUEST   AR # ___5761___

** CONFIDENTIAL **

FOR (ACTION):   JFT   START: October 9, 1991

CC (INFORMATION):   DUE: October 15, 1991
FROM: T.J. RODGERS
TITLE: FYI: DESTRUCTIVE PUBLIC WHINING

CONTENTS: There is a difference between being a noisy customer who demands perfection (which is okay) and a person who is continually complaining about the company, its environment, and systems without offering any suggestion for a viable improvement (which is not okay). To give you three recent examples:

- Complaining about the wafer starts system which is specified and operational, but not to your liking, without much forethought (or frankly even much knowledge of how it works) and with no solution offered to improve it—just public whining.

- Musing out loud "how screwed up" it was to put units into American assembly when the obvious conclusion would be a layoff in our assembly area. The comments were made in public, which is inappropriate, and when I asked what your better idea was, you had no response at all.

- Complaining loudly in my recent staff meeting about Stu's quite reasonable proposal for how we were going to do the next quarter's plan without really having taken any time to study his proposal, and without an inkling of an idea (when you were asked directly) how you would improve what you were complaining about.

The arrogance of a small company which is easy to manage is again surfacing at your operation. When you come to Cypress everything is "screwed up" and "shouldn't be that way." The fact is you run a minuscule test area and do a reasonable job at that. It is not at all clear that if you had the kind of test burden on you that Cypress has, you would perform even close to us. It is certainly clear that you do not even understand the systems for operating our wafer fabrication plants let alone how to improve them or how to manage them if you had them. In short, you do not have the accomplishment behind you to take the arrogant position that everything around Cypress is "screwed up," with the implicit assumption that your ship is very much better run.

You can complain anytime you want about lack of performance or a failure to commit. But these public musings about our systems being "screwed up" have got to stop. They are unprofessional, unwarranted, and undermine confidence

continued

in the management of my company—which I will not tolerate. You also come off pretty foolish complaining about a wafer start system which is fully documented and being run according to spec. If the system is so screwed up, why weren't you educated about it and why haven't you done something about improving it in all the time you have had to work on it?

I don't want you to sit there like Joe and watch your P&L get wiped out without complaining. But when you complain, I want you to come out with constructive criticism.

TO COMPLETE AR: FYI only.

We have a tough culture at Cypress. We are candid with each other—sometimes brutally so—because we are so determined to get the job done. However, we also have to remind ourselves about the importance of being constructive.

Growth

CHAPTER 8

Perpetual entrepreneurship: size without sclerosis

We want to be a big company. In fact, we want to be a billion-dollar company by the year 2000. There's just one catch. We don't know how to run a billion-dollar company. I'm not sure it's even *possible* to run a billion-dollar company with the speed, discipline, and energy that Cypress has shown in its first ten years. There comes a point in the growth of any organization where adding more people, more buildings, and more equipment *reduces* overall productivity. With annual revenues of more than $250 million, we are dangerously close to that point.

But we want it all. We want the muscle and staying power of a big company with the drive and agility of a startup. Over the last five years, we have pursued a model of growth that we expect to deliver the best of both worlds. The theory is simple. Rather than build one billion-dollar company, why not build a *collection* of companies—each small enough to maintain its intensity, together big enough to matter? Our system of perpetual entrepreneurship, embodied in our federation of autonomous subsidiaries, translates theory into reality.

We created this approach out of fear. Fear that we would become one of the slow-moving, self-satisfied organizations that have lost ground to the Japanese. The idea was hatched in the winter of 1986. We were in the early stages of building Fab II, our manufacturing plant in Round Rock, Texas. We had hired Clive Barton, a top manager from Advanced Micro Devices, to run the operation. Clive was smart and talented. But like so many big-company managers, he instinctively applied the spend-to-salve logic of big companies to his new assignment.

Remember the stepper story from Chapter 6 on head count and capital? (That's where we got the whole company running on just two step-and-repeat "cameras" because they cost $1 million each.) Well, it was déjà vu all over again. And Clive, because he knew so much, made incredibly detailed arguments about why Fab II needed four steppers, how this was standard industry practice, and that, if we weren't willing to make this commitment, we would never be a big-time manufacturer.

I was dejected. I couldn't face another grueling round of negotiations over resources. So I asked myself: How do we enlist Clive and his people as allies rather than adversaries? How do we persuade them to direct their considerable energies and intelligence toward meeting our targets rather than telling us why they can't be met? In short, how do we get them to think like entrepreneurs?

That last question answered itself: *You can't expect people to think like entrepreneurs unless you make them entrepreneurs.*

I presented Clive with a deal that I was willing to take to my board of directors. We offered to create shares in an independent subsidiary called Cypress Semiconductor Texas, Inc. (CTI). The stock would be worth $1 per share if the company met the ambitious long-term performance goals we had established. Then we offered Clive options on 2 million shares of CTI stock and millions more stock options to CTI's current and future employees. The exercise price on this employees' common stock was 3 cents per share.

Suddenly the plant's capital-equipment requirements took on a different look. Each stepper was no longer worth $1.2 million. (The price tag had increased since 1983.) Rather, at CTI's initial share price of 20 cents (for preferred stock for investors), each stepper was worth 6 million *shares*—three times as much as Clive received.

The resource exercise took on a new dynamic. "How many steppers do you need?" we asked Clive. "We're ready to write a big check and buy a lot of your stock. After all, just one extra stepper is three times more valuable than the two-million-share contribution you will make by busting your ass for four the next four years. So you must really need those steppers."

"We'll have to think about that," came the reply. We got an answer a week or so later. Now CTI needed only two steppers, the same answer we arrived at three years earlier.

From that day forward, the men and women of Cypress Texas began thinking like entrepreneurs. In fact, they became productivity zealots. Their new mindset became clear a few months later, when Cypress San Jose was recruiting Mark Allen, vice president for worldwide manufacturing, from National Semiconductor's operation outside Dallas.

"I'd like to work with Cypress," Mark said, "but I'm worried about your finances."

"What are you talking about?" we asked, genuinely mystified. "We have sales of $150 million. We have more than $100 million of cash in the bank. We are solidly profitable, growing like gangbusters. You work at National, which is in real trouble, and you're worried about *our* finances?"

Then Mark explained why he was worried. He had recently met with a chemical vendor on some National business. That vendor, who was also trying to sell Fab II some chemicals, complained about "that flaky new outfit outside Austin, Cypress."

"What's the problem?" Mark asked.

"Well, the guy who runs it told me he would be willing to consider doing business if we gave him, *for free*, enough chemicals to get his plant ramped up to volume production. If our product worked well and he liked our service, he would qualify it and give us plenty of future business. What kind of deal is that?"

Mark had understandably interpreted those bargaining tactics (to which the vendor eventually agreed) as a sign of weakness. In fact, it was a sign that Clive and his people had figured out, yet again, how to cut a tough and creative business deal (in this case, how to get several months' worth of free chemicals) with absolutely no prodding from headquarters. Clive and his people used the same approach to "evaluate" big-ticket items such as steppers and etchers. They would evaluate them for months and months before eventually agreeing to buy them—making free use of the equipment during the evaluation period.

The end result? Fab II went up in quick time (eight months) and with remarkably modest capital investment ($40 million) by industry standards. Indeed, CTI's performance was a major factor in Cypress's ability to grow so quickly and profitably in the mid-1980s— which was disaster time for the U.S. semiconductor industry. The plant now generates annual revenues of more than $200 million and accounts for two-thirds of our manufacturing output.

Cypress Texas also delivered for its people. In 1990 Altera Corporation, one of the plant's non-Cypress customers, paid $7.4 million for 7.4 million shares held by Clive and CTI's 200 managers and workers. They *had* met their original business plan. Their stock *was* worth $1 per share. The company was worth $90 million in a true, arm's-length transaction. And they reaped the rewards. Clive decided to retire. Lots of other people don't worry quite so much about sending their kids to college.

Cypress too has benefited financially. Since the original investment deal, Altera has increased its ownership stake to 17 percent by acquiring 7.6 million more CTI shares from Cypress San Jose. Thus, we and CTI's employees have collected $15 million and still own more than 80 percent of our Texas company.

The story of Cypress Texas underscores an important point. Our subsidiaries are not "pseudo" startups with "phantom" stock. They are real, live, independent companies. They have their own business plans, with performance milestones, funding schedules, and market valuations. They have their own shares. Their people hold options on a big chunk of those shares. They have their own lawyers, who negotiate with our lawyers. They have their own boards of directors. Cypress holds seats on these boards (just like any other venture capitalist), but the boards also include genuine outside directors.

At the same time, the startups operate under the Cypress umbrella. Their presidents integrate their strategies into our strategies. Their financial results are included in our financial results. They sell their products through our sales force. They build their products in our factories (although, as we've explained, they can go outside if they get a better deal). And they plug into all of our management systems.

This combination of autonomy and cohesion is what gives our federation model such power. The challenge, of course, is making it work.

BREAKAWAY PERFORMANCE AND THE 10,000-WATT SPOTLIGHT

The subsidiary strategy is a good bet to be our central engine of growth through the 1990s. Why? Because startups are uniquely structured to generate "breakaway performance" of the sort demonstrated by Cypress Texas. I don't know exactly why startups turn talented men and women, with a healthy dose of ambition, into absolute fanatics about success. But I do know that the energy levels of a startup, the sense of mission, the unwavering determination not to fail, are unlike anything you will find in any other environment. People truly can do the impossible if they commit themselves to doing it. Startups create that commitment.

ACTION REQUEST	AR # __2198__
FOR (ACTION): BOB	START: November 11, 1988
CC (INFORMATION):	DUE: November 15, 1988
FROM: T.J. RODGERS	
TITLE: THE $10 MILLION HOUSE	

CONTENTS: Right after Apple went public, Steve Wozniak sold a lot of his stock and bought a house for $500K. He later calculated that his house had

continued

really been a $10M house because he sold his stock early and cheap. Your stock option is at $6.25, Cypress's stock is currently at $8.25. If you were to sell 70K shares to raise $140K in cash, it surely would be one of the worst economic decisions you ever made in your life. Thinking about selling now ascribes a National Semiconductor mentality to our stock. I firmly believe that within the next five quarters, our stock will see the bright side of $20 a share. That same 70K shares would then be worth $1.4M—think about it.

If you want to get into a house, given your newly high income and another raise coming up, and given some creative work on loans which you could support because of your new income, you should be able to do it without throwing away a big chunk of your net worth at bargain basement prices.

TO COMPLETE AR: If you are interested in exploring concepts like the one outlined above, see me and I will sit down with you and Stan.

The right way to think about entrepreneurial rewards. Fortunately, "Bob" did not sell any of his Cypress shares until 1991—when the price hit $24.

We work hard at Cypress. By most big-company standards, we work extremely hard. When I arrive at seven forty-five A.M. the parking lot is already filling up. If I look out my office window at six-thirty P.M. (I usually don't leave until eight or nine P.M.), the parking lot is still half full. Cypress people want to achieve, they push themselves, they enjoy what they do.

But we don't work today with anything like the take-no-prisoners intensity of our startup days in the mid-1980s. We just can't conjure up that same desperate effort. Back then it was normal for me to arrive at work and find engineers asleep on their desks. We never encouraged these all-nighters; we wanted our people to get a decent night's sleep. But the more we tried to send our engineers home, the more they insisted on staying.

In fact, I got a bum rap in our rumor mill when I tried to do something about it. One morning I arrived to find one of our best engineers, Ken Molitor, using a set of engineering textbooks for a pillow. I couldn't imagine anything more uncomfortable. We bought some cots and pillows and told the troops, "If this is really how you want to work, fine. Here's something to make your life less miserable."

(Or, to be more precise, a "little less" miserable. We put the cots in an unused part of our San Jose plant that we called "Siberia" because it was always unheated. We gave our people wool blankets and expected them to weather the elements. The cots did beat sleeping on desks, but they were no one's idea of highbrow accommodations.)

Word quickly got around to other parts of the company. "That T.J. is a bigger SOB than we thought," people said to each other. "Now he's telling engineers they have to sleep here!" Well, that was nonsense. But that was the work ethic you'd find among many of our engineers just after the startup. These people lived and breathed Cypress Semiconductor.

(A few years later, when it began to feel like Cypress was losing its resolve to do whatever it took to win, I used the by-now-forgotten cots to symbolic effect. People were whining about how hard and late we were all working to make our quarterly plan. I took the cots out of storage, put them where everyone could see them—outside the rest rooms in our main factory building—and let them speak for themselves. A local newspaper found out about the cots and had a field day with the story.)

Money was not the real motivator in the early days. Sure, the engineers sleeping on their desks had options on Cypress shares. But even if we did well enough to go public, which of course we did, they were not going to become millionaires. Maybe each of them would sell stock worth $50,000, or $100,000, or $150,000. A nice nest egg, but hardly enough riches to inspire the kind of superhuman effort so many of them demonstrated.

My cofounders and I certainly didn't start Cypress for the money. We had a much stronger motivation: We wanted to show the world (and ourselves) what we could do. Once we got the chance, we weren't about to screw it up. Especially since we never thought we would get the chance.

Cypress raised its first round of venture capital in 1983. Prior to that time, I had given up the idea of starting a company. Three years earlier, before joining Advanced Micro Devices, I had tried and failed to launch a startup. The business plan for "International CMOS

Technology" was built around the same technical revolution and product strategy that would eventually launch Cypress. But I just couldn't interest investors.

And the late 1970s were healthy times for our industry. U.S. chip companies were not yet feeling the bloody impact of Japanese competition. By 1983, with much of the industry in retreat, I had grown truly depressed. "If I couldn't fund a company back then," I told myself, "it will never happen now that the industry is under attack from Japan."

Then one day I got a call from a New York venture capitalist named Stanford Fingerhood. He was doing reference checks in connection with a potential investment in a chip startup. The people he wanted to talk about were good engineers who used to work for me, but they certainly couldn't run a company. I didn't want to trash them, so I delicately asked Stanford to describe their business plan. They wanted to build CMOS Read-Only Memories (ROMs) and Small-Scale Integration (SSI) logic products.

These products were easy to design and build. "Yeah, they can probably pull it off," I said tepidly. Then I asked, "But if you're willing to invest money in semiconductors, why don't you invest with me? I could do a hell of a lot more with it than those guys."

Stanford couldn't generate the funding I needed, but he did set me up for lunch with Ben Rosen. Ben, the chairman of Compaq Computer, is one of the greatest venture capitalists around. His firm, Sevin Rosen Management, was the financial force behind Compaq, Lotus, Convex, and many other high-technology success stories. I knew Ben from the 1970s, when he was a silicon analyst at Morgan Stanley and I was running the VMOS technology group at Advanced Microsystems. We got along well back then, so I felt pretty good about the meeting.

I flew to New York and described my plans. "I'm not sure I like the concept," Ben said, "but I believe in you. I think you could run a company. You need to meet my partner, L.J. Sevin, right away."

L.J., who founded Mostek, the big Texas chip company, was the only member of the silicon establishment I had never met. I knew the Big Three at Intel—Bob Noyce, Gordon Moore, and Andy

Grove—because I had interviewed with them. I worked for Jerry Sanders at AMD. But I knew next to nothing about L.J.

I told Ben I couldn't go. I had to get back to work.

He wasn't taking no for an answer. "Gee," he said, "you look kinda sick all of a sudden."

Message received. I called AMD and charged off a sick day. I hopped on a plane to Dallas. On the flight, I took out a calculator and generated a seven-page business plan. I estimated the market for one industry-standard Random Access Memory (RAM) chip, newly introduced in CMOS technology, did a cost of manufacture, some overhead estimates, and a profit projection. Then I scaled up the economics of that one product to show what a company with a portfolio of comparable niche products might look like. By the end of the flight, the business plan looked pretty good.

L.J. met me at the airport in his Texas-size Cadillac. I handed him the handwritten plan. He read it, then issued what, to my eager ears, sounded like a ringing endorsement: "Hey, this isn't as screwed up as I expected it to be!" I went back to AMD and waited.

Three months (and endless questions) later I got a phone call from L.J. I was in the middle of my staff meeting at AMD. He wanted me to meet him at the Santa Clara Marriott, a favorite hotel for money types who come to Silicon Valley. "We've decided to support you," he reported. "You can use my name."

That was on a Thursday. I was ecstatic. "Great! I'll quit right now."

"No," L.J. cautioned. "You've gotta see the lawyers. I want you to know how to quit, to find out what you can and can't do."

L.J. and I spent three hours on Saturday morning with Larry Sonsini, one of the savviest business lawyers in Silicon Valley. Larry read me the riot act about the right way to leave a company without triggering a lawsuit over trade secrets or some other intellectual-property dispute. He told me not to take any documents, no matter how innocuous. He told me the right and wrong things to say. It was a tutorial I have since given many times.

L.J. quietly said he expected me to follow the letter of the law Larry had just handed down. If I screwed up, there would be no money, no L.J., no company. He also said I should tender my resignation personally to Jerry Sanders, the CEO of AMD.

I went back to the office on Monday. It turned out that Jerry was holding a "strategic planning session" with his vice presidents. In Bermuda. That was after a board meeting with his directors. In Munich. AMD's crack discipline and Spartan culture had obviously started to slip. I wasn't about to wait two weeks for Jerry to return.

"That's it," I announced. "I quit."

Jerry got word and ordered me to fly immediately to Bermuda. It was the first time I had ever flown first class at penny-pinching AMD. I worked all day Monday, flew to New York on the red eye, slept on a bench for two hours at Kennedy Airport, and landed the next morning in Bermuda to see Jerry.

I was still wearing the same suit I had gone to work in on Monday. The weather was hot and tropical, and the suit was sticking to my back. Jerry was in white Bermuda shorts, knee socks, and a bwana shirt. He and two of his top lieutenants spent the next three and a half hours beating the crap out of me.

To end the pain, I said I'd think about staying. I was a lousy liar. I got back to California the next day, my worn gray pinstripes barely intact. AMD had already changed the locks on my office door. The lawyers were already reading through my files, getting ready for war. My secretary was asking if we would grant founders' shares to the new company's earliest employees. (We did, and the capital gains helped her and her family buy their first house.)

So I quit for good. It was November 1982. I spent the next four months fine-tuning the Cypress business plan. In March three AMD colleagues joined me (along with cofounders from Intel and National), and we filed our incorporation papers.

Cypress Semiconductor actually existed. When AMD threatened to sue me, my cofounders, and Cypress as a corporation, it hit us. *We were on our own.* It was as if we had cast a 10,000-watt spotlight on ourselves and our company. And the whole world (or at least the part of the world we cared about) was watching.

That "spotlight effect" runs through the ranks of most startups. Typically, the president is a refugee from a big company who thinks he or she can do a better job—and wants to prove it. The president recruits managers with that same mindset. These managers almost always move up a big notch in authority when they sign on—authority they were denied at their old company. In other words, a whole bunch of people finally get the responsibility they thought they deserved all along. They develop an I've got-to-make-it-happen mindset that becomes infectious.

I've seen that mindset flourish in our Ross Technology subsidiary. Roger Ross and his team put Cypress in the microprocessor business, one of the most exhilarating parts of the semiconductor world. We funded Ross in 1989. It took the company only $7 million, thirty engineers, and eighteen months to design its first microprocessor, called SPARC. This small band of entrepreneurs (most of them refugees from Motorola) went head to head with many powerful competitors, including Fujitsu, one of the world's biggest electronics companies. And they won. When Toshiba, another Japanese giant, selected a microprocessor for its first-generation SPARC laptop computer, it chose Ross's chip over Fujitsu's chip. A few years later Fujitsu itself chose Ross's microprocessor as the "brains" for a line of fault-tolerant computers for the Japanese banking industry.

There are all kinds of "technical" factors behind Ross's achievement. In an age of superfast workstations and computer-aided design tools, disciplined teams of talented specialists can compete and win against big-company bureaucracies. It is easier to coordinate thirty or forty highly motivated engineers—all working in the same room, all working off the same database, all following the same design rules—than to coordinate hundreds of engineers scattered around the country. When it comes to high-tech design, small really is beautiful.

But there is a deeper reason behind Ross's success. I'm convinced Ross did what it did because no one else thought it was possible. When a group declares, "We are going to design with thirty people a chip that would require two hundred people at Motorola or Intel," a powerful sense of camaraderie takes hold. People *will* themselves to succeed. In fact, you have to watch them closely. Startups can become unrealistic about their capabilities and turn down resources

ACTION REQUEST   AR # ___4736___

FOR (ACTION):   SUBSIDIARY
                  PRESIDENTS   START: September 20, 1990

CC (INFORMATION):   DUE: September 25, 1990

FROM: T.J. RODGERS

TITLE: THE PRESIDENT: KEEPER OF THE PROFIT & LOSS

CONTENTS: Attached you will find two documents that I wrote concerning the hiring freeze in the beginning of the quarter. The first, a memo, was a very clear-cut statement that we had to shut down and the reasons for it. It was sent to the vice presidents and all of their managers so that the communication was direct. The managers got it so that the vice presidents had the best possible argument against the inevitable backlash. When I wrote that memo, I tried to indicate that I thought there would be a backlash and that we could not live with any exceptions to the rule. I did that to avoid the inevitable period of wheedlers that would follow.

The second, an AR, is a reiteration of the first memo (Cypress people never hear what you say the first time; they always must test to make sure that what you said is true). In this AR, I indicated in fairly harsh terms that it would not be okay to continue arguing and debating about the hiring freeze. The fact that I was the first to perceive the need for the shutdown, that I knew the communication had to be written and firm, and that I knew a second communication would be needed separates me from the vice presidents who align themselves clearly on the other side of the line, arguing against me for resources regardless of what the company could afford.

Each of you is having a disappointing financial quarter this quarter. Ross has slipped back into the red for the first time in several quarters. Multichip has had yet another customer disaster and has been flat now for three consecutive quarters. Aspen continues to lose money, quarters after it was supposed to have turned profitable. On a relative basis, the financial quarters you are having are more disappointing than the financial quarter Cypress is having—the financial quarter which caused me to shut down hiring for the company. In other words, as presidents of your respective companies, your hiring freeze memo should have come earlier and been even more harshly worded than mine. But, there were no memos from you. You chose to align yourself with the vice presidents, trying to break the embargo. The line of management was clearly drawn between me and you and the vice presidents as a group. In some cases, you even used the unfair advantage you have relative to the vice presidents to apply extra pressure on me: board meetings turned into hiring pitch sessions. Instead of holding the line with your managers and supporting those managers to hold the line with those below them, your managers were allowed to turn into pitch men for extra resources.

In retrospect, all our companies are damned lucky not to have fifty or sixty or seventy extra people that we cannot afford. Even if we would not be facing a layoff, certainly those people hired in an ordinary manner would not have been the carefully scrutinized, critically needed people we have been adding in the recent quarter.

In your jobs as presidents of your companies, you are responsible primarily for the profit and loss statement. I am obviously interested in other things like technologies, new products, and yields, but you are ultimately responsible for the financials. The next time we have to draw lines around Cypress, Mr. Presidents, you should be on my side of the line.

TO COMPLETE AR: FYI only.

Sometimes our subsidiary presidents slip out of their entrepreneurial mindset into a resource-wheedling mode. This memo reminded them which side they're on.

they desperately need. There is a fine line between bravado and recklessness.

But bravado matters—perhaps more than any other factor. That is why big companies, even Cypress now, can't ever truly replicate what goes on in startups, even with "intrapreneurship" programs and skunkworks. Sure it's possible to design bonuses, phantom stock, and other incentives that mimic the financial rewards startups create. But money alone doesn't inspire their relentless drive to succeed. *It is impossible to create the energy of a startup unless you create actual startups.* So that's what we do.

A VENTURE CAPITALIST FOR YOUR OWN PEOPLE

One big benefit of being so committed to the startup model is that we get good at it. We learn how to evaluate new business opportunities and add important new categories of products to our portfolio—products we couldn't design on our own. Sometimes, as with Cypress Texas, we initiate a startup. Other times, as with Ross Technology, outside entrepreneurs look to us as a strategic partner and a source of funding. In either case, we make the same decisions that all venture capitalists make: how much equity to provide, how many shares to issue, how to value those shares, what performance timetables to demand.

We have developed a standard methodology for creating, funding, and valuing new businesses. Each of our subsidiaries has gone through this process. Each has produced a business plan based on the methodology. And each works to achieve the same "moment of truth" as Cypress Texas: building a company whose true value on the open market translates into a share price of one dollar. (We issue the right number of shares to create that one-dollar target.) At that point, Cypress agrees to turn some or all of those shares into cash to reward all the company's employees.

We use a few basic guidelines to evaluate opportunities. We are interested only in businesses that can generate, at a minimum, annual revenues of $20 million and pretax profits of 20 percent within three years. We prefer to own between 80 percent and 90 percent of the companies in which we invest. We expect a minimum return of 5:1 on our investment. That is, if we invest $10 million, we expect our stake in the company to be worth at least $50 million when it "goes public" or otherwise cashes out.

A 5:1 return may sound generous. But it is substantially less than the 10:1 return venture capitalists demand. Venture capitalists understand that most of the companies they fund will crater. Many others will be mediocre. They stay ahead of the game by cashing in on the handful of companies that meet or exceed their 10:1 target. These huge capital gains average out with their losses to create a reasonable rate of return.

We don't need those kinds of returns because we don't throw money at companies and then walk away if things get tough. We fund startups based on Cypress's long-term strategy and market position, not just financial returns. We stick by the companies we sponsor. Which makes it all the more important that we succeed.

Some of our subsidiaries would not be alive today without that grind-it-out commitment. Aspen Semiconductor, which we founded in 1987, is already on its third president. In 1990, when Tom North agreed to take the reins, the company was way behind plan and on the verge of failure. Most investors (and a few Cypress directors) would have pulled the plug. Instead, we revised the business plan and approved a new infusion of equity. Today Aspen is running on plan. It is an important source of revenue and profits for Cypress.

We also have some basic guidelines on personal wealth. Our first step in starting a new business—nothing happens unless there is agreement here—is to determine what rewards the founding team expects if the venture succeeds. It's true that money is not the prime motivator in startups. But no one launches a startup without some expectations about the ultimate payoff. And people can have wildly unrealistic expectations.

Most startups have a lead founder and four or five cofounders. We believe a lead founder should expect a capital gain of about $1 million to $2 million when the company "goes public" or lets its people cash out. The cofounders should expect to make about $500,000 each. There's nothing particularly scientific about these numbers; they represent the basic pattern of rewards for success in Silicon Valley.

We often must adjust the expectations of our entrepreneurs. Given our own history, however, we're on pretty solid ground. Let's say a founder expects to be worth $5 million the day after an initial public offering (IPO). "No deal," I reply. "I got $4 million for starting Cypress. The vice presidents each got $1 million. Your little company won't be worth nearly what Cypress was worth. Let's get real."

Cypress was, in fact, a kind of Cinderella story. We received founders stock in 1983 at a price of 3.33 cents per share. Our initial investors paid nearly 67 cents for their preferred stock. We went public in 1986 at $9.00 per share. So our initial investors saw a nearly 14:1 return on their money. At that point, the company was worth $270 million.

Cypress's top team didn't end up with much of a claim on all that IPO wealth. We had to raise about $40 million in equity to build the company to the point where it could go public. We acquired those funds in four venture-capital rounds. We raised $7.5 million in the first round and immediately gave away 70 percent of our shares. (The day after we raised that $7.5 million, I owned only 5 percent of Cypress's total shares.) We managed to reserve 25 percent for current and future Cypress employees. We also managed to limit our dilution in the next three rounds. Indeed, when we went public, Cypress employees as a group still held 25 percent of the company. My share, as CEO, was diluted to 2 percent of the IPO.

Two percent probably doesn't sound like much. But we cut the best deal we could. I was an unproven engineer with an unproven technology who needed $40 million. What would you have demanded in return for funding a "company" with no technology, no products, no sales force, no factory, seven employees, AMD lawyers breathing down its neck, and my dining room for its world headquarters? Our sponsors understandably insisted on a big share of the returns in exchange for their cash. So do we when we operate as a venture capitalist.

An organization is more than its founders. We want everyone in our startups, from the chief design engineer to a junior clerk, to hold potentially valuable stock options. All of our companies set aside a fixed pool of options for current and future employees. The size of that pool reflects the number of people they plan to hire and a preset schedule of expected capital gains based on starting salaries.

We believe that individual contributors should expect to make, on average, a capital gain of $50,000 to $100,000 when their company goes public. This average incorporates lots of variation. A circuit designer will receive more options (and thus make larger capital gains) than a shipping clerk. Senior managers will receive options that will generate capital gains of a multiple of their salary, junior people a fraction of their salary. People who join early will receive double the options of people who join late. Still, $50,000 to $100,000 is a good rule of thumb for setting company-average expectations.

Of course, these evaluation guidelines are the preliminaries. The main event is funding and executing a business plan to build a company that *delivers* those capital gains to its people, meets Cypress's investment-return criteria, and emerges as a technology force in world semiconductor markets. Our approach to funding startups differs sharply from traditional venture capital.

Most entrepreneurs fund their companies the way we funded Cypress. They write a business plan and shop it to venture capitalists. They secure a first round of financing, hire some people, design a product. Then they go out for a second round. Maybe they work with the same investors, maybe they look to other venture capitalists, maybe they find a strategic partner. They use their second-round money to commercialize the product and sign up customers. Then it's time to build a factory. Which means it's time to find still more investors.

And so it goes, round after round. The search for capital is plagued with chronic uncertainties: Will we raise the money we need? From whom? At what price? What will our company be worth if we succeed?

These uncertainties do create strong incentives to perform; it's tough to fund a company that's failing. At the same time, they often distract entrepreneurs from the nitty-gritty (and all-important) details of building their business. Who has time to worry about hiring the right people or cutting favorable deals on capital equipment when there's still more money to be raised to make the payroll?

ACTION REQUEST	AR # __899__
FOR (ACTION): *RO	START: November 4, 1987
CC (INFORMATION): NRB	DUE: November 10, 1987

FROM: T.J. RODGERS

TITLE: THE HALF-MILLION-DOLLAR DIODE

CONTENTS: The Schottkey diode you are using only once in the RAM cell is going to be a half-million-dollar device, unless we can figure out how to avoid going into a full platinum silicide/titanium-tungsten/aluminum metal system, just for one passive component used one place in an integrated circuit.

continued

> The alternatives are PNP loads in the cell and titanium/n-Schottkey barrier diodes.
>
> TO COMPLETE AR: Determine whether or not your company needs to spend one million shares of stock for a single diode.

How to make engineers think like entrepreneurs. Our Aspen subsidiary had incorporated a neat piece of technology in one of its new chips—technology that cost a small fortune. Aspen shares were worth fifty cents each in late 1987. Since this engineer held options on 400,000 shares, my logic was persuasive. He found a way around the diode.

We do it differently. We create a business plan that forecasts revenues, expenses, head count, cash flows. These forecasts answer all the questions any business plan answers: How much will the company lose before it makes a profit? How quickly will it make a profit? How much cash will it burn in the process? How much will the company be worth if it succeeds?

Then we take a critical next step. Cypress agrees to provide *all* the funding required to execute the business plan. Thus, we liberate our entrepreneurs from the money chase. But we provide the equity funding in distinct stages that relate directly to how the business plan unfolds. We project how much new capital the operation will need each quarter. We project the "price" of that capital—the number of shares Cypress receives in return for it. And we establish quarterly performance milestones to measure the company's progress along the way.

These three factors—staged investments, estimated share price, and performance milestones—work together to create a "dynamic" funding schedule. If, at each stage, the company meets its performance milestones, Cypress invests the planned amount of capital and receives the planned number of shares. If the company lags its milestones, Cypress invests its money but receives more shares. If the company beats its milestones, we receive fewer shares. If the company beats its milestones so much that it actually needs less money than planned, Cypress receives still-fewer shares.

This internally consistent funding schedule takes the company from initiation to IPO—and creates well-defined benchmarks along the way. It eliminates distractions without diminishing incentives. Our entrepreneurs don't worry about locating their next big source of capital; they can spend all their time focusing on the nitty-gritty details that can be the difference between success and failure. But they do worry about the *price* of that capital. Naturally, they want Cypress to receive as few shares as possible in return for our capital; it leaves more for them and their people. So they work hard to meet or beat their performance milestones every quarter.

Consider again the performance of Ross Technology. We approved Ross's business plan in May 1989. We agreed to provide total funding of about $13 million. The goal, by the end of 1991, was to create a company with annual revenues of $40.5 million and pretax profits of $12 million. We also agreed to value the company at four times sales. In other words, if Ross achieved its revenue plan, the company would be worth $162 million by the end of 1991.

Our target share price is always one dollar. Thus, we authorized 162 million Ross shares. The plan projected that Cypress would receive 152 million of those shares in return for its $13 million. Ross's founders and employees would own the remaining 10 million shares.

But those were projections. The actual number of shares we received each quarter reflected Ross's actual performance. We established quarterly performance milestones and set estimated preferred share prices for our funding along the way. For example, we invested $5.6 million in the summer of 1989. In return, we received 69 million shares (8.1 cents per share). Nine months later we injected another $1.4 million. Because Ross met its intervening milestones, we received only 12.5 million shares (11.2 cents per share). The better Ross performed, the fewer shares we received. Meanwhile, the share price kept climbing toward its one-dollar target.

In the original plan, Cypress also agreed to conduct a partial buyout at the end of 1991—provided, of course, that Ross met its performance targets. It turns out the company's actual 1991 revenues exceeded the target (despite the short-term reversal we described in Chapter 6). So the buyout price wasn't $1 per share. It was *$1.25* per share. Cypress spent $5 million to purchase 4 million shares from Ross's founders and employees—turning some of their hard work into hard cash. We also agreed to conduct another $5 million buyout in 1993.

A FEDERATION OF ENTREPRENEURS

We are in the early stages of building our federation of entrepreneurs. But the model is already showing results. Our product subsidiaries—Multichip Technology, Aspen, and Ross—now generate one-third of our revenues. They are experiencing heady growth. Aspen's revenues went from $4.3 million in 1990 to $24.3 million in 1991. Ross's revenues went from $16.8 million in 1990 to $52.3 million in 1991. Meanwhile, our manufacturing subsidiaries (Cypress Texas and Cypress Minnesota) continue to drive down production costs and drive up quality.

Indeed, let's "fast forward" six or seven years to the end of the decade. Here are the outlines of what we hope our federation looks like:

Cypress Semiconductor, the parent company, has just crossed the billion-dollar revenue mark. Most of these sales come from entrepreneurial subsidiaries. Ross Technology now generates revenues of several hundred million dollars. Its shares are publicly traded, although Cypress still owns a majority interest. Aspen has passed the $100-million mark. New subsidiaries, each responsible for different product categories (video signal processors, data communications chips, other yet-to-be identified niches) are growing and well into the black. These highly focused "product companies" are hotbeds of innovation. They concentrate on design, engineering, and marketing strategy.

We also have state-of-the-art manufacturing operations that build chips on a profit-and-loss basis. These companies are hotbeds of efficiency. They compete with each other to win business from the product companies. They also sell their manufacturing capacity to non-Cypress companies. This helps keep the factories full, lets them test their costs and quality levels against real competition, and, as with Altera, may generate valuable outside financing.

Finally, we have a "distribution company" that sells the chips our product subsidiaries design and our manufacturing subsidiaries build. This central marketing operation lets us take advantage of our worldwide sales force and leverage our multiproduct clout with big customers. It is not a subsidiary. But it does operate on a profit-and-loss basis. It charges the product companies through negotiated allocations. Its managers work to minimize costs, maximize market position, and run a responsive organization.

In essence, then, Cypress functions as a self-contained market economy rather than a self-centered bureaucracy. Member companies specialize—in design, manufacturing, sales. They negotiate—over price, delivery schedules, cost allocations. And their people benefit directly from success—through stock options and bonuses tied directly to their autonomous operations.

The billion-dollar federation also transforms the role of Cypress headquarters. I am no longer a hands-on, micromanaging CEO. I become a roving "on-line director." I stay current with developments at our member companies through computer-based management systems. I help out with big problems or big opportunities, represent Cypress to important customers, and champion projects that require intense cooperation among the companies.

The corporate staff plays a similar value-adding role. Cypress's vice president of quality reports to me and has a "dotted line" relationship with the director of quality in each of the subsidiaries. This vice president, who has installed major quality programs at Cypress, helps install similar programs at our subsidiaries. He tracks quality levels across the company and becomes a source of valuable benchmarking data. His job is to assist, not to control.

So too the CFO. He is a financial strategist. He negotiates with subsidiaries over equity funding and buyouts. He looks for ways to exploit Cypress's financial clout on behalf of the subsidiaries. He is also a tough-minded auditor. (Startups can get pretty "creative" with accounting principles.)

Meanwhile, the subsidiaries are out competing. They can adopt different management styles, different cultures, different policies on company meetings, vacation, overtime. But one important bond holds them together: *They all use the core management systems we've developed at Cypress.* Our practices become "templates" that free entrepreneurs to develop new technologies, perfect new products, and beat the competition. They concentrate on innovating; we teach them blocking and tackling.

Thus, Ross recruits people based on the Cypress hiring specification. Aspen organizes its work with the Cypress goals system, and its goals database merges seamlessly with the main corporate database. Cypress Minnesota allocates head count and justifies capital spending with the same procedures and productivity indices that we use. All our new companies grant raises through the focal-review system.

Achieving this managerial cohesion is much tougher than it sounds. The very qualities that inspire our rogue entrepreneurs to conquer the world make it tough for them to embrace any systems. These people don't like rules and procedures. When they see a barrier to progress, they go over or around it and get the job done. That's fine. All too often, though, when they see a rule that exists for good reason, they break it anyway—just because they like breaking rules.

Some of my most blistering memos and meetings have been attempts to get our subsidiaries to conform to Cypress ways of managing. Two years ago, for example, when we started the TAB module project described in our "Work" section, we discovered that Ross had never implemented the Cypress goals system. The company had a rickety little database that resembled the goals, but it never took it seriously or integrated it into our goals database. TAB couldn't work without that integration. We had several "attitude adjustment sessions" to win them over. (Which means we yelled and screamed and damn near killed a few people until they agreed to play by the rules.)

Another one of our subsidiaries was running chronically late with new products. We badgered them, we met with them, we offered to help. Then we discovered the operation had never implemented Cypress's goals-based approach to New Product Plans—a religious commitment at our company. This memo was one small part of our "persuasion" campaign.

ACTION REQUEST   AR #   5699

FOR (ACTION):   ABC   START: September 19, 1991

CC (INFORMATION)   DUE: September 24, 1991

FROM: T.J. RODGERS

TITLE: TRULY FOLLOWING CYPRESS SYSTEMS—NPPs

CONTENTS: For a long time, your company has paid lip service to following many of the Cypress systems. The ones where I have a choke hold on you—the ones which prevent you from getting resources—are followed. The other ones are not. My recent example on how your goal system is not truly integrated into our combined corporation's is a case in point. The NPP system problem uncovered in the board meeting is another case in point.

Your company has a terrible record in developing new products. (Frankly, I am somewhat disappointed that these major problems have not been forcefully and directly brought to the attention of the board of directors.) In my 20 years of experience in research and development, I have discovered that having a written commitment with details in it is the only way to break through the typical smoke and bullshit that excuses lack of new product performance. Of course, you have binning distribution problems which are nobody's fault. You have set up a system which allows people to blame their problems on that nebulous area perched between groups. Until you start following more rigorous development methodologies, you haven't got a chance in hell of producing a moderately complicated product like the DRAM controller board.

TO COMPLETE AR: Start following the absolute letter of the NPP law immediately. Every product that you are working on should have a complete NPP in document control with a schedule which you are currently following. When there are changes in an NPP, a trouble meeting should be held in which root cause corrective actions are defined and assigned. At or before the next board meeting, I would like to receive a copy of an NPP for every product currently under development at your company. You will note that the NPP milestones cover complete production status with full yields. Therefore, any product which is "in production," but not truly meeting all of the NPP milestones, needs an NPP generated for it.   *continued*

At that same board meeting, I would also like to see a brief presentation which shows the actual performance of your new products versus the NPPs that were created for them (at least the ones you have). I am interested in only two comparisons between the actual products and their NPPs: cumulative revenue to date and first sample delivery. These two milestones will give me the information I need to know on whether or not your research and development has delivered to the promises it did make. Obviously, if there are discrepancies between the NPPs and actual performance, I would like to hear the analysis you have performed and the corrective actions here about that analysis and the corrective actions you have assigned to eliminate the problems from your company permanently.

Despite these headaches, the federation approach delivers big benefits to both sides. Perhaps the most important benefit is that it clarifies organizational boundaries. These boundaries unleash "creative tension" that helps resolve conflict and eliminates bureaucratic wrangling.

Internal friction cripples organizations. Haggling between sales and manufacturing, or between product lines, saps energy, wastes time, and creates lingering mistrust. The federation approach transforms internal friction into external *negotiation*. When we disagree, it is usually not one department squabbling with another. It is one real, live company negotiating with another real, live company. Our subsidiaries place purchase orders, submit bids, establish delivery and reliability schedules. Such market-oriented transactions make it easier for people to split the difference and go on about their business. The key issues become price and performance rather than ego and bureaucratic politics.

A few years ago, for example, Ross Technology and Cypress Texas complained that our corporate payroll operation was too slow and too expensive. They pushed for better service but still weren't satisfied. As divisions of a big company, they would have either suffered in silence or waged the occasional (and fruitless) memo war. As autonomous subsidiaries, they simply took their business elsewhere.

Of course, their defections made the payroll operation even less efficient. It was now spreading its fixed costs over fewer checks. That shock therapy created strong incentives for payroll to improve—

which it did. What could have been a lingering source of internal frustration became a self-reinforcing improvement loop.

Autonomy also creates heightened awareness of financial value. Companies organized by product lines or divisions seldom appreciate what their individual operations are really worth—in other words, how much Wall Street or a competitor would pay to acquire an operation's assets and revenue streams. That lack of appreciation is a license for headquarters to run roughshod over small (but valuable) business units. "Who are you to question us?" demands the arrogant corporate staff. "You're one puny division in this giant organization."

Our subsidiaries have their own business plans and stand-alone valuations. Cypress Texas, for example, is not just a factory. It is a *business* with a market value, based on the Altera transaction, of nearly $90 million. The people of CTI expect to be treated like a business, not a branch plant. This independent valuation enhances their clout in San Jose.

The federation strategy also creates meaningful career opportunities for our best people. The runaway success of the early Cypress "raiding parties" confirmed what we already knew: When it comes to attracting talent, startups have powerful advantages over big companies. Of course, as your startup succeeds, you become one of those big companies. Which creates a choice: Do nothing and export talent to a new wave of startups, or create your own startups and let your people pursue their dreams without leaving the fold.

Tom North, the president of Aspen, is a case in point. Tom was Cypress's manager of product marketing before he took the reins at Aspen. I'm convinced he would not be part of Cypress today were it not for that opportunity. Tom is a small-company, startup guy. He simply won't tolerate the slower pace and bureaucratic give-and-take of a big company. As Cypress grew, despite all our efforts to stay lean and focused, we could sense Tom's growing frustration. Now, because of Aspen, Tom gets to run his own show. And Tom's show remains part of the Cypress federation. Everyone wins.

BREAKING UP IS GOOD TO DO

Our federation of entrepreneurs has made important strides since its creation in 1986. In fact, it has influenced how we organize and manage the core Cypress organization. Over time, as we became more and more enthusiastic about the performance of our subsidiaries, we grew less and less satisfied with our product-line operations in San Jose. It seemed as if years of success had begun to dull our hunger.

The behavioral differences between our startups and our product lines were hard to miss. Twice a quarter we would hold board meetings at Ross, Aspen, and the other subsidiaries. These sessions felt like "real" board meetings—because they were. Our startup managers really worried about money. They really worried about balance sheets. They really worried about performance milestones. You could sense the urgency.

Then we would hold "operations reviews" for our four product lines in San Jose: SRAMs, PLDs, PROMs, and Data Communications. These reviews felt more like bargaining sessions—because they were. Sure, managers paid close attention to their group's capital productivity and head count. (Our resource-allocation systems saw to that.) But they paid only lip service to profitability. An important ingredient was missing.

We decided to act. In April 1990 Cypress adopted a new structure designed to re-create the atmosphere of our startups within the core business. We reorganized our four product lines (as well as our San Jose factory) as stand-alone profit centers. These groups now have their own income statements, their own balance sheets, and direct responsibility for their operating results. They also have their own "boards of directors." These boards include their top managers, me, and an outside director from the Cypress board.

These profit-and-loss organizations are not subsidiaries. It was too radical a step, even for us, to dismantle a company it took nearly a decade to build. We realize the atmosphere and incentives of this new P&L structure may approximate, but never quite match, the supercharged environment of our subsidiaries. Still, the impact of these reforms has been dramatic.

We are also clear about their limits. Only genuine startups can inspire "breakaway performance" of the sort that drove Cypress in its early days and that has motivated Cypress Texas, Ross, and our other subsidiaries. That's why we expect these and other yet-to-be-created startups to account for much of our growth as we advance toward becoming a billion-dollar company. If we succeed—and we will accept nothing less—it will be as a federation of entrepreneurs. It's the best way we know to achieve size without sclerosis.

CHAPTER 9

Killer software: oversight without bureaucracy

Growth requires oversight. The more products a company builds, the more people it employs, the more facilities it owns, the more countries in which it operates, the more difficult it becomes to guarantee that important activities are being done right—the way you used to do them. Which is why growth often leads to bureaucracy. How can you be sure things are being done right without a layer of managers who track performance, collect and relay information on performance, and otherwise maintain organizational standards? In other words, how can you maintain oversight without an army of bureaucratic overseers?

We have developed a set of computer applications that help track and improve performance without bureaucratic monitors. There are certain things in our business that we don't want to happen. We don't want products shipped late. We don't want customer orders sitting unattended. We don't want slow-moving inventory. As Cypress got bigger and bigger, we started bumping into these and other execution problems. We wanted to fix them without unleashing a bureaucracy that would create new problems.

That's where "killer software" comes in. Killer software operates behind the scenes. It sorts through electronic databases to detect whether key departments violate reasonable and previously agreed upon performance targets. It warns the department electronically when performance begins to slip toward unacceptable levels. If the group fails to act—if the warning goes unaddressed—the software automatically shuts down the group's computers. Material can't be moved. Units can't be shipped. The group can't continue with daily activities until it eliminates the problem.

This approach may sound severe: Big Brother shuts you down—no trial, no mercy. And it is severe. *But that's precisely the point.* The severity of the consequences means people rarely allow performance to slip to a point that triggers the software. In the rare cases when the software does shut down an area, the penalties inspire a massive effort to solve the problem.

Some commentators have dubbed killer software a "unique management experiment" with all kinds of futuristic implications. But if you think about it, killer software is little more than an electronic version of a traditional management tool—the red lever on the Japanese assembly line. Why do Toyota and Honda encourage front-line workers to pull the lever and stop the entire assembly line the moment they detect quality defects—an action that costs tens of thousands of dollars a minute? Because that stoppage is so catastrophic it creates enormous pressure to analyze the defect and never let it happen again (in quality terms, a "root-cause corrective action").

Sure the Japanese are willing to shut down their assembly lines. But they are not willing to shut them down twice for the same reason. That's the paradox: The fact that management is willing to shut down the line means it rarely shuts down.

The process of manufacturing computer chips is not linear, like an auto assembly line. Our people can't just pull a lever and shut down the factory. But we *can* shut down the computers that run the factory. These shutdowns are painful, they hurt the company, and they are career-threatening if they become common events. We are willing to accept the dislocations because they force us to get to the root cause of problems and fix them forever.

In fact, that's how killer software got its name. As we described the original concept to our computer specialists, Greg Belt, our MIS manager, got more and more intrigued. "You mean you want the computers to shut down a whole operation?" he asked. Right. "Automatically?" Right. "Even at two in the morning?" Right. "Wow!" he exclaimed. "This is going to be "Killer Software from Hell.""

Some people misunderstand killer software in much the same way they misunderstand the Cypress goals system. Killer software is not designed to pressure people or "speed up" operations. It is not, in that sense, a productivity tool. It is a quality tool that improves execution without imposing bureaucracy. It flags a pre-defined, mutually-agreed-upon definition of unacceptable performance and guarantees that immediate steps are taken to resolve it.

It is also an experiment. Cypress has developed literally hundreds of killer-software applications over the last five years. Many have worked spectacularly. Others have worked, but we have found better ways to maintain performance standards. A few have been disasters. Killer software is not a "magic bullet" that eliminates all quality and execution problems. But it helps us watch literally thousands of the mundane aspects of our business and prevent surprises.

Like the goals system, killer software began as a noncomputerized solution to a common managerial headache. If you understand the logic of this story, you will understand the basic logic behind killer software as it became electronic and permeated the Cypress organization.

It was the spring of 1988. The vice presidents were late submitting quarterly performance reviews—again. I was frustrated. Actually, I was outraged. We were re-creating at Cypress a management failure that had afflicted the two big companies where I had worked—and nearly every other big company I knew about. Few things are as demotivating as late performance reviews. What kind of message does it send when the boss is "too busy" to conduct reviews? Good people are eager to know where they stand relative to their expectations and to their peers.

· For five years we had been urging people (without much success) *always* to do their reviews on time. We tried tracking the details.

Human resources generated quarterly reports of late reviews sorted by vice president. If any manager was late with a review, his vice president's name would appear on the list along with the late managers who reported to him. I would badger the VP about on-time reviews and expect the issue to go away. But I could never get all reviews done on-time automatically. I had to burn valuable time listening to excuses so predictable I could usually pick them up in midsentence and recite them.

As the years went by, the problem of late reviews just would not disappear. The 1988 list was the worst ever. As my pupils started dilating and the veins in my neck started bulging, I yelled, "What do you people want me to do? Cut off your paychecks until your managers do their reviews?"

The light went on. Diatribe ended. I stopped the meeting and called in the director of human resources. He got his instructions: "The VPs with late reviews have two weeks to persuade their managers to do their reviews. After that, make a list of all VPs with late reviews and notify payroll to cut off their checks. Don't come to me—just do it. Have one of your clerks deal with a payroll clerk. Make it automatic."

Naturally, the vice presidents scrambled to get their act together. Two of them had "minor exceptions for good reasons." The vice president of quality, a Cypress founder, headed straight for my office. "My check got cut off yesterday!" he reported. "I know reviews are important, but we don't want to carry this paycheck business too far. I have mortgage payments and tuitions. This isn't fun and games."

"You're right," I replied. "Reviews *are* important. They are *not* fun and games. And there is no excuse for one of your managers being late. You won't get another paycheck until your manager does his reviews. I'm prepared to watch your kid drop out of school and your house be auctioned off on the courthouse steps."

For effect, I followed my macho tirade with my best impression of the vacant glare of a crazed killer, Robert De Niro style. A second vice president got the word and never even came to my office. Both VPs completed their reviews and got paid within two days.

From that moment on I have not spent one minute worrying about whether performance reviews are on time. They are almost always on time. If not, "paycheck killer software" automatically makes sure delinquent reviews get fast action from a vice president.

(By the way, as these words are being written, *my* paycheck has been shut off. I'm late with performance reviews for a few of my vice presidents. Payroll delights in testing the CEO.)

This little story captures all the basic principles behind killer software. We identified an execution problem that is not make-or-break for the organization—no company ever went bankrupt because of late performance reviews—but that can do real damage over the long term. (Make-or-break problems have a way of correcting themselves.) We quantified a performance target to which no reasonable manager could object: Who disagrees that quarterly reviews should be done on schedule? We gave people time to whip their operations into shape before the system went on-line. Then we implemented an automatic, behind-the-scenes, no-exceptions monitoring device with real enforcement clout. The penalties it imposed were severe enough to make sure the problem got immediate attention—and got fixed.

HOW THE SYSTEM SHOULD WORK: TWO "KILLER" APPLICATIONS

The best way to understand the electronic version of killer software is to walk through a few of its most successful applications. Consider, for example, the first manufacturing process to which it was applied—a process called "Mark-QA." To "mark" a chip is to stamp it with basic information—the Cypress logo, a part number, other specially requested details—after it has been manufactured and assembled. "QA" (quality assurance) represents the chip's final pass/fail electrical check before it gets shipped to customers. It should take one day, and certainly no more than three days, for any production lot to leave the manufacturing line, get marked and tested, and then be on its way to the final customer.

During the late 1980s, however, as we scrambled to push more and more product through the factory, the Mark-QA process began to slip. It took an average of six or seven days rather than three. Worse, the performance distribution around that average was scattered. Some chips would get marked and tested in under a day. Others would sit around for twenty or thirty days. In the language of statistical-process control (SPC), both the "mean time" of the process and the "standard deviation" around the mean were increasing. In more familiar language, our Mark-QA performance was unequivocally unacceptable.

There were plenty of excuses for the delays. Small lots sometimes got misplaced in the frenzy of activities. Small orders sometimes got ignored as the Mark-QA area emphasized high-volume shipments to big customers. The list of little execution screw-ups was endless, just like the list of late-review excuses.

Customers sometimes got frustrated. They would check on the status of an order. We would report that their chips had been manufactured and assembled, that they were sitting in Mark-QA, that they should arrive within four days. Three weeks later the customer would call again: "Where are our chips? You said they would be here eighteen days ago and they still haven't arrived."

Everyone knew this couldn't go on. Our first response was a classic bureaucratic approach. We assigned a clerk to analyze the Mark-QA inventory every day. This clerk would identify lots that were not moving fast enough and notify Mark Allen, our vice president of manufacturing. (At that time we were small enough that he could intervene.) Mark would spend up to an hour a day analyzing the clerk's report, meeting with managers from the factory, engineering, and production control, and rescheduling overdue lots. His top-down intervention would cut through the red tape.

It was an important job that had to get done. But it burned a lot of valuable time. We asked ourselves: Why do this manually? Why do it bureaucratically? Why not assign a computer to identify problems and force accountability? These commonsense questions led to the first electronic version of killer software.

Here's how it works. Every four hours, a computer scans barcoded information for every lot in the Mark-QA inventory. It knows the maximum number of days that lots are allowed to sit before moving to the next step. It looks for lots that are about to exceed their "trigger limit." If it finds them, it generates a warning: "The following lots will trigger killer software within the following time frame." These warnings begin two or three days in advance.

People use the warning reports to schedule their activities and make sure that in-jeopardy lots get marked and tested first. If the group fails to react, if those in-jeopardy lots exceed the trigger limit, the computer discovers them on a subsequent scan. It then invokes its "can't-ignore" response. The next time someone in Mark-QA tries to use the area's computers to move lots, they will not work. Instead, they will flash a message: "Your area has been shut down by killer software. The following lots have exceeded their cycle-time limits."

Mark-QA can't mark or test any parts until it addresses the problem lots and notifies the system. The computer screen will list the lot numbers in violation, the device types, and how long they have been sitting in excess of the limit.

Two points merit emphasis here. First, killer software is not designed around "gotcha" surprises and unexpected penalties. It generates regular and timely warnings about lots that are falling behind schedule. These warnings serve as an important management tool that keeps the process moving and helps prevent shutdowns.

Second, the "trigger limit" is neither punitive nor unrealistic. No one objects to the target embedded in the software. It represents a commonsense signpost for the edge of reasonable performance. Killer software merely automates common sense.

In Mark-QA, for example, we arrived at the trigger limit through an iterative process with which all the area's managers agreed. Before we applied killer software, we examined the Mark-QA inventory to quantify the backlog problem. It was like turning over rocks in a damp garden and looking at whatever crawled out. We discovered some truly absurd situations—such as "unshipped lots" that were more than a year old.

We set the first "trigger limit" at 150 days—just below the worst of the worst. About twenty lots violated that limit. We gave Mark-

QA one week to deal with those lots: "Get them shipped, get them off the system, but get them cleaned up." One week later we turned on killer software. Then we announced plans to lower the trigger limit to eight days, its current limit. That does not guarantee good performance. But it automatically eliminates terrible performance.

Killer software is not designed to make people sweat. It is designed to eliminate preposterous outcomes—the "tail end" of the performance distribution. The penalties are severe because we want the organization's response to avoid the trigger limits with energy. If problems get bad enough to trigger killer software, people should treat them the way the FAA treats an airplane crash. They should rush to the scene, sort through the debris, figure out what went wrong, and make sure it never happens again.

(By the way, eliminating the tail end of the performance distribution uncovers lots of undiscovered quality problems that must get fixed in order to avoid more encounters of the wrong kind with killer software. If you want to discover problems you thought never existed, just put a killer-software limit on accounts receivable and watch the cash come rolling in!)

We used the same approach with order entry—another big success. Cypress receives hundreds of customer orders every day. But an order does not officially enter our backlog (and thus get scheduled for production) until it goes through a series of computerized quality checks. We need to be sure the ordered part has been released for production. (Customers can receive samples of chips that are not yet in volume production.) We need to be sure the price is within a valid corporate pricing structure. We need to be sure the customer's required performance specs match the performance specs of the chips they ordered.

Orders that pass these computerized checks get "uploaded" to the backlog and scheduled for production. Orders that are held in the "uploader" sit there until they get fixed. Perhaps the sales department has to renegotiate the price. Perhaps an engineer has to revise certain performance specs. Most changes can be made in a day. Even the biggest changes (those that require engineering reviews) can be made in a week.

Every so often, as our business exploded in the 1980s, orders would get lost in the shuffle. A ten-unit problem order would sit in the uploader for weeks without being approved. These breakdowns didn't happen every day, but they happened often enough to be noted in our customer satisfaction surveys.

Once again we decided to implement killer software. We set a trigger limit for the maximum number of days a problem order could sit in the uploader. The initial trigger was again absurdly generous (forty days), but we gradually worked our way down to the current limit of ten days. Again, everyone agrees that no order should remain unscheduled for more than ten days. (More than 95 percent take one day or less.) It is a reasonable standard for minimum-acceptable performance.

ACTION REQUEST	AR # 6117
FOR (ACTION): RXR	START: March 16, 1992
CC (INFORMATION):	DUE: March 23, 1992

FROM: T.J. RODGERS

TITLE: GET RID OF THE COMPUTER PHONE MACHINE!

CONTENTS: Roger! What are you doing? Nobody at Cypress can call your company anymore after 5:00 or 6:00 P.M. because you have got a goddamned computer answering the phone. I will pay $50,000 for it if you promise to stomp on it in the middle of a company meeting! Communication is one of our most important problems, let's not let computers "improve" that problem.

TO COMPLETE AR: FYI, but please get rid of that Son of a Bitch.

One of life's less-urgent headaches.

As with Mark-QA, the software scans the uploader and alerts the marketing manager when problem orders are approaching the trigger. If the order remains uncorrected beyond the ten-day limit, the system shuts down the department's computers. Talk about serious consequences! I have never heard reports of an actual order-entry shutdown. But if it happened, you can bet people would scramble to get things fixed—and to get the order-entry computers back on-line.

Killer software also creates incentives for different parts of the company to work together quickly, without political wrangling. Who would think of appealing to "higher authorities" to resolve a squabble when everyone appreciates the gravity of a killer-software shutdown? Its warning reports increase the clout of junior managers working to fix problems before they become crises.

ACTION REQUEST   AR #   7006

FOR (ACTION):   RTW   START: February 14, 1992

CC (INFORMATION): VPs AND SUBSIDIARY
                   PRESIDENTS   DUE: February 24, 1992

FROM: T.J. RODGERS

TITLE: KILLER SOFTWARE FOR SMALL ORDERS

CONTENTS: The definition of a "small order": an order with 50 or fewer units or an order with a value less than $1,000. The purpose of this AR is to put killer software on the shipment of those orders that we have neglected terribly. The killer software for these orders will shut down the ability to ship the product that has a late order. Thus, if a 10-unit order for the 7C45X is late, no 7C45Xs will be allowed to ship until the small order is shipped. The trigger limit will be 60 days (this is more stringent than the original 90 days I discussed), and there will be a 3-week grace period to clean up the backlog prior to turning on killer software.

TO COMPLETE AR:

1.   After the 3-week grace period, turn on killer software as described above.

2.   Please attach your list of 500 old small-line-item orders to the copies of this AR which go to the product control managers.

3.   Also, as a separate item, please run a report of current inventory versus your latest small-line-item report to see what could have shipped but was just ignored. Send a copy of that report to me, the product-line managers, and the production control managers for every operating group at Cypress.

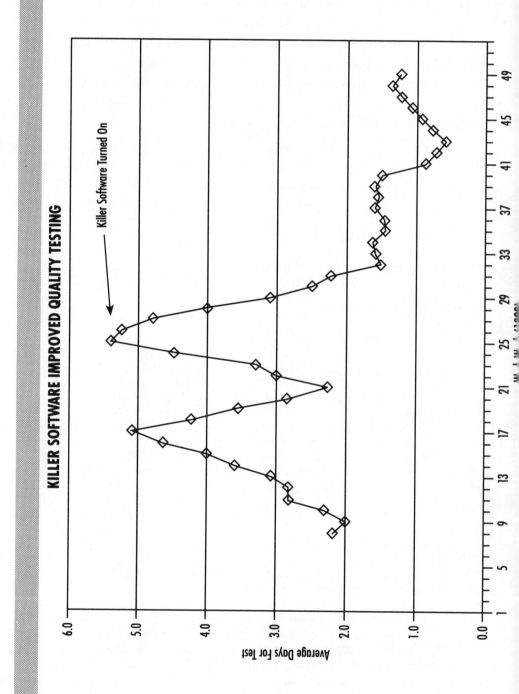

KILLER SOFTWARE HELPED RESOLVE PROBLEM ORDERS
Total

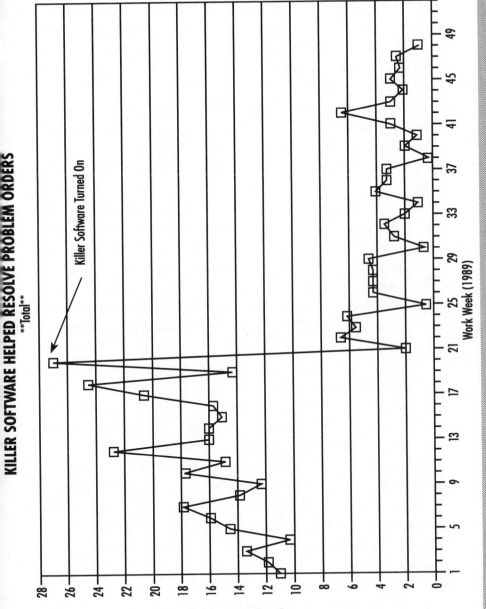

Killer Software Turned On

Average Days For Problem Orders

Work Week (1989)

In the case of order entry, for example, resolving a problem order may require help from a salesperson in another country. It may require an engineering review or a change in product specs. All too often, these stretched (and sometimes faraway) people are "too busy" to attend to the order. A marketing manager will use the warning report to tell a harried engineer: "We have one day before killer software bites on this order. Just sign right here, where I've written 'too busy to help.' "

Over time, the mere prospect of killer software became a strong incentive to improve performance. In the winter of 1992, for example, another classic problem began to surface in our factories. They seemed to be ignoring small orders so as to pump through high-volume orders and post bigger production numbers. That kind of myopic attitude (which makes sense to an overburdened factory) hurts the company's reputation for on-time delivery and great customer service. It is truly penny wise and pound foolish. Ten-unit orders are the forerunners of ten-thousand-unit orders.

In a memo, I insisted that manufacturing apply killer software to the small-order problem. In reality, the memo was less an edict than a wake-up call: "Get your act together or killer software will help run your factory."

Soon after the memo went out, a self-appointed committee of production control managers came to my office. "Your killer-software idea is the wrong way to solve this problem," they said. "We have a better way." They demonstrated a clear intent and method to solve the problem. We agreed not to implement my system.

Killer software's impact in our factories and offices has been dramatic. By focusing on the tail end of the distribution—the real disasters—we have greatly improved overall execution. Two nearby graphs tell two typical success stories. In the spring of 1989, for example, the average cycle time for the quality-assurance test on commercial parts exceeded five days. We applied killer software that June. By October the average cycle time was less than one day. The same goes for order entry. Before killer software, the average time for the few orders that got "stuck" in the uploader was twenty-five days. (That's how long it took, on average, to review the spec, or work out the pricing problem, or otherwise get the revised order into the backlog.) Four months after killer software, the average time in the uploader was less than one day.

There is a long list of documented successes. But the ultimate success was our big-picture execution. A year after we introduced killer software, Cypress's overall performance-to-schedule (delivering what customers want when they want it) reached levels approaching 95 percent. Not perfection by any means, but a substantial (and important) improvement for a fast-growing company struggling to meet the demand for its products.

HOW THE SYSTEM SHOULD NOT WORK: APPLICATIONS WE KILLED

It's hard to argue with killer software's results during the first generation of applications at Cypress. And the more applications we wrote, the better we got at writing applications. Our computer specialists could develop most killer-software programs in less than one week. Even the most complex applications took less than a month. We were ecstatic. Killer software meant we could have great execution, immediate attention to quality problems—and no bureaucracy.

In fact, we were *too* ecstatic. We began proliferating applications across the company. It became a reflex: Identify a problem, develop a killer-software application to solve it. Meanwhile, we began to allow less tolerance between a group's average performance and its shutdown trigger performance. Trigger limits got screwed down tighter and tighter.

The worst problems were in our San Jose factory, where we installed more than eighty applications. Instead of applying killer software to a few key areas, we attached trigger limits to virtually every step in the manufacturing process. There were limits on how long a wafer could reside in each of its 100 manufacturing steps in our wafer-fabrication plant. The result: Killer software became a tool to speed up performance rather than to eliminate absurd outcomes. It was no longer a "red lever." It was an accelerator switch.

That was a big mistake. We ran into all the problems you would expect with a speed-up tool. Rank-and-file people hated it because it hurt quality. Too many of them had to make unpleasant (and unproductive) choices: Do we move chips that aren't quite right or do we fix them and suffer through a killer software–imposed shutdown? Worse, there was no time to understand performance failures and develop root-cause solutions. Instead of triggering occasional earthquakes, killer software triggered small tremors every day. It created more problems than it solved.

We overdid it. Our motivation was right: We had grown so big so fast that we simply had to develop new ways to guarantee good quality and crisp execution. And we desperately wanted to avoid top-down bureaucracy. The idea was to take a system that had worked well in a bunch of different places and apply it everywhere as a speed-up tool. It was a bad idea.

We got rid of much of the second-generation killer software in our factories. In its place we relied on an even more powerful tool—market forces. Chapter 8 explained how and why we turned Cypress into a self-contained market economy in which our factories negotiate price, performance, and delivery schedules with our product lines. That profit-and-loss reorganization had a huge impact on day-to-day performance. Indeed, it made much of our second-generation killer software obsolete.

Why? Because our factories now *lose revenue* when their production schedules fall behind. Late wafers are sold to the product lines at a discount from the negotiated price—2 percent per day up to a maximum discount of 28 percent. People are committed to great performance because their profit-and-loss results depend on it. No amount of electronic intervention can substitute for market discipline.

We made a similar change in our test area. For eight years, our San Jose plant ran with one centrally managed test operation. This group was responsible for conducting a complex series of electrical tests on all four categories of our chips: SRAMs, PLDs, Data Communications, and PROMs.

The group always faced intense and competing demands from other parts of the Cypress organization. Naturally, each product line wanted its chips tested right away. But certain chips (especially SRAMs) are inherently easier to test than others and also move in high-volume batches. Test managers wanted to test as many chips as possible—the better to post big performance numbers. So they tended to pump out as many SRAMs as possible and leave the "tougher" chips for later.

This was not only unfair but unproductive. Our most profitable chips are usually our most specialized chips—those that are harder to test and move in smaller batches. Thus, the area had a built-in bias against our most lucrative products.

This problem became a big source of organizational discontent. So we decided to implement killer software. The system we developed required that all chips move through the test area on a FIFO (first-in, first-out) basis. If a small lot of PROMs arrived before a huge lot of RAMs, the PROMs would have to be tested first. What could be simpler? Who needed a new layer of management when behind-the-scenes computer technology could prevent people from picking and choosing the easiest-to-move material and require them to do the right thing?

The system was simple, all right—too simple. There are plenty of circumstances in which FIFO is *not* the right way to run a test area. There are rush orders, emergency orders, orders on which we want to deliver great turnaround to an important new customer. We had taken an impossibly complex situation—a huge operation responsible for testing hundreds of different chips—and imposed a set of inflexible rules.

It didn't work. And it didn't work because it didn't match the basic role of good killer software: to identify performance targets with which no reasonable manager could disagree, and to create powerful incentives to operate within those targets.

Thus, as with manufacturing, we adopted an *organizational* solution. We divided up the test area and delegated control to the product lines. Today our PROM group no longer pleads with a centralized test operation to move its chips. *It does its own testing however it sees fit.* Business logic—not a set of inflexible rules—determines what gets tested when.

Two of the lines (PLDs and SRAMs) kept the killer software in place after the reorganization. These are products for which FIFO testing makes perfect sense, and the product-line managers liked the commonsense discipline the software imposed. The other two lines eliminated the application because it did not meet their needs. They developed their own tools to track and maintain good execution.

That's fine. Our basic goal is to maintain tough performance standards without bureaucratic meddling. Killer software can't substitute for decentralized management and profit-and-loss accountability. Nothing can. Still, within Cypress today, there are more than one hundred active "triggers" for killer software—in areas as diverse as planning, sales, assembly, and final test. They are there because killer software works. It is a critical part of our antibureaucracy toolkit. Indeed, we recently moved 80 percent of our test area to Bangkok, Thailand. The fourth action of the Bangkok plant manager—after installing the equipment, hiring workers, and translating his specifications into Thai—was to turn on killer software.

Killer software is just one of the tools we use to fight big-company disease. On the surface, the following memo is primarily about responding to emergency ("lines down") customer requests for Cypress parts. But it's really about accountability—and the commonsense attention to detail that separates crisp execution from self-satisfied inertia.

We solved this problem and moved on to others. And there will always be *plenty* of others. The battle against sloppy performance and unresponsive bureaucracy never ends.

ACTION REQUEST	AR # 5673

FOR (ACTION):   ALL VPS   START: September 16, 1991

CC (INFORMATION):   DUE: September 24, 1991

FROM: T.J. RODGERS

TITLE: LET'S GROW UP

CONTENTS: I have now spent several days thinking about last Wednesday's Ship Review. It's hard to remember the last time that I was so completely depressed over the future of our company. Not the near-term future success—making the next quarter or two—but the long-term prospects for our company. The last time I was this disillusioned about our future was about three years ago, due to a similar set of circumstances. Our orders were down. Our business with major customers had stagnated. We were begging our customers for turns and pull-ins. At just that time, I discovered that we had <u>hundreds</u> of unshipped sample requests for products that were declared to be <u>production products.</u> We were not shipping samples and begging for orders at the same time. It was the fifth time I had stumbled in an anecdotal way onto the samples issue. I had complained about the samples problem in my staff meeting many times. Yet I found out that every product line had dozens of unfilled sample requests, some of them as old as two years! How could high-level managers in a highly regarded company be so foolish as to not ship samples to the customers from whom they were begging for more orders?

As is my style, I micromanaged a solution to the problem. Dick Gossen came up with the concept to solve the problem—the "samples czar," a solution that seemed to work much better than the solutions attempted in the other product lines. We appointed sample czars in each product line and the numbers improved rapidly. However, I did not bail out of the problem when the numbers started to get better. I continued to manage the problem (long weekly meetings) until a system was in place that gave permanent measurement and visibility to sample status. You have all seen the samples report. Recently I had to start writing notes to several of you again because the samples report showed that you were not shipping all production samples. One of you "had trouble making the product," but still managed to ship tens of thousands of dollars worth of production. Another of you had a production control manager that "dropped the ball," but I noticed that before you did. This most recent samples fumble was minor and we are again on track with nearly zero "defects," that term meaning a sample request for a production product which is currently unshipped. My concern for the company's long-term future at that time was obvious: How could I have turned over daily operation of a company to managers who collectively do not ship samples to their customers—or who do not even know or measure that they have not shipped samples to their customers? How far could the company grow before I become incapable of managing all the details?

I get a continuing barrage of complaints. TJ overmanages. TJ micromanages. TJ's meetings are too long because he covers too much detail. The product lines should have more autonomy to prevent their initiative from being stifled. But what would happen if I turned some of those details loose?

<u>Think about</u> yield improvement. We all know that yield loss is our largest cost of quality, but my unclosed AR's on getting yield analysis are over one year old.

<u>Think about</u> last-minute rescheduling. Our customers have told us on dozens of occasions that they can accept schedule changes but not abrupt schedule changes just prior to shipment. I have reinforced those comments in my meet-

continued

ing on many occasions. Yet I continue to get complaints from the field that we jerk around shipment schedules only days before committed shipment dates, or even after the shipment date. That flow of information on late reschedules from the field comes from my initiative, not the initiative of the product lines, marketing, or manufacturing. Currently, a report is being generated that will list completely and automatically the schedule jerk-arounds suffered by our customers. Again, the push behind the report comes from me. Once the report comes regularly, I will begin to micromanage a solution to the problem, hammering on the causes of the problem until they are root-cause eliminated. Then the reschedule report will become another weekly status memo that will show zero defects or initiate action.

Think about customers' lines-down situations. The only thing that infuriates our customers more than last-minute reschedules is our shutting their lines down. What would happen to Monsanto the second time their shipments shut down our line? The issue has been discussed in my staff meeting on numerous occasions. Manufacturing announced that the data they get relating to lines down is so erroneous that they were no longer reacting to it. I then sent an AR to marketing and manufacturing asking them to create a system to solve the problem (copy attached). I was later assured by those groups and the product lines that a working system to react to lines down existed and that I could stop worrying about it. Autonomy requires trust; I stopped worrying about lines down without my usual check to make sure that a system was really in place and really did work.

Then what happens? Joe Smith complains that we are not serving a lines-down customer. When I ask marketing into which manager's group the lines-down information comes, no one seems able to answer. When I continue to probe, I am told that the lines-down information is Bob Jones's responsibility, but he no longer works for the corporation. When, after several frustrating minutes of evasive answers, I finally identify the marketing manager who is responsible for lines down, I find out that our marketing group does not even keep a comprehensive guaranteed-correct list of lines-down reports. Marketing drops a piece of paper over the edge of the Grand Canyon and hopes that somebody will take care of it. There is no follow-up to make sure that a lines-down problem has been fixed. There is no list of the commitments that have been made to our customers to fix lines down, or data to show whether or not the promise has been kept, or trend charts to show that the defects levels are dropping. Marketing fills out a form and drops it over the edge of the Grand Canyon.

Meanwhile, manufacturing has decided not to respond to the lines-down report. Of 50 lines-down requests, manufacturing decides to shaft the customers associated with 25 valid requests in order to "show the product lines and marketing" that they are not going to be jerked around by the other 25 erroneous requests (killer software at its finest). Although manufacturing pays lip service to serving our customers, product with a burn-in window problem is currently expedited with a higher priority than lines-down material. The product lines and marketing are blackmailed with a threat to their customers who are in a lines-down position in order to get them to make their error-laden lines-down reports more accurate. They fail to respond to the blackmail, and manufacturing follows through the promise.

The product lines (apparently with the exception of SRAM) cannot say exactly how many lines-down situations there are and exactly how and when they will be alleviated. Even with the president's urging, the product lines have failed to work in cooperation with marketing and manufacturing to develop a system that automatically reacts to customers' lines down. There are no graphs that treat "lines-down" as a "defect," with a goal to drive the number of defects to zero. There are no metrics presented in any of the product line board/operations meetings to indicate that there is a problem with regard to lines down or that the problem is being solved. The product line board meetings are cookbook presentations in which the head cook (me) happened to forget the lines-down page.

TO COMPLETE AR: There are two aspects to solving this problem. First, we should use every means and all the adrenaline at our disposal to make the problem go away immediately. Here I will give credit to the SRAM group, which knows its current situation and has complained publicly that the factory is not responding.

Second, we must put a systematic solution on line. By "system," I mean a solution like the one to the samples problem. At one time, I had to spend two hours a week trying to make sure that our company shipped samples. Now it takes me 30 seconds per week to review a clean samples report or about two minutes to send a note or an AR if the samples report is not clean.

If you were me, would you turn over Cypress—your major life project—to people who hadn't already answered the questions in this AR? If you want not to be micromanaged, earn it.

CHAPTER 10

adversity

We're proud of the quarter-billion-dollar company we've built at Cypress. And we believe in the business principles and management systems behind our success. But nothing we believe can guarantee uninterrupted growth. In a world of relentless and exacting competition—a world in which new and nimble competitors are always looming on the horizon—the real test of an organization's character is not how effortlessly it handles prosperity. It is how confidently it works through adversity.

We are emerging from our first test. For a solid year—from the winter of 1991 through the winter of 1992—Cypress experienced flat revenues and declining profits. The third quarter of 1991 was the first time in four years that we reported lower revenues and profits than in the immediately prior quarter. In the second quarter of 1992, we posted our first-ever loss ($1.7 million) as a public company. We ended 1992 with lower annual revenues than in 1991—the first year we actually went backward in sales. Grim statistics.

These tough times were new and unsettling for us. Most organizations react to adversity the way most people react to a life-threatening disease. First there's denial: "Sure we had a bad quarter, but we'll bounce back." Then there's rage: "How can this be happening for three quarters in a row? Why aren't people doing their jobs?" Finally there's acceptance: "The world *has* changed. We *are* a different company than we used to be. We need to understand the changes and devise a new game plan."

The tough times also punctured our aura of invincibility on Wall Street. For eight years, runaway growth was virtually automatic at Cypress—almost like a law of nature. Every quarter seemed to bring news of record sales, record profits, record productivity. Cypress stock, which first sold for 67 cents in a 1983 private financing, went public in 1986 at $9 per share, and climbed as high as $24 per share by the middle of 1991. As our performance faltered, so did the price of our stock. By the middle of 1992, Cypress shares were selling *below* their IPO price. It was as if, in Wall Street's eyes, we had come full circle.

We understood the market's harsh verdict. We were, after all, reporting very un-Cypress-like results. On the other hand, our results were hardly without precedent. Nearly all of today's most powerful and prosperous technology companies have "stalled" at some point in their history. Intel, the $5-billion dynamo of our industry, barely broke even in 1985 and lost more than $200 million in 1986. It is now the world's most profitable chip company. Compaq, the computer manufacturer launched in 1982, reached $1 billion in sales faster than any company in history. It stumbled in 1991, recorded its first-ever quarterly loss, and has roared back. The list could go on.

These setbacks, however traumatic, are like a rite of passage from entrepreneurial adolescence to corporate adulthood. Indeed, for technology companies, they reflect a certain arithmetic inevitability. The high-technology market isn't like the market for toothpaste or soda pop. Companies don't introduce new products and then expect to sell more and more of them forever. High-tech products hit the market, experience meteoric growth, and then crash to earth at the hands of new and better products. Most companies, including Cypress, are in the business of making their own products obsolete before someone else does. We race against ourselves as well as our rivals.

Which means, from the point of view of growth, that young companies have an important advantage over established companies. A young company, by definition, sells nothing but new products. Its overall growth rate reflects the combined growth of its various products, each of which is soaring. It's like adding booster engines to a rocket. That's precisely how Cypress took off so dramatically in the 1980s. Every time we introduced new products (and we introduced twenty or thirty every year) we compounded more growth on a growing base of products. Revenues increased by nearly 200 percent in 1986 (to $51 million), by 80 percent in 1988 (to $140 million), and by 43 percent in 1989 (to $200 million).

After five or six years, however, the mathematics of growth changes. The company has begun making its first wave of products obsolete; its mature-product revenue actually begins to decline. The company's overall growth rate now reflects the still-meteoric growth of its newest products, plus the modest growth of products that are a few years old, minus the *shrinkage* of products that are more than five years old.

The "rocket" days are over. Now growing the company is like building a skyscraper on quicksand. You race to add new floors just to keep the building at the same height. Fail to add a floor soon enough—arrive to market late with a few new products—and the top floor starts to sink.

We recently documented this skyscraper-on-quicksand effect at Cypress. Our products grow and decline with statistically predictable life cycles. A new chip that generates, say, $2 million in sales one year after introduction will generate, on average, $12 million in sales in its third year and reach a peak of $14 million in the fourth year. That's a compound annual growth rate of more than 60 percent!

Then the fade begins. Eight years after introduction, this same chip generates only $4 million in annual sales. Ten years out the chip is back where it began—with sales of less than $2 million. Unless, in the intervening years, we have introduced a hot new chip to ride the next growth wave, the decline creates a "revenue gap" that reduces our overall corporate growth rate.

This life-cycle dynamic is as unforgiving as it is unchanging. In 1991 our seven product lines generated record total revenues of $287 million with 232 chips, each packaged, on average, in five different package types—a total of 2,500 distinct product-package combinations. Nearly 50 percent of our revenues came from products *three years old or less.* More than 70 percent of those revenues came from products four years old or less.

The lesson is clear: To grow, Cypress constantly must reinvent itself. Of course, as the company gets bigger, so do the challenges of reinvention. Our "innovation engine" must work harder and faster all the time just to stay on track. We have to create more new products, to create new products more quickly, or better still, do both at the same time. If the "innovation engine" sputters, even momentarily, so does the company.

None of this is meant to excuse or explain away our one-year stall. We've never been willing to think of Cypress as "just another company," and we never expected the tough times we encountered. In fact, success itself helps bring on the tough times. We got distracted from our most urgent strategic demand—ever-accelerating innovation—and we paid the price.

Here too our experiences were not without precedent. A young high-tech company almost always develops more new products than it can build right away. Venture capitalists expect their startups to lose money for their first few years. So management has the luxury of pumping all kinds of resources into R&D without triggering the wrath of its sophisticated investors. This deficit R&D spending generates a valuable "excess" backlog of innovations that launches the rocket at the IPO.

Once the company's first products hit the market, though, management changes its focus. It races to draw down that backlog. After all, the only constraint on growth is what the company can actually build and ship. Production, not innovation, begins to occupy center stage. The company enters a manufacturing sprint.

Our manufacturing sprint ran from 1985 through the middle of 1991. We had so many products in the pipeline, and so many customers eager to pay a premium for them or complaining about shortages, that we devoted ourselves to our factories. The more chips we made, the more we sold. So we focused on making chips. We added production capacity in San Jose. We built a plant in Texas. We bought a manufacturing facility in Minnesota.

Our single-minded commitment made sense in the short term: What was more important than growing the company? But it took a toll in the long term. Time and again, when we faced choices about resources (people, computers, access to the plant), the demands of "getting more product out the door" took priority over getting new products out of the labs. Why should we invent more chips we would not ship? Slowly, unintentionally, but quite devastatingly, our R&D people became second-class citizens.

The results began to show financially by the middle of 1991. Several important new products were late—a few as much as one year late. The delays left many existing products open to intense price competition, since our three- to five-year-old products were no longer clear-cut performance leaders. Don't get the wrong idea: Cypress was still churning out lots of industry-leading chips in the many niches in which we operate. But in a business as brutal as semiconductors, just a few slips can be the difference between runaway prosperity and high-profile adversity.

I was slow to recognize this self-imposed distraction—even though I was growing more and more frustrated with our failure to meet new-product timetables. Toward the end of 1991, I held a one-on-one meeting with Tony Alvarez, our vice president of research and development. There was one issue on the agenda: How and why had Cypress stopped executing on new products as crisply as it once did?

Tony updated me on his group's progress on several key technologies. He reviewed some of the technical hurdles that had slowed them down. Then he got down to business. "The real problem," he said, "is that this company has developed a deep-seated bias against research and development. We are never going to get back to our old form until we eliminate that bias."

I was floored. "What the hell are you talking about?" I angrily objected. "This company *lives* for new products. Our entire strategy is premised on constant innovation. My whole career has been spent developing new products. How can you accuse Cypress of having a bias against R&D?"

He patiently explained how so many decisions over several years had made life harder and harder for our design engineers. He also politely pointed out that I had concurred and sometimes even driven those decisions, and that the R&D rank and file saw *me* as a major obstacle. These people had been so productive for so long that we had started taking innovation for granted—and starving out innovators. Our manufacturing sprint had left our "innovation engine" out of gas. Tony was dead right. VPs who are willing to say you are full of crap are invaluable.

It was at that point—that moment of recognition—that our comeback began. In the past eighteen months, Cypress has rededicated itself to R&D and innovation. We created the top-ten program to enhance the visibility and clout of our most important new products. We initiated a campaign to slash R&D cycle times by 50 percent. I even agreed to personal, weekly oversight of three critical R&D projects—including our program to develop the world's smallest, fastest one-megabit SRAM memory chip. It wasn't long after I took on those projects that I got a taste of biases Tony had described and vowed to eliminate them: "Whaddya mean, you're not going to run my wafers!"

SACRIFICE, BACKLASH, COMMITMENT

It's one thing for management to understand the causes of hard times and begin the work of correcting them. It's quite another for the organization to maintain its composure and commitment during the comeback. For a company as visible as Cypress, adversity imposes real psychological costs. Competitors and critics gloat. Supporters disappear—or at least become decidedly less public in their support.

The real impact was more serious than just a psychological slap on the wrist. Cypress paid a stiff price for its temporary stumble. We were forced to abandon our "only-in-America" manufacturing policy—a real defeat—and relocate our packaging and test areas to Thailand. We announced the first layoffs in our history. We suspended the focal-review process, which meant our people did not get their 1992 raise. Our people also stopped getting their quarterly profit-sharing checks. (From 1989 through 1991, we paid out $9 million in profit sharing—real money. But the plan only kicks in when we post record quarterly revenues and operating profits exceed 10 percent of sales.) The erosion of our share price eroded the value of millions of outstanding stock options.

Many people wondered how we would react to this first-ever wave of bad news. It's fun and exciting to be part of a winning team—even a team as demanding as Cypress. But what about a team that seems to have lost its touch? Would our people stand by a tightly managed company? Or would they jump ship for younger companies still riding the growth rocket? Would middle managers stand by our systems? Or would they abandon the systems the moment performance faltered?

The answers came quickly—and loudly. Morale remained reasonable—our people weren't happy about events, but remained determined to succeed. Employee turnover stayed at 8 percent, as low as at any point in our history. People rolled up their sleeves, worked harder, and fought through the adversity. It became more obvious than ever that financial rewards, however important, played a modest role in what drove our people. They are motivated by pride, a sense of purpose, an appetite to succeed—and a commitment to preserving our legacy of achievement.

That said, we also set clear limits on sacrifice. Late last year we announced that we would reinstate the focal-review process in 1993 and grant raises after a one-year hiatus, *regardless of the company's performance.* We settled on a 5 percent corporate average raise. That meant adding $5 million to annual operating costs. Therefore, we made a second announcement: If granting raises meant violating 1993 profit targets, Cypress would fund the raises with a second round of layoffs.

The logic behind these announcements may seem puzzling: Why not maintain the no-raise policy and avoid layoffs rather than impose layoffs to fund raises? The answer goes back to our merit-based philosophy of reviews and rewards. Top performers are as prepared as anyone to sacrifice. But they are not prepared to sacrifice for-ever—especially since they know, in Silicon Valley at least, that they can move two miles up the road (or across the street) and get a big raise, a nice package of stock options, and a fresh start. *Hard times can't become a long-term excuse for not rewarding outstanding per-formers.*

I learned that in the mid-1980s, when the big chip companies in Silicon Valley were experiencing a crippling downturn and Cypress was a beneficiary of the phenomenon. Back then I interviewed every recruit before we made a job offer. One week I interviewed five peo-ple from Advanced Micro Devices. For two years, in the name of "equitable sacrifice," AMD had imposed a no-raise, no-layoff policy. All of the recruits I interviewed were vocally unhappy, and all were unhappy for the same reason.

One young finance manager explained his discontent. "I have an MBA from Berkeley," he said. "I was one of thirteen MBAs hired the year I graduated, from some of the best schools in the country, to introduce more high-level analytical capabilities to AMD. Yet I have not had a raise since I started. That's bad. What's worse, I sit in an office with four other people. If two of those people left tomorrow, no one would notice. They are deadwood. It offends me not to have had a raise for two years while those turkeys collect paychecks."

We won that smart young analyst away from AMD. His discon-tent was a classic illustration of the "distillation effect." Imposing an indiscriminate salary freeze is like placing a vat of crude oil on an open flame. For a while nothing much happens. But the longer you maintain the freeze—the longer you heat the crude—the more quickly you boil off the valuable, volatile elements like gasoline. Boil the crude long enough and all that's left in the vat is tarry sludge.

So we faced a choice: Maintain the salary freeze beyond one year and start to lose our top performers, or impose merit-based layoffs (if needed) and lose our lowest-ranking performers. It's an unpleas-ant choice—no one likes to inflict pain—but it's not a difficult one. We made it.

So much for money and financial sacrifice. What about our management systems? Did people lose faith? Did they rebel?

Hardly. The principles and systems that served us so well during our eight-year climb also helped mitigate our one-year stall. Indeed, we can look back on the hard times as an affirmation of the values that guide this company. Whatever the management system—hiring, goals, new product planning, resource allocation, killer software—people used them even as they worked to improve them. But most of all, they stood by them.

Which is not to suggest there was no backlash. We have always had revolutionaries and renegades at Cypress—people who never liked a particular system, who complained loudly about it, who tried to buck it or get around it. That's not all bad. Renegades are innovators. Most of us were renegades at our former companies. As the revenue stall persisted, however, our most vocal renegades turned up the volume.

To be honest, even I had some quiet doubts. I began to wonder if we had outgrown some of our management systems, if they had become too rigid, if our people had lost their commitment to making them work. Many of them do impose limited (but necessary) rules and procedures. Had I turned healthy discipline into stifling bureaucracy? Had our commitment to blocking and tackling sapped our imagination? Had our belief in "commonsense" management somehow reduced our creativity?

The PO-Commit system was an early test. Middle managers at Cypress have always been strong supporters of PO-Commit. They like it because it tells them precisely how much they can spend each week and guarantees that their purchase orders will be approved quickly and predictably (within five working days). A few of our vice presidents have never liked the system. They believe that PO-Commit dilutes their authority, that it suggests the CEO does not "trust" them with budget autonomy.

In the spring of 1992, some of these critics suggested that we abolish the system. Others lobbied for exemptions. I worked hard to reestablish managerial buy-in. In fact, I wrote a fifteen-page memo that reminded our top managers of the origins, evolution, and effectiveness of the PO-Commit system over our first eight years. I agreed to make a few simple and sensible changes—changes designed to speed up approvals for urgent purchases without diminishing our ability to hit weekly budget targets. But I also declared that the sniping had to end. We were not going to abandon a budget system that had served us so well for so long.

"The PO-Commit system represents many person-years of evolution by some relatively high-powered system architects," my memo concluded. "There is no group within Cypress that has an alternative system with the sophistication of our system. We burn a lot of energy whining about the 'president signing for pencils' when that statement is not true and merely panders to sympathetic ears. The system should be improved. Improving the current system will require much less energy than creating multiple systems from scratch.

"We need evolution, not revolution," it continued. "We currently have wafers with defect densities that are a threat to our business, microprocessors that are a year late, process technologies that are a year late—and a group of managers apparently intent upon reengineering a PO-Commit system that works well. We ought to put our energies into adding real value, not shortening one two-hour PO-Commit meeting to one hour."

That's basically the attitude with which we approached all our systems. We scrutinized the rules and procedures they imposed, listened to the critics, and agreed to changes that made sense. But we also drew the line. Temporary business setbacks would not become an excuse to sabotage well-designed management tools with proven value.

Sometimes we made mistakes. More often than not, however, we made mistakes when we backed off the systems rather than when we stuck by them. In the spirit of attacking bureaucracy, we inadvertently re-created some of the very problems our systems were designed to address.

Consider head count. Chapter 6 described the company's frustrating (but ultimately successful) head count–and–capital negotiations during the third quarter of 1991. Soon after that meeting, we realized that Cypress was in for several lean quarters—that revenue might actually shrink rather than just grow more slowly than before. Which meant, of course, that we would enter a zero-hire, capital-starved mode. The logic of the system demanded it.

Thus, the fourth-quarter head count–and–capital meeting was even more bruising than the meeting the quarter before. After hours and hours of wrangling, I got fed up. "This is bullshit," I declared. "We know we can't add to head count, so what are we arguing about? It's a waste of everyone's time to submit head count requests and hold negotiations just to keep saying 'no.' That's enough."

I walked out. We suspended the head count–allocation process until further notice. In a period of flat or declining revenues, it seemed more like a ritual (and a painful one at that) than a system. Why go through the motions? We didn't hold another head count–and–capital meeting for nine months.

That decision was a *huge* mistake. By failing to conduct the negotiations, by failing to argue for as long as it took to reach consensus around the harsh reality of our revenue stall, we left unchecked the expectations of managers whose operations were still growing. These managers (and there were plenty of them) no longer felt the tough zero-sum logic the system imposed on all parts of the company. Middle-management myopia began creeping back in: "Everyone says Cypress is facing hard times, but my operation will grow by 10 percent. Why can't I hire people?"

The lack of consensus allowed the company to slip back gradually into "hallway requisition" mode. I would arrive for work and find three or four people hovering outside my office. "I need ten minutes with you," a factory manager would say. "I must have six operators or one of our lines is going to shut down." Or, "I need five minutes," a product-line manager would say. "Let me tell you why we're not going to make our numbers unless we get the people we need."

It was as if I had built a "gun-to-the head" shooting gallery and handed our managers nickel-plated revolvers. In the spirit of getting tough, I left myself wide open to special pleading—precisely what the head count–and–capital system was designed to prevent.

The memos that follow capture my growing frustration with my own decision to retreat from the system. A few weeks after we canceled the fourth-quarter head count–and–capital meeting, I approved a major investment in new test equipment. As with so many ad hoc negotiations, I approved the decision based on bogus argument, knowledgeable that I didn't have the data to refute. (With a room full of allies, I *would* have had the data.) This memo corrected the mistake. We returned the machine to its vendor.

ACTION REQUEST   AR #   5896

FOR (ACTION):   JMT   START: November 20, 1991

CC (INFORMATION): MKA, MHM, HC   DUE: November 26, 1991

FROM: T.J. RODGERS

TITLE: JUSTIFY THE STS ON A ZERO BASIS OR SEND IT BACK

CONTENTS: I made the mistake of yet another hallway capital purchase because I was told that the STS was a required test capability. I was told that we needed a more accurate STS to enhance our current base of STS testers. No way in hell would I have ordered that machine as a sort tester for Minnesota.

TO COMPLETE AR: Either that tester is justified, or it is a toy of the product line. Either it goes into the test area (they agree to pay for it) or we send it back. Which will it be?

I wrote the head count memo a few months later—after having spent lots of hallway time beating back "special-case" requests for new people. I couldn't always stand my ground, however, which meant we wound up making a bunch of hires we should not have made—hires that would not have been made under the formal system. This memo put an end to the lobbying.

After nine months, we came to our senses. We reinstated the head count–and–capital negotiations and got back on track. The meetings were even more bruising than they were before we suspended them (because we now dealt with "negative" numbers—attrition

```
** COMPANY CONFIDENTIAL **

            ACTION REQUEST                AR #    6072

FOR (ACTION):      VPS & SUBSIDIARY
                   PRESIDENTS              START: January 30, 1992

CC (INFORMATION):                         DUE: February 3, 1992

FROM:    T.J. RODGERS

TITLE:   FYI: WE ARE IN A PERIOD OF ZERO HIRES & ZERO OVERTIME

CONTENTS:     Just a reminder. We are trying to fight a layoff. I am totally
unsympathetic—even hostile—toward well-reasoned arguments why we need
to replace a critical etch engineer or a great marketeer. I will be monitoring our
attrition as it turns over. We will try to fill critical requisitions by transferring
people on the inside—and then not replacing them. The vice presidents and I
discuss every turned over person every week. We do not need any data-filled
memos to help us do our thinking.

As an obvious second point, there is to be zero discretionary overtime. Wouldn't
it be preposterous for us to be finally forced to lay someone off, so that another
person in the company could work overtime? I just assume this zero-overtime
policy has already automatically happened and will not check on it.

TO COMPLETE AR:      FYI only, but I need your total support on this issue.
```

and possible layoffs). But we all had new appreciation for their value.

PLANNING FOR CORPORATE ADULTHOOD

Our management systems reflect creative thinking and hard work by lots of dedicated people. Eight years of spectacular business results speak directly to their value. One year of disappointing results does not mean the systems aren't right. They are *dead right*. And they have played a crucial role in our comeback.

But there are genuine differences between life as a company on the fast track from $0 to $250 million and life on the bumpier road from $250 million to $1 billion. That's especially true with strategic planning and resource allocation. It's the one area where we have modified our earlier systems to reflect our strategic rite of passage.

Our original approach to planning and resource allocation was designed for a young company in an environment of runaway growth. As we've said, the seeds of business failure are sewn in good times, not bad. Our job was fairly simple: Be sure, as the company grew explosively by 40 percent or 50 percent each year, that we made tough, smart, well-documented decisions that held spending increases below the rate of revenue increases. So long as we contained runaway costs, profits would take care of themselves. So we focused on revenue per person, capital productivity, and other deliberately simple performance measures designed to control the prosperity illusion.

But what happens when explosive growth is no longer so automatic? When it is no longer unthinkable for revenues to grow modestly for a quarter or two as the company launches itself onto its next high-growth trajectory? In short, how do you plan for life as an established enterprise rather than a skyrocketing startup? Our systems weren't equipped to answer those questions because those questions weren't part of our world. Now they are.

The new approach grows directly out of the "money" systems described in Chapters 6 and 7 — and it uses them to make real-time tradeoffs over people, capital, and operating expenses. We still hold our head count–and–capital meetings and PO-Commit budget reviews. Today, however, these negotiations and reviews are part of a broader planning framework that ties them together and incorporates high-level financial goals.

The following flow chart outlines the framework. Planning starts with the big-picture external goals in loop 1: What do we want our shareholder value to be and by when? That share-price goal immediately feeds back into business-performance targets. We know the standard price-earnings ratios Wall Street assigns to chip companies like Cypress. So if we set a target share price, we know the earnings per share we must deliver to achieve it. Based on the number of shares outstanding, we can calculate the total profits we must gen-

CYPRESS SEMICONDUCTOR:
FINANCIAL/STRATEGIC PLANNING PROCESS

CYPRESS
STRATEGIC PLANNING PROCESS
G = Goal
A = Assumption
C = Calculation
I = Index

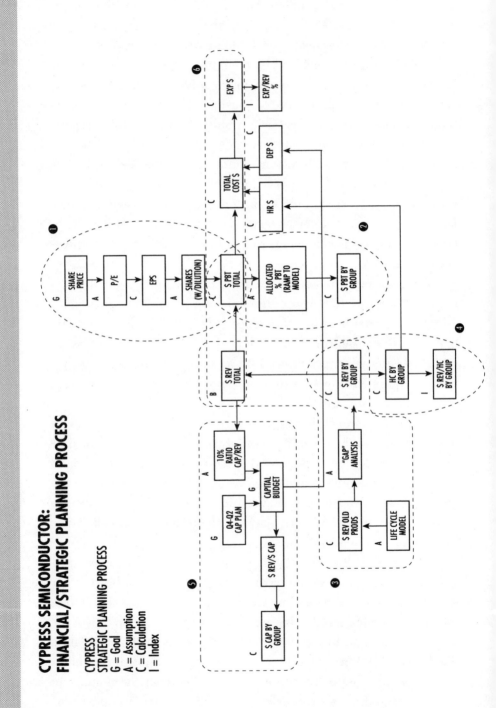

erate to deliver our target share price. This operating target—profits before tax (PBT)—becomes the common denominator behind all subsequent revenue forecasts and resource negotiations.

This represents a major shift for us. For most of our history we managed for revenue. We made profit-sharing checks depend on revenue targets, offered as "fat" a product catalog as possible to increase revenue, and measured our internal sense of momentum based on revenue. Now we manage pretax-profit dollars. The new focus forces us to get rid of empty calories—products that don't generate the margins we need—and focus on high-growth, high-profit chips.

The next step (loop 2) is to allocate the corporate PBT target among our product lines and subsidiaries. This step is key—and it incorporates both top-down "assignments" and horizontal negotiation. We know the profit margins our product lines and subsidiaries should be able to deliver. Top management uses those expected margins to set profit goals for each operation. However, we are prepared to modify the initial goals based on reasonable objections. We convene a meeting of our vice presidents and subsidiary presidents and ask them to "sign up" for their targets or explain why they can't.

The meeting works under Cypress's familiar zero-sum logic. It revolves around the nonnegotiable target for corporate profits calculated in loop 1. Thus, if one vice president insists that his operation can't reach its assigned PBT target, another operation must agree to exceed its initial target. This means all the vice presidents have an incentive to help find ways for reluctant colleagues to hit their targets. We don't leave the room until each operation has signed up for profit goals that together allow the company to reach its overall PBT goal.

The profit targets established in loop 2 also set implied targets for revenue. After all, if each product line knows how much profit (in dollars) it must deliver, and if it also knows the profit margins it expects to register, a revenue number falls out. The question, of course, is whether the product line can actually deliver on that revenue number.

Loop 3 answers that question in a two-stage process that incorporates the skyscraper-on-quicksand dynamic described earlier. The first step is based on history: What revenues do we expect from "old" products according to the statistical model of product life cycles? The model is valuable because it forces us to recognize and quantify the irreversible decline of once-fast-growing chips. It disabuses managers (including me) of congenital and damaging overoptimism about the performance of old products.

The second step focuses on new products: What are our best estimates of the revenue we can generate from our about-to-be-introduced chips? How confident are we of these estimates? What are the jeopardies—what can go wrong? We review each new chip from each product line and agree on detailed revenue forecasts.

Then comes the all-important reconciliation: Do the two distinct forecasts (for old and new products) together meet each product line's total revenue target? If so, the planning portion of the exercise is over. If not, we conduct a "gap analysis" to figure out how to meet the target. Can we assign a few more engineers to a new product and accelerate its introduction? Can we push harder on a few old products and bump them above their statistical life-cycle curve for just a quarter or two?

At this point, the framework has produced two sets of dollar-based targets: revenue by group and profit by group. The targets reflect very different logic. The profit figures are driven by external goals for share price and expectations about product-line margins. The revenue figures are driven by history (the life cycle of old products) and by our ability to deliver new products on time. We then subtract each product line's profit target from its projected revenues and calculate its total allowable spending. This figure represents a binding budget constraint under which the group must operate.

Now it's time to move into the details—which is where Cypress's familiar resource-allocation systems kick back in. There are, after all, three basic ways for the company to spend money: on people, capital, or operating expenses. The next three loops draw on our "money" systems to reach the detailed tradeoffs that allow us to live within our means.

Two points deserve special emphasis. First, as we emerge from our stall, we have adopted even-tougher expectations about organizational productivity. For example, we have currently agreed to limit the growth of dollar spending on people to 40 percent of the growth of revenue (loop 4). In other words, if quarterly revenues increase from $70 million to $74 million (6 percent), then head-count spending can increase only from $26 million to $26.6 million (2.4 percent). This is a brutally tough constraint—much tougher than in our startup days—that will remain in place during a "get-well" phase.

We convene a head-count meeting and conduct the negotiations required to work our way down to the 40 percent limit. It's the standard routine: Our vice presidents and managers present their requests for people, use revenue-per-person and department-specific performance indexes to justify their requests, and cut deals in real time. Under the new framework, however, revenue per person is a reality check rather than an end in itself. We are prepared to accept a modest erosion in the index if that erosion reflects, say, substituting low-cost labor (Bangkok) for high-cost labor (San Jose). We will accept a modest erosion if adding ten people means not spending millions of dollars on a new piece of equipment. The real goal is staying within that 40 percent head count–to–revenue dollar limit.

The get-tougher dynamic also applies to the capital negotiations in loop 5. We have agreed to limit quarterly spending on new equipment (or, to be precise, net additions to depreciation) to 10 percent of revenue growth. If we expect revenues to increase from $70 million to $74 million ($4 million), then total depreciation charges can increase by only $400,000. (In other words, based on five-year depreciation, we can afford $2 million in new capital purchases.) Again it's the same drill: The vice presidents negotiate, make their productivity-based evaluations of each proposed capital investment, and work out the tradeoffs.

Then come operating expenses (loop 6). The company's global expense budget essentially writes itself. After all, we have already established corporate and product-line goals for revenue. We have agreed to must-achieve targets for profit before taxes. We have reached negotiated spending agreements on head count and capital. The corporate (and product-line) budgets for operating expenses are whatever resources are left over. If the expense targets are so tight as to be unachievable, we know the capital and/or head-count plan is wrong. So we start over. We then conduct the BOQ reviews, approve budgets, and guarantee that total expenses stay within the required corporate limit.

This planning framework has become a remarkably powerful unifier up, down, and across the company. If we are late with a new product, we can go back to the revenue forecast, calculate the delay's effect on the "gap analysis," and estimate how it will lower our profit before taxes—and thus everyone's stock price. If a vice president insists on buying a new machine, we can add its depreciation charges to the existing model, run the calculations, and estimate that machine's impact on the stock price unless corresponding cuts are made. It allows us to trade off among the three spending categories—people, capital, operating expenses—and still meet a tough corporate budget constraint.

The model is admittedly less simple and intuitive than the old system. But so is Cypress.

Conclusion

america can win

The men and women of Cypress spend long days (and plenty of late nights) figuring out how to do more with less, how to stay ahead of the pack in new-product development, how to maximize quality and minimize cycle times. Part of what drives us is the simple adrenaline rush of competition. Part of it is a healthy ambition to achieve and make money. But part of it is something deeper. We know—even if we don't talk about it very much—that Cypress is a small player in a big unfolding drama: the new world of global competition.

It matters who wins that competition. The winners get the highest standard of living, the most prosperous communities, the best schools, the widest opportunities for their people to apply their talents and realize their dreams. Sure we want Cypress to win. But we also want America to win. And there is every reason to believe we will win, so long as we understand what makes us strong.

The United States is the best country in the world in which to start and grow a company. What's more, the economic and technological changes reshaping the logic of competition play directly to our strengths. Companies that are losing (and there are plenty of them) are seldom losing because our economic system is poor or because our foreign rivals are competing unfairly. They are losing because they are being outmanaged.

Too many Americans, and far too many American managers, accept an altogether different proposition: The United States is on a trajectory of decline. They point to the agonizing retrenchment of General Motors and the U.S. auto industry. They cite the slow-but-steady dismantling of IBM, once the world's most profitable and admired corporation. They fear the commanding presence of foreign (mainly Japanese) companies in high-profile industries such as consumer electronics and machine tools.

These developments are real and troublesome—as is the pain they inflict on American workers and communities. But they are only part of the story. America is not in decline. *America is being rebuilt.* In industry after industry, a new generation of companies is taking the lead. This process of "creative destruction" is bad news for old-guard companies that can't match the organizational capabilities of their dynamic new rivals. But it is great news for the United States and its future role in the world economy.

Think about computers. Fifteen years ago, the leaders of the computer industry were IBM and the five giant "BUNCH" companies: Burroughs, Univac, NCR, Control Data, and Honeywell. Today the BUNCH has been virtually eliminated from the scene and even mighty IBM has stumbled. But the United States, driven by the rise of young companies such as Apple, Compaq, Dell, Gateway, Silicon Graphics, Microsoft, Sun, and Thinking Machines, has maintained or increased its global dominance in virtually every important segment of computer hardware. America's computer pioneers did not lose to the Japanese. They—and Japan—lost to a new guard that is very much made in America.

Or think about biotechnology. For the past decade, Japan's vaunted industrial policy machine has declared that it will be a world biotech leader. But its giant (and globally uncompetitive) pharmaceutical companies, centralized government agencies, and scientific establishment have been no match for a wave of startups in cities like Boston, Houston, San Diego, San Francisco, Seattle. There are now nearly 250 publicly traded biotechnology companies in the United States. Several of them (Amgen, Chiron, Genentech, Synergen) have become powerful enterprises with market values worth billions of dollars. The biotechnology revolution is at hand, and American companies are in the vanguard.

Let's be clear. For all of our deep-seated economic and social problems—the decline of public education, the harrowing condition of our inner cities, the corrosive effects of the national debt and deficits—America's long-term competitive strength is wide and deep. The global economic landscape has changed. The economic model with which Japan scored so many victories in the 1980s—a model premised on cheap capital and fabulously disciplined mass manufacturing—is giving way to a new logic of competition. This new logic emphasizes creativity over size, innovation over monopoly. A world in which the power of scale gives way to the capacity for change is a world in which America will flourish.

At least that's the promise. Delivering on the promise requires that as companies and as a country we have the courage of our convictions—that we recognize and leverage our home-grown strengths. Of course America should learn from Japan. But *imitating* Japan is to mistake the past for the future. There are new rules for success in global competition, and American business is writing them. We hope, in a modest way, that this book has sketched some of those rules.

NEW RULES FOR GLOBAL COMPETITION

I am enthusiastic about America's competitive promise because I see it unfold every day in my own industry. Indeed, there may be no better case study of the new logic of global competition than semiconductors. If you understand the powerful forces reinventing our business, you will understand how the entire world of business is changing—and how America can win.

Most everyone who follows the "competitiveness debate" has some familiarity with the U.S.-Japan rivalry in computer chips during the 1980s. And most everyone has heard the conventional view of America's "crisis." In 1982, the doom-and-gloom story goes, the United States held 54 percent of the world semiconductor market while the Japanese held 34 percent. By the end of the decade, the Japanese held 49 percent while the U.S. share had slipped to 37 percent—an almost total reversal. The bleak conclusion: America's position in semiconductors, the core technology of the information age, had suffered the same depressing fate as its position in autos, tires, and other "basic" industries.

This declinist scenario is startling, to say the least. It is also incomplete and misleading. The sky has not been falling on the U.S. semiconductor industry. Some of the apparent erosion represents genuine setbacks. Some of it is localized—as with Japanese dominance in chips for consumer electronics, where U.S. companies never played much of a role. But much of the "decline" is a statistical illusion—a function of volatile exchange rates that distort figures on market share and say little about U.S. technological prowess.

The real story of the 1980s was neither the humbling of the United States nor the triumph of Japan. It was the rise of a new generation of semiconductor companies that successfully took on the giants in both countries. Cypress is a member of this new generation. There are many others: Altera, Cirrus Logic, Cyrix, Lattice, LSI Logic, Micron Technology, Xilinx, the list could go on. These new companies, and others like them, helped America hold its ground in world markets even as many of the American giants faltered. And they will extend our market power in the 1990s.

It is certainly true that Japan came to dominate some segments of the chip market in the 1980s—especially DRAMs, the ubiquitous memory chips that store information for computers. DRAMs are the single largest segment of the world market, and Japan builds about 75 percent of the newest-generation DRAMs. But DRAMs are also a brutal commodity business in which even the most efficient Japanese producers suffer from cutthroat domestic rivalry and fierce competition from elsewhere in Asia.

The financial realities are grim indeed. The Japanese collectively invested $4 billion to design and build their latest-generation DRAM chips. They have yet to make a dime of profit on all that investment.

A 1992 Goldman, Sachs report estimates that from 1982 through 1991, the period of Japan's DRAM triumph, its semiconductor companies generated combined cash flows of *negative $5 billion.* Some triumph!

Now consider microprocessors, the "electronic brains" behind the computer revolution. Microprocessors remain the most technologically exciting and consistently profitable segment of the chip business. Their design and production is thoroughly dominated by American companies. Intel, one of the pioneers of our industry and the inventor of the microprocessor, was the most profitable chip company in the world in 1991 and 1992. And when you look at the array of technologies driving the next stage of the computer revolution (digital signal processors, video compression chips, multimedia architectures), innovative American companies lead the way at every turn.

My conclusion: Viewed as a country or as a group of companies, the United States is positioned precisely where it should be. We are dominating the high-value, high-margin, innovation-driven parts of the business. We are not winning everywhere, but we are winning where winning makes sense. And we are winning because of the explosion of entrepreneurial innovation in the 1980s.

Our industry has experienced real problems over the last ten years. But the most severe problems were concentrated in the large, established, high-profile companies associated with the industry's early days—companies that faced the need to change or become dinosaurs.

America's much-lamented decline in DRAMs helps tell the story. Intel invented the DRAM in 1971. It eventually lost its market lead to Texas Instruments, which, in turn, lost its lead to Mostek, which, in turn, lost its lead to Japanese suppliers. Note that Intel started to lose DRAM share long before the Japanese took over. Over time, American companies collectively lost market share because of Japanese efficiency, automation, and quality. (And because the Japanese cut their prices and broke the law by dumping parts below their costs.) As their share declined, many of these American producers left the DRAM business altogether.

There is, however, one company in the United States that still prospers making DRAMs—a $425 million, new-generation company based in Boise, Idaho, called Micron Technology. That 1992 Goldman, Sachs report estimates that Micron may be the lowest-cost DRAM producer in the world—*and the world's only profitable DRAM producer.* How does lean, flexible, hungry Micron hold its own against the Japanese juggernauts while multibillion-dollar American giants hemorrhage red ink and throw in the towel? Just posing the question suggests the answer.

I do not believe the old-guard companies will disappear. In fact, some of them have begun to recover. National is again in the black—a major achievement. Advanced Micro Devices, thanks to its aggressive challenge to the Intel monopoly in personal computer microprocessors, is setting records for sales and profits. And Intel, never a dinosaur, is the most profitable semiconductor company in the world.

Still, we are in the midst of a changing of the guard. The balance of power in semiconductors will shift away from the big, established companies toward smaller, nimble companies focused relentlessly on innovation, quality, and value. The main engines of growth, innovation, and profitability in our industry will be the new, dynamic, entrepreneurial players.

What explains this dramatic shift? More than any other factor, the accelerating power of computer technology. Our industry is essentially overthrowing itself. Thanks to the relentless advance of semiconductors, computers have become so powerful that they allow us to reinvent how things get done. Small groups of self-motivated engineers can achieve more, faster, and better results than large groups of average engineers working in gigantic organizations. Corporate size is no longer an intrinsic asset in competing with Japanese conglomerates. In many cases it is a liability.

I think back to my first job in Silicon Valley, as a chip designer at AMI. My biggest bottleneck was getting access to the central Burroughs mainframe that ran the rudimentary calculations I had to make before I could work with draftsmen who toiled for months, drawing by hand the circuits I was designing. Eventually I solved my computing bottleneck. Rather than work standard hours, I came into the office at noon and stayed until early morning. Right after five P.M., when the bureaucrats left, I would buy a six-pack of beer and head for the computer room. In return for liquid refreshment, the technicians put my runs on the top of their priority list.

After a while the AMI brass caught on. So I hired a hacker who rigged the priority matrix in the Burroughs mainframe. If my runs went in at, say, priority six, they would be bumped up the queue to priority one. (Not only that, but my projects were only charged priority six usage rates.) Eventually the operators got wise to my new gambit, so I had to resume my visits to the package store.

That was the frustrating, cumbersome, centrally controlled environment in which chips were designed when I started in this industry. Big companies dominated because only big companies could afford the costly mainframes and armies of engineers and draftsmen required to develop new products. Contrast that with 1988, when Cypress introduced its first microprocessor, SPARC. It took thirty engineers just eighteen months to design that fabulously intricate chip. Designing SPARC in my AMI days would have required several years and hundreds of engineers. More likely it would have been impossible.

The drastic compression in design time and cost is a function of the vast and decentralized computing power at our disposal. We used a distributed network of Sun workstations to design SPARC, which was to become the heart of computers twice as powerful as the most powerful Sun computers available to us in that design effort. Today our design efficiency is much greater than it was in 1988. Last year, for example, we introduced a new class of microprocessors called the hyperSPARC. These chips are three times faster than our original microprocessors, and they represent a quantum advance in design complexity. Yet it took less time to design the hyperSPARC than the original SPARC. And we spent under $10 million—less than what a Japanese behemoth spends on office supplies in a month.

We are describing an exponential curve: designing new, more powerful chips in record time for workstations that we then use to design more powerful chips even more quickly. The ultimate implication of this curve is the demise of command-and-control economics. Back in 1974, my work was held hostage by my superiors, who could make or break me by controlling access to a mainframe. Now, with a workstation for every engineer in the Cypress design department, I have very little control over who does what when. Not that I want such control, but even if I did want it, I couldn't exercise it. If I tried, a bunch of my designers could simply move over to workstations in another company or buy their own workstations and pursue their design vision independent of Cypress.

The age of the corporate battleship is over. We have entered the age of the cruise missile—small, smart, targeted, powerful, inexpensive. We can't beat Japan's corporate giants with a handful of American giants trying to build factories that are bigger and more automated than Japan's. We need hundreds of small, flexible, innovative companies waging slashing raids at Japan's weakest points. In the semiconductor business, brains will win out over brawn.

What goes for our business goes for the economy as a whole. Think, for example, about a much more prosaic industry—steel. The very forces reinventing competition in computer chips are also at work in steel. America spent much of the 1970s and 1980s wringing its hands at the "demise" of the steel industry. And with good reason. U.S. companies lost billions of dollars, laid off hundreds of thousands of workers, and seemed powerless to combat low-cost, high-quality imports.

Today? The industry has emerged from the darkness. The U.S. market position in steel doesn't compare with our global leadership in computers or biotech, but the trends are headed in the right direction. In 1991 the average number of person-hours required to make a ton of steel was 50 percent lower than a decade earlier. We even exported 6 million tons of steel that year—six times as much as in 1986. All told, our companies now rank among the world's most efficient producers.

The primary engines of America's comeback in steel have not been the sprawling, old-guard, integrated giants like USX, Bethlehem, and Inland—companies that have spent most of their recent history retrenching and lobbying rather than expanding. America's comeback has been led by the minimills—a new generation of companies formed over the last two decades. Minimills now control a greater share of the U.S. steel market than imports, and their market share has increased every year for the past ten years. The five largest steel producers account for only 40 percent of U.S. production, down from 60 percent a decade ago. They are expected to account for less than 25 percent by the year 2000.

What explains the growth and prosperity of minimill operations like Nucor, Chaparral Steel, Birmingham Steel: tough-minded management, intense worker commitment, creative and flexible use of capital equipment, constant experimentation and improvement.

Winning companies in all kinds of industries embrace new organizational capabilities. They are agile and responsive. They maximize speed, deliver unique value, and race to make their products obsolete before others do it for them. They function as loose federations of business units, each independent, all working in tandem, linked by computers and telecommunications, operating as strategic alliances.

These are precisely the capabilities of the emerging companies in our industry and the big, powerful flagship companies of the new American economy: Federal Express, Microsoft, Wal-Mart. These are emphatically *not* the capabilities of most of the old-guard giants in semiconductors or elsewhere. That's why the future rests with the new guard—and why America's future can be so bright.

A GAME PLAN FOR AMERICA'S COMEBACK DECADE

If there is a new logic to global competition, and if a new generation of companies is leading America's resurgence in industries from biotechnology to steel, what does that mean for U.S. competitiveness? How can Washington help companies win in world markets and help build a higher standard of living for American workers?

Tough questions—and the central economic questions facing America in the 1990s. As a country, we are at a moment of truth. America can embrace the familiar and bet on its sagging old-guard companies with the damaging mix of subsidies, trade protection, and unfair tax breaks that masquerade under the euphemism of "industrial policy." Or we can embrace and enhance America's unique strengths: our system of entrepreneurial capitalism and our national commitment to creativity and diversity. If we do, the 1990s will be remembered as America's comeback decade.

The sober reality, of course, is that government has always been better at protecting the familiar than encouraging the new. As we search for ideas and solutions for the 1990s, we can look back to a classic model from the 1980s—a fabulously instructive example of how *not* to help an American industry become more competitive. Once again the example comes from semiconductors. But the same basic story (with different characters and plot twists) could be told for countless other industries—from autos to steel to machine tools.

In 1987 a worried U.S. government approved a five-year, $500 million subsidy for Sematech, a chip-industry consortium based in Austin, Texas. The worthwhile goal was to spur America's semiconductor "comeback" against Japan. Sematech set up shop, hired hundreds of engineers and researchers, and commissioned a red-white-and-blue logo to remind everyone of its patriotic mission.

There was just one problem. Nearly all of the founders of the subsidized consortium were charter members of the old-guard chip establishment—many of the very companies that were losing to Japan. There are more than two hundred semiconductor companies in the United States. Yet only twelve joined Sematech and only eleven are still members. Every one of these companies has revenues of more than $1 billion.

Why such an exclusive club? Why haven't more of America's two hundred chip companies signed up for the free money? Because Sematech's dues structure was designed to exclude smaller companies. The group postures that its dues are set equitably at 1 percent of a company's sales. But it also sets a $1 million dues floor. That means a $20 million company must pay annual dues of $1 million—5 percent of its sales, perhaps all of its profits, and five times the percentage dues for a company with revenues of more than $100 million. Sematech also sets a dues ceiling of $15 million per year. That means a member with $3 billion in sales pays dues equal to one-half of 1 percent of sales—or ten times less than the dues rate for a $20 million company. The absurd (but all-too-predictable) result: Sematech effectively excludes the very American chip companies that are bringing energy and innovation to our industry.

I could go on for pages about why Sematech is the wrong answer to the wrong problems in our industry. Indeed, I have been called to Washington three times in the past few years to testify about the consortium and other misguided proposals to prop up the chip establishment. I certainly prefer that Washington spend $500 million on Sematech than on needless irrigation projects or more subsidies to tobacco farmers. But in its organizing structure and practices, the program represents a classic misreading of the sources of America's economic strength and how Washington can help build it. If Sematech is an example of American industrial policy, then we should immediately adopt a 100 percent laissez-faire approach. We can't afford much more "help" like this.

I first testified against the Sematech pork barrel in 1989. The chip-industry establishment said I was crazy. The media labeled me a gadfly and rabble-rouser. *Business Week* called me "The Bad Boy of Silicon Valley." *Time* called me an *"enfant terrible."* The *New York Times* said I was a "maverick."

But I was also right. In 1990 America actually won back market share from the Japanese for the first time in six years—a major achievement. Yet that year six of America's eight largest chip companies lost money. America again won back share in 1991. Yet that year Texas Instruments and National Semiconductor, both of which rank among the top five U.S. chip manufacturers, generated combined losses of $550 million. In 1992, America took back more market share—and Intel surged past its Japanese rivals to become the world's largest chip company.

What was Sematech's role in all this? Not much. Does anyone believe that a big-company consortium in Texas had anything to do with Intel's remarkable dominance—as opposed to the guts, brains, and drive of Andy Grove and his team?

Misdirected policies like Sematech look even more counterproductive in light of the damaging legal assault being waged by the chip establishment against the companies that have led America's revival. Even as they collect government subsidies, many of the big companies in our industry—all of them members of Sematech— have been abusing the patent laws to wage war against their new-guard rivals. This litigation brinkmanship is an outrage. It is a huge diversion from the business of competing—a diversion that our Pacific Rim competitors manage to avoid. No policy to promote American renewal can ignore the legal wars.

Semiconductor technology advances at breakneck speed. Companies race with one another to master the latest process improvements or perfect the newest wrinkles in circuit design. A hot new chip may depend on dozens of patents both internal and external to the company that invented it. Thus, patents have always been intrinsically less valuable in this environment than in an industry like pharmaceuticals, where developing a new drug can require hundreds of millions of dollars and ten years of work. What good is seventeen-year legal protection when chip technology can be obsolete in eighteen months?

From the industry's earliest days, then, Silicon Valley's pioneers adopted a live-and-let-live posture on intellectual property. Companies knew that patent advantages were at best temporary. So they filed for patents, but they liberally swapped patents with other companies, granted licenses to rivals as well as allies, and threw as few roadblocks as possible in the path of innovation. Sure companies sued each other, but only if their "family jewels" were threatened or if a rival company committed an egregious violation. This antilitigation ethos helped everyone focus on what mattered: building new and better chips and winning in the marketplace, both as distinct companies and as a critical American industry.

No more. The walls of my office aren't decorated with expensive art or glowing testimonials. They are decorated with framed pages from thirty actual or threatened lawsuits against Cypress since we began in 1983. We have been sued by nearly all of the Big Boys: AMD, Motorola, National, Texas Instruments. Yet we have never lost a single case. (We did settle one case for $4 million because it would have cost us far more to litigate it to victory.) Are our lawyers that good or are we being harassed by wasteful litigation?

We've already discussed Cypress's strategy for long-term growth, our creation of a "federation of entrepreneurs." This strategy means we are always looking to start new companies—which means we are always within minutes of being sued by an established company. In our industry, it has become almost as certain as death and taxes: Start a new company, expect a lawsuit.

Consider again the story of Ross Technology. In the late 1980s, we were eager to enter the microprocessor market. I learned from a venture capitalist that a well-known design guru, Roger Ross, was looking to leave Motorola and raise money for his own company. I telephoned Roger and explained our federation of entrepreneurs: "Why start your own company? Cypress will fund you. Our sales force will sell your chips and our plant will build them. But you can run your own operation as a legitimate startup with a real founders' stock reward."

Roger bought the idea. He and four colleagues left to establish the company that developed the SPARC chip we discussed earlier. They were sued immediately by Motorola, both as a corporation and as individuals. Big companies hate it when good engineers leave to start new companies—*even though virtually every major advance in our industry has come from startups.* And they use lawsuits, which almost always allege theft of trade secrets, to scare off investors and persuade other engineers not to join.

The Motorola suit was a typical warning shot fired across our bow. We settled it the usual way, with no money changing hands, a temporary no-hiring agreement, and an agreement not to disclose the terms. Both sides went on with their affairs. The suit caused Roger's people some worried nights, cost us thousands of dollars in legal fees, but had no impact on the new company's plans. It was a classic piece of useless litigation.

Motorola's garden-variety harassment suit pales in comparison to what happened next. Soon after the settlement, Ross Technology hired *one* engineer from AMD. The company immediately turned around and sued us and him. The suit alleged the standard litany of traitorous activities, starting with theft of trade secrets. Fortunately, AMD's lawyers made an embarrassing mistake that I dubbed "Xerox litigation." They simply took the earlier Motorola lawsuit, which had named five defendants, removed their names, inserted the name of the engineer we hired from AMD, and then refiled the lawsuit. *They literally copied Motorola's legal document.* But they didn't even have the plagiaristic skill to change all the verbs and pronouns from the plural to the singular!

The filing would have flunked fourth-grade English, but it had a potentially great return on investment. The logic was as simple as it is destructive: "Let's sue just like Motorola did, copy Motorola's documents to minimize legal costs, let Motorola bear the burden of the litigation, and accept whatever settlement Motorola hammers out of Cypress."

We arrived at the preliminary injunction hearing ready to fight. We won the round and AMD's lawyers indicated they were ready to compromise. We decided to offer a face-saving settlement that spared big legal expenses and allowed both sides to claim victory. The settlement had no impact on our hiring plans.

I settled the case by inventing the "selective no-hiring agreement." Essentially, we proposed that AMD name seven of its 18,000 employees who would be off-limits to Cypress for the next six months. We did not expect AMD to give us the names of their key employees (that wouldn't have been very bright of them), so they agreed to create a confidential list and have one of their officers hold it. If Cypress decided to hire someone from AMD, I would contact the designated AMD executive. If our new recruit was on the list Cypress would wait the required six months. If not, we were free to make the hire.

This absurd settlement was an appropriate end to the ludicrous "Xerox" litigation. A few months after the settlement, we decided to hire another AMD engineer. I telephoned the designated AMD vice president to see if the new recruit was on the list. I was told that the list was lost and that the VP had resigned. Why had he resigned? To become president of Actel, a hot Silicon Valley startup! I never found out whether AMD sued him for theft of trade secrets (or perhaps the list). We went ahead and made the hire.

This story would be funny if it weren't so infuriating. American business complains endlessly about the damaging impact of our legal system on industrial competitiveness. CEOs recount antilawyer statistics like the plot from a horror movie. You know the mantra: The United States has more than 800,000 lawyers, Japan has fewer than 15,000. Law firms gross more than $100 billion a year in revenue. The annual number of legal filings in state courts alone exceeds 18 million per year.

I agree that America has become too litigious. And I have no quarrel with reforms to curb ambulance-chasing tort lawyers and their financial-market equivalents—securities lawyers who file class-action suits the minute a company's stock drops unexpectedly. But in our business, and in many high-technology businesses, big companies aren't innocent victims of abusive litigation. *They are among the worst abusers.*

No company has been more abusive than Texas Instruments. TI is a classic semiconductor dinosaur; it registered operating losses (a total of nearly $500 million) for six quarters in a row in 1990 and 1991. However, as an industry pioneer, TI holds a vast store of old and largely forgotten patents. How has the company responded to its chronic problems? By opening up its legal vault, dusting off its patents, and terrorizing every chip company in sight.

TI has actually transformed its legal department into a profit-and-loss center. Lawyers get assigned specific patents with marching orders to maximize revenues. The company's litigation terrorists generated revenues of $172 million in 1990 and $256 million in 1991. One high-ranking executive has quipped that Texas Instruments should consider selling off its factories and building a business around its patents. The returns are so much higher.

This is a business perversion of the most damaging sort. Had our industry's pioneers hectored each other the way TI does today, America never would have developed its leadership position in semiconductors. TI's strategy creates incentives for its lawyers to sue with impunity, almost without regard for the merits of the case. If it costs an average of $2 million in legal fees per suit, and the company only wins one of five suits, all it needs is a $10 million judgment to break even. It also creates incentives for outrageous royalty demands. Remember, the goal is not to protect intellectual property. It is to maximize revenues from intellectual property, however dated.

Last year, for example, in one of our few intellectual property cases that has actually come to trial, I spent nine full days in a Dallas courtroom with the TI executive who runs the company's $3-billion chip division. We could have spent those precious days working to beat the Japanese. Instead, we argued over a patent on an obsolete testing method that even TI admitted it no longer used. Cypress didn't use it either. But since our chips included the capability for our customers to use it, we were accused of "contributory infringement."

The entire suit should have been good for a laugh. But TI was asking a jury in its home state to give it $26.4 million of Cypress's money—resources we needed to keep pace with our well-financed rivals. Fortunately, even the hometown Dallas jury got the joke. The jury deliberated for only five hours before throwing out the TI patent on multiple grounds. It was a total victory for Cypress. But the victory came at great cost, including the $40,000-per-day trial, countless days of my time in depositions and legal strategy sessions, and nine full days in court. What a monumental waste of resources!

The semiconductor establishment can't sue its way back to prosperity. Success depends on innovation, not litigation. That's a principle too many old-guard companies have forgotten. In the process, they have slowed down the rate of growth and change in our business.

These backward-looking legal war games are bad for America. Washington could make a much bigger contribution to America's future in semiconductors by curbing the legal abuses of the chip establishment than by subsidizing it through Sematech. For example, Congress could pass legislation requiring plaintiffs to pay the legal fees of defendants in failed intellectual property actions. That certainly wouldn't end the litigation wars. But it would make these skirmishes less appealing to the big-company bottom line. It might even make some CEOs think twice before they drag successful competitors into court.

''SOAK THE RICH''

I don't pretend to have a convenient five-point program to enhance America's economic leadership. In fact, I don't believe in such programs. As illustrated here, well-intentioned "industrial policies" often inflict damage their architects never anticipated. Washington should stay away from the intricacies of our business or any other—the dynamics are just too complex. It should focus instead on the *infrastructure* of competition—those factors of production that help all companies equally.

Politicians love to give speeches about infrastructure: deteriorating highways, falling bridges, aging railroads. But the real threat to our country's economic future is the condition of our *financial* infrastructure—the scarce supply of reasonably priced capital that successful companies need to build their manufacturing muscle. If Washington adopted policies designed to lower (and keep low) the cost of capital and extend the time horizons of investors, it would make a genuine contribution to America's entrepreneurial advances in the 1990s.

The ambiguous and overused term cost of capital means different things to different people. Troubled companies often use it to explain away bad management or poor investments. But in Silicon Valley, the sector of the economy I know best, the capital problem is real and severe. And much of the problem can be traced directly to Washington.

The single most damaging tax the federal government imposes on high technology is chronic, massive deficit spending. Last year, H. Ross Perot spent tens of millions of his own dollars to explain how $300-billion federal deficits steal resources from future generations. He's right; it's a scandal. But do we also take seriously the deficit's staggering here-and-now impact on America's entrepreneurial, high-technology companies?

Any college freshman understands how competing for money with a government that soaks up $300 billion a year drives up the cost of corporate borrowing. During the early 1980s, when America's worldwide semiconductor market share did experience real declines, our companies were paying 12 percent interest while the Japanese were paying 4 percent. The disparity has closed during the recession, but our Asian rivals consistently get more money more cheaply than we do. This "financing gap" is a huge competitive burden for fast-growing companies.

A similar financing gap applies to equity. As Washington borrows to finance massive deficits, long-term interest rates tend to exceed their natural levels. So investors gradually move their money out of stocks and into high-yield, safe, government-secured debt. As investors sell off their high-tech stocks to load up on debt, equity prices (as expressed in price-earnings ratios) sink, which makes it more expensive for companies to raise capital by selling shares. It's like a double whammy: Long-term interest rates are too high, stock prices too low.

During the semiconductor decline of the early 1980s, the average price-earnings ratio for a high-tech issue on the New York Stock Exchange was about 15. In Tokyo it was about 60. That meant U.S. companies had to sell four times as much stock as comparable Japanese companies to raise the same amount of money. Even if the equity gap has closed somewhat in recent years, how can our companies compete over the long term in the face of such a massive financing imbalance?

Venture capital remains America's high-technology saving grace. No good engineer in Silicon Valley will be refused his or her first $10 million to prove the feasibility of a new technology or product. The problems start at the next stage, when the company needs its second or third $10 million to build a plant and acquire real manufacturing muscle. This is when young companies must turn to the public capital markets—or to cash-rich foreign operations eager to acquire valuable American technology at bargain-basement prices. This is where the "equity gap" bites.

What's worse, American companies must sell their undervalued shares to investors obsessed by short-term forecasts, short-term performance, short-term profits. Plenty of executives bash Wall Street to gloss over their own failures. I don't object that our investors expect us to perform every quarter. After all, what is the "long term" if not a series of short terms? Even if Cypress were still a private company, I would measure our results quarterly and demand that we make those targets.

I don't even object that Wall Street punishes us when we disappoint it—as we did during our one-year stall. But when Wall Street treats our shares like chips in a casino, when financiers buy and sell stock based on what they bet will happen over the next few days, speculation has gotten out of hand. I don't blame investors, I blame the system. The system is what we have to change.

The short-term casino mentality of our financial markets is real, hurts American manufacturing, and is encouraged by our current tax system. Consider one experience from the summer of 1991. The second quarter of 1991 was the single best quarter in the history of Cypress Semiconductor. We were bursting with pride over our performance. We always release our quarterly results over the business wire and then hold a nationwide teleconference with analysts and money managers. For our second-quarter teleconference, I gathered a thousand Cypress people in an auditorium to listen in and get educated on the fickle nature of our stock markets. Participating in the call were sixty-five of our major investors, accounting for more than half of our outstanding shares.

These investors spent literally thirty seconds talking about what we had achieved in the quarter. They spent five minutes talking about our long-term strategy. The next ninety minutes of questions concerned what would happen over the next $89\frac{1}{2}$ days—when our next quarterly results would appear. How were yields in our plant? Did we expect to see the normal summer lull in orders? Our people left that session surprised and dispirited. But this is the financial environment in which we must operate every day.

Most of our investors are smart and well meaning. They are forced into the quarterly mentality so as not to suffer a disadvantage relative to other investors. Indeed, when we finished the teleconference, our share price shot up $2. Was Wall Street endorsing our performance and long-term prospects? Not exactly. Our stock rose because of "short covering" by two groups of speculators who had sold our shares in advance of the teleconference—in essence betting that we would report bad news rather than good news. How does such behavior help us or any other company compete?

Washington can take two steps to restore our financial infrastructure. After twelve years of the most reckless fiscal behavior in American history, we simply must pass a balanced budget amendment. No industrial policy or national investment strategy or trade negotiation—no matter how brilliant—would have the same energizing effect on American entrepreneurship as a return to fiscal sanity. It is a prerequisite for economic leadership.

Second, Washington should restructure the capital gains tax to punish short-term speculation and encourage long-term investment. Notice I said *restructure*, not reduce. A majority of Americans have been convinced that any reduction in capital gains is a "tax break for the rich." That's why we should *increase* taxes on assets held for less than six months by imposing a 50 percent surcharge over the nominal capital gains rate. This surcharge would be a stiff disincentive to unproductive speculation. It would allow us to "soak the rich"—or at least the rich who play hunches, trade on rumors, and churn investments to the detriment of the American economy. In return for this penalty on speculation, capital gains taxes on assets held for more than three years would be totally eliminated. Assets held between six months and three years would be taxed at the current income tax rate.

Think of how radically this simple reform would change investor perspectives. A short-term speculator would pay a huge tax relative to someone willing to invest over a three-year period. Somehow I suspect our quarterly conference calls would take on a different character if this provision were in place. The questions would revolve around determining whether our company was positioned, managed, and funded to be a leader for the next three years rather than the next quarter. Which, of course, would make it easier for us to raise capital with the long term in mind—and to compete more effectively against our better-financed foreign rivals.

IT'S TIME TO WIN — NO EXCUSES

So there you have it. A program for American renewal that revolves around cutting the deficit and restructuring taxes on capital gains. Hardly the stuff of brass bands and whistle-stop tours, especially with all the energetic talk these days about critical technologies, government-funded investment in human capital, high-speed rail and fiber optics, and countless other agendas for renewal. I wish we could propose a razzle-dazzle game plan that would capture the imagination of Washington and help put America back on track. But those of us out competing every day understand that there are real limits to Washington's potential contributions to our success — and countless opportunities for mischief and missteps.

America has plenty of work to do on the economic and social problems we have ignored or created for ourselves over the past fifteen years. Ultimately, though, the economic battles of the 1990s will be won or lost in America's factories, labs, and offices — not in the halls of Congress or the corridors of the White House. That's good news. Hundreds of American companies are competing with fervor and daring, dominating markets, rewriting the rules of competition in their industries. There's no reason hundreds more can't do the same. All it takes is vigilant, disciplined, tough-minded management — the subject of this book.

Let's end where we began: *The United States is the best country in the world in which to start and grow a company.* There are problems, to be sure, but they can be addressed by some commonsense improvements to our system — a few of which have been suggested here. Every failing CEO who uses America as a scapegoat for poor performance supplies to his or her entire organization a clear leadership message that failure is tolerable, even expected. That is a message no organization can afford to hear.

It is time to get back to the business of winning — No Excuses.

WARRANTY REGISTRATION CARD

Where had you heard about this book?

☐ Magazine ad   ☐ Magazine article   ☐ Newspaper article

☐ Review   ☐ Saw in store   ☐ Personal

☐ Gift   ☐ Other   recommendation

☐ Retailer recommendation

Age of reader: _____

Have you ever purchased any other Currency business books? _____

If yes, please specify titles: _____

_____

What are your favorite business books? _____

_____

Would you be interested in (5 being the most interested):

Currency catalog and newsletter	1	2	3	4	5
Business book audio tapes	1	2	3	4	5
Business book video tapes	1	2	3	4	5
Executive summaries of the book	1	2	3	4	5
Chapter excerpts	1	2	3	4	5

Name: _____

Address: _____

City: _____ State: _____ Zip: _____

Your job title: _____

Industry: _____

Function: _____

Company size: ☐ Small   ☐ Medium   ☐ Large

Please fold and seal before mailing

WE'D LIKE TO HEAR FROM YOU . . .

We take pride in our books. Please help us continue to address issues that are important to you. Let us know what you think of *No-Excuses Management* and any other Currency books you own. Thank you.

_____

_____

_____

_____

Currency is interested in quoting our users in future promotional materials. If your comments are used, your name will appear with your quote. Please check the box that follows if you DO NOT want us to print your comments. ☐

Diskette Copyright Information:
"Goals" © 1992 by Avantos Performance Systems
"Focal" © 1992 by Cypress Semiconductor Corporation

The enclosed Focal Demo is licensed only to the purchaser of this book for his personal use. The purchaser owns the book and the media containing the software, and the software is merely licensed to the purchaser of the book. It may not be distributed, sold, rented, or leased.

Doubleday, Cypress, and the authors specifically disclaim all other warranties, expressed or implied, including but not limited to implied warranties of merchantability and fitness for a particular purpose with respect to the disk, the programs therein contained, and/or the techniques described in the book, and in no event shall Doubleday, Cypress, and/or the authors be liable for any loss of profit or any other commercial damage, including but not limited to special, incidental, consequential, or other damages.

Note:
Doubleday warrants that the physical disks within are free from defects in materials and workmanship for a period of 60 days from the date of purchase. If Doubleday receives notification within the warranty period of defects in the material or workmanship, Doubleday will replace a defective disk. The remedy for breach of this warranty will be limited to replacement and will not encompass any other damages, including but not limited to loss of profit and special, incidental, consequential, or other claims.

This diskette includes demos of two *No-Excuses Management* software systems. The demos only run on IBM-compatible computers. One requires Lotus 1-2-3 version 2.01 or higher. The other requires 3 megabytes of available hard-disk memory and VGA graphics.

CURRENCY

DOUBLEDAY